Date Due

	GOB Jan 80	Kirkton	
Kirkton APR. 6	APR. 16 1978		
May 5		June 2	

971   Morton, W. **25239**
Mor   This land, these
         people.

1 Lair Atkins 2995			
APR. 6 1978	1536	MAR. 8	
APR. 18	0578	769	
May 1943		APR. 16	

25239

971   Morton, William Lewis, 1908-
Mor   This land, these people; an illustrated
         history of Canada   [By] W. L. Morton &
      L. F. Hannon. Agincourt, Gage, 1977.
         248 p. illus.
         Includes bibliography.

      1. Canada – History. I. Hannon, Leslie F.
      II. Title.
      0771593325   0350583

               15.   6/HE/CN

This Land, These People

This Land, These People

An Illustrated History of Canada

W. L. Morton & L. F. Hannon

Gage Publishing

Agincourt

Gage Publishing
Copyright © W. L. Morton and L. F. Hannon, 1977
No part of this book may be reproduced in any form without
permission in writing from the publisher.

Canadian Cataloguing in Publication Data

Morton, William L., 1908-
  This land, these people
Bibliography: p.
Includes index.
ISBN 0-7715-9332-5
I. Canada – History. I. Hannon, Leslie F., 1920-
II. Title.
FC164.M67   971   C77-001508-5
F1026.M67

Design: Allan Fleming
Photo Research: Honor de Pencier

Printed and bound in Canada

CONTENTS

Books by W. L. MORTON
The Progressive Party in Canada
Manitoba: A History
One University: A History of the University of Manitoba, 1877-1952
The Canadian Identity
The Kingdom of Canada
The Critical Years: the Union of British North America, 1857-1873

Books by L. F. HANNON
Forts of Canada
The Discoverers

Fix your eyes on the greatness of your country
as you have it before you day by day, fall in love with her,
and when you feel her great, remember that her greatness was won by men with courage, with knowledge of
their duty, and with a sense of honour in action,
who, even if they failed in some venture, would not
think of depriving the country of their powers but
laid them at her feet as their fairest offering.
PERICLES

This Land, These People

PART I

The overwhelming land

A most remarkable community

The history of Canada is the story of how a great country has influenced its people and how the people have adapted their lives to the part of the land they live in – or changed it to suit their lives. The Canadian experience has not yet been deeply examined by Canadians themselves. The Canadian drama has in the past lacked a Canadian audience. This book is evidence that this is now changing, that Canadians are trying to set their own values and to judge their experience for what it seems worth to themselves. To do so they need, among other things, to know how they came to be what they are. No one quite knows yet.

It is one of the fascinations of Canadian history that so much of it remains to be explored. At the moment, none the less, two great features of that history seem to stand out. One is the mixture of peoples. Most Canadians are of either French or British origin, but many others – making up almost a quarter of the whole – descend from all the nations of Europe, others from

Asia and Africa. And, since Canadians did not purposely destroy the peoples they found here, the Indians and Eskimos survive and enter into Canadian life in their own time and on their own terms. This mixing of peoples, which has been happening for more than two hundred years, still goes on. It is now part of the Canadian way of life.

What do peoples so diverse have in common? Their pasts, on the whole, divide more than they unite, as do those, for example, of the British and the French. No common ideals, as in the United States or in Soviet Russia, bring them together. It was once conventional to say they were all subjects of the Queen, giving a common allegiance. Now the stress is rather on their common citizenship; all are equally citizens of Canada, and share a common experience of Canadian life. Whether they like it or not, Canadians have to learn to live with other and different people – never an easy thing to do.

The other great feature of the Canadian experience has been the awesome grandeur of the land itself. The vastness of the country, the sweep of the inland plateau and plain, the extremes of climate, the cold embrace of the Atlantic and its chill inlets of the Bay of Fundy, the Gulf of St. Lawrence and Hudson Bay, all these, and the Rocky Mountains, towering over the river valleys and plunging towards the sea, make the land overwhelming in Canada.

Geography is as important here as history. To understand the story, one must study the stage upon which the drama is enacted. One must see how each different part of the country has affected the people who live there, and how the parts have contributed to the history of the whole.

The largest region in size and the strongest in its effect on the people is the Canadian Shield, called Precambrian by geologists, one of the most ancient of geological formations. Some rocks in Manitoba are reckoned to be among the oldest in the world. Through the original granite, quartz and mineral ores boiled up from below

The awesome grandeur and vastness of the land have always been inescapable elements of the Canadian experience. Photo by JOHN DE VISSER

in the fiery ages of the earth, and the composition of the Shield is now such that one scientist has called it 'a geological salad.' This vast complex stretches from the coast of Labrador and the North Shore of the St Lawrence, by Lake Superior to the mouth of the Mackenzie River, in an enormous horseshoe around Hudson Bay. It makes up roughly one-half of the land mass of Canada.

Across the Gulf of St Lawrence to the south and east is quite a different land. It is the northern end of the great Appalachian fold along the Atlantic seaboard from Georgia to New England and the South Shore of the St Lawrence, spilling into the Atlantic in the peninsula of Nova Scotia and the island of Newfoundland. In it also there are ancient rocks, but none so old as the Precambrian, for in it are coal and oil, secreted in the rocks after the Precambrian was formed. The Appalachian fold thus joins the Canadian Shield as a steel beam joins a concrete abutment, different yet part of the same structure. Canada shares with the United States a geological formation that played a very similar role in the histories of the American and Canadian people.

Just as the great arc of the Shield abuts across the St Lawrence on the Appalachian fold from the south, so, across the Mackenzie, it rests on another great fold from the south: the Cordilleras, generally synonymous with the Rocky Mountains. There the likeness ends, however. The Appalachians are old and soft and worn. The Cordilleras are new and hard and jagged. They are a recent upheaval of the earth's crust caused by the drift of the continent westward and the unimaginable weight of the Pacific Ocean. This enormous upheaval runs from Alaska through the Rockies and the Andes to Tierra del Fuego at the tip of South America.

In the east, Canada is thus almost sombrely ancient; in the west, it is, geologically speaking, brand and shining new, a land formation restless and not yet wholly settled into place.

That is not the end of the natural wonders. These great rock formations were not so long ago (as geologists think) islands reaching above rolling seas. Slowly between the Shield and the Rockies, and the Shield and the Appalachians, the basins filled with earth washed down, and, more important, the sea bed rose in one of the imperceptible constrictions of the globe. The sea bed and tidal flats, century by century, turned to sodden marsh, then to dry land, until today Ontario farms lie green where once the waters washed, and the roll of the prairies in Saskatchewan recalls the long billows of the vanished interior sea.

Canada was shaped, however, not only by fire and global pressure, and the wearing of the sea. In long cycles of Ice Ages, glaciers formed over the one-time mountains of the Shield and even over the Rockies themselves – the remnant of one may be seen today between Banff and Jasper. The frozen rain of thousands of years, the glaciers moved under their own pressure

southward from their centres of greatest weight across the Shield and the Rockies. They became ponderous planes shearing the rocks down, enormous chisels gouging the valleys deeper and wider. The mountains of the Shield were ground down, their rocky cores polished smooth except for the long grooves cut by pebbles set in the moving ice. The mountains of the Rockies were cut apart and separated like an old man's teeth. The debris was pushed into the seas. And when the glaciers retreated, melting, they cast behind them the eskers and the drumlin ridges that mark the Canadian countryside.

The last Ice Age ended perhaps a mere ten thousand years ago, only twice the recorded history of man. What emerged was the Canada of today, the Canada of the worn-down Shield, of the newer Rockies.

The remorseless forging of the land, the comparative nearness in geologic time of the great glaciers, makes a dramatic but sobering story. And, as they come into the consciousness of Canadians, the sombre tundra and the perpetual ice of the Arctic increase this sense of a life dominated by land and climate. It is a climate of extremes. The southernmost point of the country is at 42° N, almost halfway between the equator and the North Pole. Much of Canada is north of 45° and the vast bulk well beyond 49°. Thus winter and its cold dominates half of the year in all but a few small and favoured regions of Canada. Yet the winter's cold is balanced to some extent by the summer's heat. Canada is one half of the continental land mass of North America and, because it is so far north, its summer days are long. Summer is thus as hot as winter is cold. In much of the country, only those things survive that can stand great heat and great cold.

For the majority of Canadians, of course, this part of the Canadian experience is no longer vital in their daily lives. They now live in a few large cities. While cities develop each its own character, city life is much the same the world over. A city is an artificial way of life, rich in all that living together can provide, poverty-stricken when any of its citizens fail to have a part in the benefits of the city life – when concentration becomes congestion, when the city fragments into suburb and ghetto. There, perhaps, is the third great feature, if not yet explored, of the Canadian experience: the growth of the big cities and their place in the life of Canada.

It could be that Canada is the most interesting country in the world. The foreigner will likely think differently but, still, it is quite possibly so. Certainly few countries have been more fortunate in their history, and few are happier in their present circumstances. But the true interest of Canadian history is much deeper than the fact of good fortune. Not only is Canada the heir of two of the greatest countries of Europe at the height of European civilization, it now draws strength and inspiration from all of Europe. Not only is it the sheltered neighbour of the world's most powerful and dynamic society, the United States, which has infused Canada

GOKSTADSKIBET

with much of its own vigour, Canada is also in itself a most remarkable community of people who have shared the common experience of Canadian history without losing their historic identities or suffering the loss of their properties, their ways of life, or their self-respect.

Canadians have made Canada what it is. It is not an idea imposed by government, or maintained by propaganda; it is what Canadian men and women have felt and done, what Canadian men and women still feel and do.

Yet it is not mere feeling and blind action. Out of the Canadian experience come the things that give Canadian history its exceeding interest. You only have to look at how Canada has lived and lives today to see them – although we do not all see them in the same way.

One is the strong sense of history, of continuity with the past, among Canadians of the past and present. Canadian history has no breaks; Canadians desire none. Yet neither has it any goal, the fulfilment of a Canadian dream, or a dictatorship of the proletariat. It has never been primarily a refuge or a retreat, a means of escape from the present and the future. Canadian history has been a continuity, but a continuity of change. Canadians, therefore, have never denied their past, but have found in it a means of possessing the future.

The growth of Canada depended in large part on the trader, lumberman, farmer, industrialist, and banker – but no less it sprang from the toil of the workmen and from the spirit and resource of unsung women. Their efforts have too often gone unacknowledged. Their types and their callings, however, are known in nature and detail: the fisherman jigging for cod on the Banks; the trapper on snowshoes with his toboggan on his trapline; the *voyageur* bent sweating under the tumpline with its piled packs on the portage; the shantyman hacking and hewing with the broadaxe in the winter pineries; the prospector in the mountain creek or on the muskeg of the Shield; the British or German

artisan in the new factories; the hired man stooking the endless rows of sheaves; the navvy digging the St Lawrence canals or building the railway embankments. These men with their hands built Canada, took wages, and are unsung. But their work should be remembered by those who ride the roads they opened. Others made Canada possible by their wit – these men built it with their hands.

Canada's place on the globe is, of course, remote from the ancient centres of civilization and still marginal to the new centres of power, but the very remoteness seems to create a response to the challenge. Particular places in Canada can seem very far from anywhere: a rural village under the cliff of Gaspé, a trading post on an Arctic inlet of Hudson Bay, a mine on a mountain slope of British Columbia. Yet in fact Canada is open to all the world. Canadians live more than other peoples in the world at large. It was not by chance that it was a Canadian, Marshall McLuhan, who coined the term, 'a global village.'

By creating a working society out of diverse people, Canada has not only dealt with the accidents and mere happenings of the past; it has also, without intending to, entered on an experience in human society that is part of, and also anticipates, what seems likely for all people everywhere. Men and women are ever more aware of one another, and must reconcile their differences and expand their likenesses. This is what most Canadians are seeking to do, to have fellowship without race, to be a nation without nationalism.

In this way, by its own experience Canada enters the human dialogue. That experience could be a significant contribution to the present fiery debate on how men are to share a burdened planet. Within the chafing limits of a single volume intended for the general reader, the authors pose the questions: What is Canada? How did this country grow to its present state? Why does the Canadian act the way he does? While their nerve holds, they offer some uncertain answers.

PART I

Chapter One
New world in the north

The deeply laden Viking freighter, full of sawn timber, tools, pottery, grain and other goods from Norway, reefed its painted sail and held well offshore as her captain, Bjarni Herjólfsson, studied the strange coastline. It was early autumn in the year 986. For many days his ship had been blown before a storm out of the north, and dense fogs had concealed the sun and his guiding pole star. When the sun finally broke through, Bjarni knew he was far to the south, in unknown waters.

He was a resourceful man, cautious, steady in a crisis. He had brought his *knorr* safely halfway across the northern Atlantic to Iceland on his regular every-other-summer schedule only to find that his trader father, Herjólfr Bárdarson, had left for Greenland in the colonizing expedition led

This elegant Viking ship suggests the slender, open Knörr vessel used by exploring Scandinavians who ventured as far as North American shores. Photo courtesy OSLO'S UNIVERSITY MUSEUM OF NATIONAL ANTIQUITIES VIKING SHIP MUSEUM

by Eirikr Thorvaldsson – better known as Erik the Red. Sailing on to join his father, Bjarni probably followed instructions left for him at Reykjavik, describing the destination near Cape Farewell on the Greenland shore. Bjarni also knew of that land's high and snowy peaks because they could be seen in the west from Iceland's own mountains on a clear day.

The land he had raised was, however, thickly forested and definitely not mountainous. It could not be any part of Greenland. Keeping the coast on his left hand, he sailed northwards and, after two days, closed on another wooded shore. Greenland's south-western fiords were fringed with some dwarfed trees but there had been no reports of timber fit for the masts of ships.

Ignoring the grumbles from the crew about short rations and scarcity of fresh water, Bjarni pushed on until a third land could be seen from the pitching afterdeck. Mountains stood behind this bleak coast and glaciers could be seen – but they were obviously too far to the west. The latitude was about right, though, and Bjarni now ordered the helmsman to set his steerboard to take the ship to the east. After four days in rough seas, the expected icy mountains of Greenland were at last seen as a towering barrier ahead and Bjarni thankfully went into the land, his instructions bringing him very close to where his father anxiously awaited.

On the evidence of the Norse sagas, Bjarni and his crew were thus the first Europeans to sight the Canada-to-be. These detailed and absorbing folk tales outlining the discovery of north-eastern America five hundred years before Christopher Columbus sailed west for Spain were told for generations in Greenland and Iceland before being first written down in the thirteenth century, but they are now universally accepted as being based on fact. Two collections of the surviving manuscripts may be seen today in Denmark.

It seems, then, that this continent was discovered by accident. Erik the Red, now the Jarl (Earl) of Greenland – he had deliberately given the huge island that name so as to attract settlers – may himself have crossed the intervening strait to what would later be called the Cumberland Peninsula of Baffin Island. The great Viking surge that had sent the feared dragon ships with their helmeted warriors up the rivers and around the entire coasts of Europe was still in spate, and it should be remarked that the intelligent Northmen often colonized what they seized. The several Atlantic sagas tell the essential story in different ways, mixing some fantasy or hearsay in with the actual mariners' accounts, and academics have never agreed totally on their interpretations; the versions are simply irreconcilable on many points.

The chronicle of Bjarni's lucky strike is recounted in the *Graenlendinga Saga*, which lists six Viking voyages to the American mainland over a thirty-year period. He had not, of course, touched ground anywhere on the new lands but his observations and records were still clear enough, fifteen years later, to guide the man who is now conceded to be the true discoverer. Leif, one of the three sons of Erik the Red, bought Bjarni's proved *knorr* in the spring of 1001, and, with a crew of thirty-five, set out from Brattahlid, the family estate in the Julianehaab fiords, to claim the lands in the west. He adopted the sensible plan of sailing Bjarni's course, but in reverse. In this way he came first to stony Helluland (our Baffin Island, only 250 miles west of Greenland), then to Markland (Labrador, close to Hamilton Inlet), and finally to the hotly disputed Vinland – most likely somewhere between the tip of Newfoundland and Cape Cod; he stayed the winter where 'no frost came and the grass was hardly withered.' Trying to pinpoint the actual site of Leif Eiriksson's 'Wineland' still keeps a fair body of scholars and amateur enthusiasts busy. At least twenty places have been suggested, from Labrador to Pamlico Sound in North Carolina, including the St Lawrence Valley and Hudson Bay. There is no general agreement, although excavations since 1961 at L'Anse-au-Meadow, near Newfoundland's Cape Bauld, are accepted as having uncovered a small Viking settlement.

Leif was followed by his brothers, Thorvaldr and Thorsteinn, and then by the Icelander Thorfinnr Thordarson, known by his nickname 'Karlsefni,' who had married Thorsteinn's widow, Gudridr. This last expedition, in 1011, was a major colonizing undertaking with three ships and up to 160 persons. After nearly three years in Vinland, during which perhaps one thousand miles

Retracing ancient voyages described in Norse sagas,
Helge Ingstad discovered a Viking settlement which in-
cluded this large house site with central fireplace near
L'Anse-au-Meadow in Newfoundland.
Photo by H. INGSTAD

of coastline was explored, the Vikings were harried into departure by the aggressive native *Skraelings* – either Eskimos or Indians, or perhaps both. The natives of the Americas had crossed the fifty-mile 'land bridge' from Siberia to Alaska during the ice ages when the seas were lowered, certainly before 20,000 B.C. Erik's lusty daughter, Freydis, who had routed a band of *Skraelings* by slapping her broadsword on her naked breasts, made a return trip with her husband Thorvard but added nothing to the discoveries except some dark tales of treachery and murder.

The Viking contact was never more than slight and the western voyages appear to have tailed off and then ceased in the early twelfth century. The Norse settlements in Greenland, which had once supported perhaps ten thousand people, themselves vanished in the early fifteenth century. As far as Europe was concerned, the brooding capes of Canada slipped back into mystery.

But the knowledge of the existence of western lands, whether written or merely passed from mouth-to-mouth, was never totally lost. Some will argue that even Bjarni and Leif were latecomers, that a populated America was already known to Celtic, Roman and even Carthaginian voyagers. Reports of skin-covered boats being washed ashore on the western coasts of Ireland and Scotland go back to antiquity. The Irish legends of the sixth century monk Brendan – he is the Celtic Sindbad – caused early cartographers to place a 'St Brendan's Isle' in the far Atlantic, and the Norse sagas repeatedly confirm the presence of Irishmen ahead of themselves in Iceland, Greenland and elsewhere. Gustave Lanctot, a towering figure among Canadian historians, put the case for an Irish religious colony on the St Lawrence in the ninth century. The village of Madoc, in Ontario's Hastings County, hints at the discovery claims of the Welsh princeling of the same name. The Scottish 'Sea King,' Prince Henry Sinclair of the Orkney Isles, led an expedition to Nova Scotia in the fourteenth century, according to a narrative published in Venice in 1558.

It must be added that no incontrovertible evidence, either in archaeological remains or written document, exists to prove any discovery voyage earlier than that of Leif the Lucky. The same has to be said, however reluctantly, about events during the suspiciously long gap between the disappearance of the Vikings and the arrival of the first of the Renaissance rovers.

When John Cabot (as the English called the Venetian, Giovanni Caboto) left Bristol in the fifty-ton *Matthew* on May 2, 1497, he knew there was land beyond Iceland and Greenland as long as he pushed far enough into the setting sun – although he was, of course, confident that it would be the edge of Asia. He was heir to all the accumulated sea lore of the northern passage: where the fitful easterlies blew in summer along the fringe of the prevailing westerlies, where he could replenish supplies with easy fishing, when he could expect the Labrador Current to push him to the south. He may have picked up an experienced pilot in Iceland. Mariners seeking the fabulous 'Brasil' had come back into the shelter of the Avon at Bristol, and tightlipped fishermen brought in big hauls of stockfish (cod) and said nothing of where they had been – the King of Denmark had banned foreigners from the waters around Iceland.

On Martin Behaim's famous globe, first shown in Germany in 1492, *Ultima Thule*, the lands west of familiar Iceland, look roughly similar in outline to the actual Newfoundland and Nova Scotia – and this before even the first voyage of Columbus. Behaim had been living in the Azores and he may have got his information from João Corte-Real, for whom is claimed the discovery of the *Terra de Bacalhão* (Codfish Land or, if you like, Newfoundland). João's sons were to play their own tragic role in the discovery story.

The two Italians, Columbus and Cabot, both in foreign service, were driven by the same inspiration – the search for a western seaway around the curve of the globe to the gold and silks of Cathay and the cinnamon and peppers of the Spice Islands. Until that time, these treasures were reaching Europe only via the tortuous overland routes through Asia and India. Columbus was first to find sponsors and ships, but he was fated to become entangled in the islands of the western Indies and he never put foot upon – or even saw, above Honduras – the mainland of North America. It was Cabot who, on June 24, 1497, came to the continent proper, landing on Cape Breton and claiming the country for England's King Henry VII.

John Cabot, the first explorer to raise a flag in Canada for the English crown in 1497, reported sailing through seas of fish off the Grand Banks which led to the first big industry in the land. Photo by M. MILNE

Cabot was undoubtedly a brilliant man in his time, well-read, much travelled; and he did not delude himself that his 'Newe Founde Launde' was the civilized and glittering China as described by his fellow-Venetian Marco Polo two hundred years earlier. He *did* think, though, that he had found Tartary, the north-eastern extremity of Asia, and that if he returned and worked his way down the coast south and much farther west, he would reach the treasure cities of Cipango and Cathay. On a second voyage, the next year, Cabot vanished from the record. If he did, as some think, coast down eastern North America to Chesapeake Bay, or even farther, it was only to learn that a huge land, indeed a New World, stood between him and the lands of silks and spices. His son Sebastian, once himself hailed as the major discoverer, today accused of merely trying to steal his father's laurels, may have made a voyage into Hudson Strait in 1509, but the evidence is thin and suspect.

The English now temporarily lost their taste, or their risk capital, for discovery and concentrated on gathering the riches of the Grand Banks. The market in Europe for dried or salted cod was insatiable. They were joined there by fishermen from all along the European seaboard, some of whom may quite possibly have been routinely harvesting these waters even before Cabot's voyage of discovery.

At the turn of the sixteenth century, the sons of Corte-Real took the Portuguese flag high up the eastern coasts to Labrador and Greenland and lost their lives in the frigid seas. Cape Bonavista (*Bõa Vista*) and Cape Race (*Raso*) are names that recall their passing, and St John's has given a prominent place to its Corte-Real statue. Jean Denys for France charted what appears to be the eastern coast of Newfoundland as early as 1506. Other great captains, including Thomas Aubert, João Fagundes, Estevão Gomes and Giovanni de Verrazzano, began to sketch in the Atlantic profile of the new lands and England's John Rut, in the *Mary Guildford*, wintered in the harbour at St John's during what was the first planned attempt to seek a north-west passage across the top of the New World.

After Ferdinand Magellan had crossed the Pacific in 1520, and Verrazzano had confirmed the substance of the New World by coasting from Florida to Cape Breton (he marked his highest latitude at 50° N), it was the French who accepted the challenge to penetrate the wide waters lying behind Newfoundland. It was the cue for Jacques Cartier of St Malo to come onstage and, with his first voyage of 1534, the traditional written history of Canada begins.

We have the Cartier journals, not telling all at the most critical times, but pithy, laconic, the calm prose of a man in command, who knew what he was to do, and could do it. And what a dramatic beginning of a history it is! No film, with all the art of the screen, could set the opening of a story more graphically: the small ships entering the Gulf of St Lawrence via the narrow Strait of Belle Isle, the sighting of the Iles de la Madeleine, the skirting of Prince Edward Island, the August heat of Chaleur Bay, the rearing of the cross with the fleur-de-lis at Gaspé, the interviewing of the Indians to discover what lay inland to the west. But, for all the romance, Cartier was working to a calculated and carefully financed plan of hard-headed men. The plan was to make a footing for France in the New World, to find, if possible, treasures such as had been found in Mexico and Peru, and to establish a base from which yet another route to Asia might be found.

What Cartier found was that behind *Terre-Neuve* lay not the western ocean open to the Orient but more land, a territory the voyage of 1535 revealed to be large enough to give rise to one of the world's great rivers, the St Lawrence, which led – he was assured by the primitive Indians desirous of pleasing the Europeans and obtaining their magical metal tools and textiles – to the kingdom of Saguenay, rich in minerals. Gold and silver would pay for the European voyages and the exploration of the river provide another stage on the route to Asia.

So bright were these prospects, so great the achievement of Cartier in ascending first to Stadacona (Quebec), then to Hochelaga on the site of Montreal, a thousand miles from the open ocean, that the collapse of this great enterprise in the next seven years is surprising and mysterious – perhaps mostly because it is at this point the documents fail us.

When Cartier sailed the third time in 1540 as the vanguard for the planting of a colony to be headed by the Sieur de Roberval, he ran into a series of failures that caused him to return to France even before Roberval joined him. The Indians wanted the Europeans to trade with them and settle amongst them but they were not willing to have the white men pass on to explore – and thus benefit the tribes deeper inland.

The minerals Cartier found, especially the *diamants*, proved to be worthless. The banks of the St Lawrence yielded neither gold nor iron, and 'false as a Canadian diamond' became a French proverb. Next, the rapids of the St Lawrence and the Ottawa made it evident that further penetration inland would be impossible with European boats – and it would be seventy years before Samuel Champlain would adopt the canoe. To all these difficulties were added the cold of the Canadian winter and the near-impossibility of keeping discipline and good health among an ill-assorted group of colonists far from home and caught in the grip of a winter harsh far beyond experience or expectation. The name New France had been placed on the map, but no real foothold had been made.

The continuing discovery of Canada was now to be divided between British efforts to pierce the suspected clusters of islands lying under the near-perpetual ice of the high north (as the merchants kept demanding a seaway to the Far East), and French concentration on the Atlantic shore and, subsequently, in the valley of the St Lawrence. Outside the pages of official record, the earliest whalers continued to scorn the ice of the great sea inlets above Newfoundland; many were lost but others contributed valuable items to the swiftly expanding hearsay.

One day during the winter of 1565-66, Sir Humphrey Gilbert argued before Queen Elizabeth for a determined attempt to force the North-West Passage into the Pacific, while Captain Anthony Jenkinson put the case for a North-East Passage into the Kara Sea and across the top of Russia, a route partly opened as early as 1553 by Hugh Willoughby and Richard Chancellor. Jenkinson himself had crossed Russia to the Caspian Sea several years earlier. Gilbert, who won the debate, was convinced that once a ship had safely rounded the tip of Labrador, it would find the coast sheering off to the southward, with the 'Straits of Anian' offering an open waterway to the Orient. In terms of the modern map, Sir Humphrey envisaged a Canadian northern coast that sloped from Hudson Bay to the Gulf of Georgia. It was Yorkshireman Martin Frobisher who made the first attempt.

Frobisher took the frail *Gabriel*, of a mere twenty tons, into the Canadian Arctic on the first of his three voyages in the summer of 1576, penetrating beyond Resolution Island at the entrance of what would later be called Hudson Strait. He returned in the following two years, only to waste his efforts digging for non-existent gold along the shores of Frobisher Bay on Baffin Island. His chilling descriptions of the menacing, grinding ice that beset his ships was an omen of what awaited voyagers, then and now, in the high north. 'Through the darkness and obscuritie of the foggie mist,' Frobisher wrote, 'we were almost run on rocks and islands before we saw them.'

In 1578 Gilbert himself set out for his 'Straits of Anian' but he didn't even get across the Atlantic; another five years passed before he reached Newfoundland, where, at St John's, on August 3, 1583, he formally claimed the island for his Queen and thus established Britain's first overseas colony and, in the long course of the years, Canada's tenth province.

John Davis of Devon followed Frobisher and made three important voyages in the 1580s into the waters above Labrador, leaving his name on the wide strait between Baffin Island and Greenland. He died convinced that 'there is a short and speedie passage into the South Seas.' George Weymouth, Henry Hudson, Robert Bylot, Thomas Button and others now broke their hearts and often their ships in trying to find it. William Baffin and Bylot went north in 1616 as far as Smith Sound – the frozen channel leading to the Pole around the shoulder of Greenland – and also found the hopeful entries of Jones and Lancaster sounds. This last-named was the true strait that would, nearly three hundred years later, allow the first ship to reach the Pacific from the Atlantic above Canada.

As another century turned and the shape of Canada's eastern Arctic slowly emerged as a by-product of the British tilts at the icy straits, the mainland to the south began to open to the steady gaze and unquenchable curiosity of Samuel Champlain. The French fishermen and travellers had probably never ceased venturing into the gulf and river of St Lawrence following Cartier's discoveries but the written record is bare for five decades – only voyages sponsored by kings of the realm and princes of the church were documented in those days. Official France was too occupied by the wars against the Hapsburgs and by the bitter Huguenot-Catholic struggle at home to pursue western discoveries. Nephews of Cartier had sought a fur-trading monopoly in New France in 1588 and the 'beaver frontier' was firmly established at the Strait of Canso, at Roche Percée on the Gaspé and at Tadoussac, at the mouth of the Saguenay.

From the time of his first appearance in these waters – in the summer of 1603 – Champlain brought the shores of Canada clearly into the light of modern knowledge. Where other men may have been before, leaving a few clumsy charts bearing little or no relation to the lands they purported to describe, he patiently probed and examined, took observations as fine as the astrolabe would allow, and made the accurate notes for the maps that he published with the several books of his voyages. First in the Maritimes, as the Sieur de Monts established his forts on the Bay of Fundy, Champlain mapped the Atlantic coast clear down to Cape Cod, and sailors say that small boats could still safely use some of his harbour charts today. Then, up the St Lawrence to the founding of Quebec in 1608 – the heartbeat of Canada quickening – and on by Algonquin canoe past Cartier's Mont Royal to those freshwater seas we choose in our grandeur of territory to call lakes, his sketching and writing hand never still.

Cautious and courageous, reserved and romantic, Champlain was a remarkable mixture of the attributes that some observers abroad have noted in the modern Canadian; in accepting the gruff fisherman's son from Brouage as prime national hero and founding father, Canadians may unconsciously model themselves on his virtues. But he was a discoverer, too – bringing more of the country into recognition than any other individual in any period. He never ceased dreaming of a river-and-lake route through Canada to the Pacific and his great map of 1632 was the finest achievement of its kind. When he died in the capital he had created on the noble Rock of Quebec, he had given more than thirty years of unquestioning devotion and untiring promotion to the wilderness that was the true love of his life.

It is a trip by time machine to mark out the remainder of the margins of Canada. Almost a century and a half passed between the death of Samuel Champlain and the arrival of James Cook on the rain-shrouded Pacific coast. Francis Drake had claimed New Albion on San Francisco Bay in the Elizabethan Age, and he very likely saw the thrilling mountain backdrop of today's British Columbia; the record of his northerly passage is maddeningly muddled. The Spaniards, Pérez and Bodega y Quadra, had coasted north as far as Russia's Alaska, but they never landed on Canadian soil. With Cook's appearance at Nootka Sound in 1778, on his third Pacific voyage, the most lovely of our lands was finally brought out of its long concealment. George Vancouver, who was a midshipman with Cook, returned to mark every cape and cove, and to leave his own name writ large on the country.

Few Canadians realize that Cook, acknowledged the greatest discovery captain of all time, built his reputation in Canadian waters. He surveyed the St Lawrence in advance of the river passage of the British fleet that besieged Quebec in 1759, then spent six years charting the coasts of Labrador and Newfoundland. After a happy month at Nootka, laying a foundation of friendship with the Indians that would endure, fitting stout Canadian masts into his ships *Resolution* and *Discovery*, Cook continued north in atrocious weather. He was on his way to test the ice through Bering's Strait for a western end to that elusive Arctic passage. A report by Hudson's Bay Company agent Samuel Hearne of a fringe of open water at the mouth of the Coppermine River on an arm of the Arctic Ocean had revived British hopes once again.

After the Cook expedition, only the blank between Coronation Gulf and Point Barrow on the

Champlain's astrolabe, an elegant instrument by which he determined his position by the sighting of specific stars. Photo courtesy PUBLIC ARCHIVES

Beaufort Sea remained to be sketched in. In 1789 Alexander Mackenzie was at the ocean delta of the great river that carries his name. Amid the islands above, Edward Parry in 1819 finally threaded his way west through Lancaster Sound, Barrow Strait and into Viscount Melville Sound. He penetrated within sight of Banks Island, beyond which lay the Beaufort Sea and, around the shoulder of Alaska, the boundless Pacific. But although he wintered in the passage, Parry could get no farther and returned to England in the following year after discovering and naming twenty major islands, straits and sounds. Sir John Franklin retraced Hearne's journey to the Coppermine in 1821 and followed the coast eastwards to the Kent Peninsula on Melville Sound; in 1826, he pushed westwards from the Mackenzie Delta to the Return Reef at 149° W. The gap to Point Barrow was closed ten years later by Peter Dease and Thomas Simpson. The last link in the North-West Passage – McClure Strait – was forged in 1850 during the desperate search for Franklin who had vanished amid the maze of islands in the central Arctic.

The three coasts of Canada were at last known and traced, but nearly a further century had to pass before any ship would complete the North-West Passage in a single season. That honour went to the RCMP motor schooner *St Roch*, under Captain Henry Larsen, in 1944. He travelled from Halifax to Vancouver in a mere eighty-six days and, for good measure, he went on to become the only skipper to circle North America.

PART I

Chapter Two
Overland to other oceans

The overland exploration of Canada occupied no fewer than three hundred years – and it would still be easy amid the fantastic spill of mountains, the enormous tundra, the silent Arctic islands, for a modern adventurer to place his feet where no other man has trod. In a land fifteen times the size of France, we have yet only half France's population. The great majority of Canadians live within a strip of territory less than three hundred miles from the American border, most live within one hundred miles, and the vastness that completes the map to the polar icecap is virtually uninhabited.

Early Canada was never a place for cowards, or for sybarites. It is a harsh, sometimes a cruel, country of rock and river, of endless forest, of exhausting steppes, of killing cold and scorching heat, and it gave up its secrets reluctantly and only to men of a superior breed. From Samuel Champlain in the early seventeenth century to Vilhjalmur Stefansson in the twentieth, they were almost all men lit by a flaming determination and sustained by a resolve for success that seems now to be ebbing in Western man. It is of passing interest to recall that Champlain was forty-eight at the time of his greatest journey, and Stefansson turning forty. Father Gabriel Druillettes, the explorer of the Acadian hinterland, was still travelling in the wilderness at the age of seventy.

Champlain seized the key to Canadian exploration when he adopted the bark canoe of the Indian. Ascending the Richelieu (then the 'River of the Iroquois') in 1609, he discovered at the rapids at Chambly that his European pinnace, or longboat, rowed by twenty men, could travel no farther. He sent the boat back to Quebec and, with two volunteers, continued by canoe into the lake that now carries his name.

His motives were not exactly scientific. He was out looking for blood, to convince his Algonquin allies that the French would side with them against the Iroquois and thus keep the furs flowing to the trading posts on the St Lawrence. The blood that did flow when the French musket-balls cut down the flower of the Five Nations was to be the beginning of a spreading stain that ran crimson down the St Lawrence for eighty years. After the one-sided affray near Ticonderoga, his Montagnais friends paddled Champlain back to Quebec within four days. They did the 120 miles from modern Sorel to Quebec City in two days.

The key to Canadian exploration was the Indians'
birch bark canoe which held 4 men and 250 lb.
cargoes, could be mended with forest resins, and
was portable. Photo by G. LUNNY

The lesson was not lost. As they pieced together a working knowledge of river and lake, the French would use the canoe to open half a continent. Built of cedar strips, covered with birch bark sewn with bone needles and *wattape* fibre threads, its seams waterproofed with spruce-gum chewed soft by the girls and women, the typical canoe could take the weight of four men and 250 pounds of pelts, yet could be carried by a boy along the portages. Eventually, to haul the tonnage of the organized fur trade, the *canots de maître* would be built thirty-six feet long, requiring a dozen men at the paddles. Champlain's confidence was complete in 1611 when he shot the Lachine Rapids in a *canot du nord* – and he was a non-swimmer.

Champlain's name might just as well have clung to either Lake Huron or Lake Ontario. It is a common error to think of 'Huron' as an Indian word; it derives from the French *huré* ('bristling'), and was applied to the Iroquoian Indians of southern Ontario because of the tuft or ridge of short hair they kept on their otherwise shaven skulls. 'Ontario' was not widely used until many years after Champlain's death; he called it the Lake of the Seneca. Champlain was in both lakes in 1615 – again on the warpath to cement the fateful alliance.

The narrower lands of Acadia had been soon crossed by men from the Sieur de Poutrincourt's Port Royal, by trader-fishermen venturing inland from Canso and other harbours, by the earliest priests seeking converts among friendly tribes. One *curé* miraculously learned the Algonkian language, and converted and baptized twenty Micmacs all within three weeks of his arrival from France.

As soon as his *Habitation* at Quebec was fairly established, Champlain sent Etienne Brûlé, then about eighteen years of age, to spend a winter with Chief Iroquet on the Ottawa River. He was to learn Algonkian and report on the geography. The following year, 1611, Champlain sent another youth, Nicolas de Vignau, away with Chief Tessouat to the villages on Lac des Allumettes. Having once enjoyed the limitless prerogatives of the Indian male, Brûlé was eager to go again and he went, next time, into Huronia – in total he was to spend about twenty years with the tribes. The somewhat priggish Champlain noted that Brûlé was 'much addicted to women.'

Strictly speaking, then, Brûlé and Vignau were the first Europeans to penetrate the unknown lands beyond the rapids that had barred the St Lawrence and the Ottawa since Cartier's first look into the hinterland from the top of Mount Royal seventy-five years earlier. Vignau covered the stretch of the Ottawa to the vicinity of modern Pembroke but his report to Champlain that he reached Hudson Bay remains controversial; it is generally accepted, however, that Brûlé was not only the first European to travel to Lake Huron's Georgian Bay via the Ottawa-Mattawa-French River route, but that he also was first to see Lakes Ontario, Erie and Superior. In 1615, his longest exploration took him down the Humber River to the site of the future Toronto, around the western end of Lake Ontario, up the Genesee and eventually down the Susquehanna and into Chesapeake Bay.

Unfortunately for Brûlé's fame, there is not one scrap of personal documentation for any of his travels or any official recognition; he left no descriptions, no drawings – most likely he was illiterate. Trying to hand him his due as explorer, one must search the writings of others and, even there, the references to him are few, obscure and often scathing. Champlain did not mention him by name until 1618 and the priests Sagard and Brébeuf were infuriated at the 'bad example' of French behaviour offered by Brûlé and others who enthusiastically embraced the Indian way of life. Father Joseph le Caron complained: 'The Huron girls are utterly shameless, and some of our French are more shameless than they.' In the early literature strongly influenced by the church, it is traditional that Brûlé got his 'just desserts' by being eaten by the braves of the Bear, at Toanché, on Georgian Bay, in 1633.

Champlain's own traverse of southern Ontario, from Matchedash Bay to Lake Simcoe, the Kawartha Lakes and via the Trent River to the Bay of Quinte, gives us our first written record of this fertile and beautiful territory. The battle that followed, against the Onondaga near present-day Syracuse, New York, was a defeat for the Hurons and Algonquins and their French musketeers. It marked, also, the end of all exploring for the ageing Champlain.

But his dimming eye was never off the frontier. Even as he lay dying in his Château St. Louis atop Cape Diamond, listening to Father Charles Lalement read from the *Lives of the Saints*, Champlain was still hoping to hear that Jean Nicollet, whom he had sent to probe beyond the western shore of Lake Michigan had at last found a waterway to the Orient. Nicollet was another of the young men whom Champlain had sent to live with the Indians. Rumour said that the China Sea was not far beyond Green Bay, and Nicollet was carrying a robe of damask decorated with coloured flowers and birds, fit to wear at the court of the Great Khan. He explored the Fox River, and reached some of the tributaries of the Mississippi – but the only time he wore his rich raiment he scared the wits out of the Winnebagoes, who thought a god had come amongst them.

Champlain's major contemporary competitor as a travel writer was the Récollet friar, Gabriel Sagard, who came to Canada in 1623, stayed ten months in Huronia, then went back to Paris to write a bestseller. Few writers today could match his performance on such brief research – it eventually added up to six books: *Le grand voyage au pays des Hurons*, four volumes of *L'histoire du Canada*, and a *Dictionnaire de la langue huronne*.

Where most explorers wrote stiffly at best, Sagard's stuff at times zipped along with lively material on the Indian way of life, the flowers and animals and geology of the country. He wrote of his difficulties in explaining his celibacy to the Huron girls who suggested he should marry them just for a night, or perhaps a whole week. He tried to change their wanton ways by extolling the virtue of French girls but his work was undone by some of the lay Frenchmen who said, on the contrary, that the ladies of France were much more ingenious and energetic at *l'amour*, thus spurring the native girls into spirited emulation.

The Jesuits added volumes – seventy-three in the English translation, to be exact – to the literature of exploration of the heartland of the Great Lakes, after their arrival in 1625. A wave of religious exaltation was sweeping France in the seventeenth century and the yearly accounts of the Jesuit missions, the *Relations*, edited by the Father Superior to the glory of God and King, were widely read with pious excitement – they were both inspiring and harrowing in their descriptions of hardship and even torture, and often rich in detail about the Canadian wilderness. When the French reclaimed Quebec in 1632, after its three years of English occupation, the Jesuits were granted exclusive rights in New France and the Franciscan Récollets were shut out.

Father Claude Allouez was perhaps the most peripatetic of the Jesuits, and certainly one of the most dedicated. In 1663 he was appointed to a mission made up, roughly, of the Middle West on both sides of the present border. From his birch bark chapel headquarters on Green Bay, Lake Michigan, he ranged over a 3000-mile area and was credited with personally baptizing ten thousand Indians drawn from twenty-three different nations. His diaries appear in excerpted form in the *Relations* for the years 1667 to 1676, often providing the very first descriptions of new territories. He made a canoe trip around Lake Superior and then drew the first map of that inland sea. Few Canadians even recognize his name, but Wisconsin remembers him gratefully in a statue erected at De Pere, on the Fox River.

The man who eventually subdued the Saguenay and dissipated the myth of its gold and rubies was the indestructible Father Charles Albanel, urged on by Intendant Jean Talon in 1671 to establish an overland route to Hudson Bay, by now the centre of English competition for the beaver of the Canadian Shield. Since Champlain's day, the French had sought to ascend the Saguenay but the obstacles of waterfalls, innumerable rapids, plus the unwillingness of the Montagnais to allow the Europeans into the interior had aborted several expeditions.

Albanel, with two French companions – Paul Denys and Sebastien Provencher – made more than two hundred portages and took a full year to pass from the Saguenay, to Lake St John, into the Ashuapmuchuan, then cross Lake Mistassini and descend into James Bay via the Rupert River. The cities of Chicoutimi, Kenogami, Arvida and Roberval prosper on this route today, and a rail spur runs to Chibougamau, but it remains one of the wildest and most difficult terrains in

Canada. Albanel made a return trip in 1673, carrying a letter for another footloose Frenchman who had, for the time being, gone over to the English. This was Médard Chouart, traditionally known as Groseilliers, who, with his brother-in-law Pierre-Esprit Radisson, had won support in London for their brilliant scheme to exploit the beaver trade through Hudson Bay.

The Canadian interior was now under attack from two bases. Under the Hudson's Bay Company charter issued by King Charles II in 1670, the English were astride the gateway to the Northwest by way of the Churchill, Nelson, Albany and Hayes river systems, while the French of the St Lawrence pushed out ever farther through the Ottawa River and across and beyond the Great Lakes.

From York Fort at the mouth of the Nelson, the Bay's Henry Kelsey made the journey that brought the prairies first into European knowledge. It occurred during 1690-92, but was not made public until 1749 (when the Bay company was accused of not pushing exploration) and, even then, was seldom quoted until the publication of the crudely rhymed *Kelsey Papers* in 1929. Even with his personal journal as guide, it is difficult to retrace Kelsey's steps exactly but most historians agree he travelled in 1690 by the Hayes River and Moose Lake to a bend in the South Saskatchewan River near the site of The Pas, now the administrative centre of northern Manitoba. He was then six hundred miles from Hudson Bay and he claimed the territory for his employers, calling his wintering place Deering's Point after a governor of the company.

In the summer season of the following year, pursuing his orders to 'call, encourage and invite the remoter Indians to trade,' Kelsey proceeded up the Carrot River, then abandoned his canoe to cross the muskeg lying to the south. After three hard days, he 'entered upon the first firm land, with its wild pigeons and moose, and farther south a more open prairie country which afforded an abundance of red deer – that plain abounded with buffalo.' He was the first to describe the bear and buffalo (he spelled it 'buffillo') of the Canadian West, and probably the first white man seen by the inland tribes. When he returned to York Fort in the early autumn of 1692, he brought with him 'a good fleet of Indians.'

This incredible nervy journey by a young Englishman into the heart of the Indian territories – he lived among the Assiniboines (Stoneys) and possibly the Sioux and Gros Ventres – is curiously overshadowed by lesser achievements in the Canadian record, possibly because of prejudice against the Hudson's Bay Company and its lordly governors, first among the chroniclers of New France and then, after the Conquest, by the Montreal-based supporters of the North West Company. Some of this bias still lingers faintly in eastern Canada.

Kelsey had earlier made several important explorations while still a teenager – he was only seventeen when he first reached Hudson Bay in 1684. He carried letters on foot from York Fort to the post on the Severn to the south-east; the round-trip required a month. He went north in 1689 by company ship to the Churchill – to the site of the modern ocean grain terminal – and was put ashore with an Indian companion to continue north by land. They walked about 240 miles but found no Indians with whom the company could trade. Twice captured by the French in their raids, Kelsey ended his career as governor of all the Bay posts.

William Stuart was another of Kelsey's mettle. He came out to Hudson Bay as an apprentice of thirteen or fourteen in 1691 and died in his early forties, broken by his sufferings on an epic footslogging journey to the vicinity of Great Slave Lake. This thousand-mile, year-long journey, 1715-16, was partly a search for gold or copper and partly to seek a truce between the Crees of the lower territory and the Chipewyans to the north that would allow the pelts to flow more freely to the Bay. Stuart found no Eldorado in the Barren Lands but he did succeed with his peace-making, allowing the company to eventually extend into the Athabasca region.

The Treaty of Utrecht had reaffirmed England's undisputed possession of Hudson Bay – as well as Acadia and Newfoundland in the east – and nearly forty years passed before spirited French competition from the St Lawrence prompted the Hudson's Bay Company to thrust again towards the prairies. During the interlude much new information about the country had been accumu-

The HBC's replica of the Nonsuch, a 36-foot ketch in which Groseilliers crossed the stormy Atlantic in 1668. It returned laden with furs thereby validating the Company's famous charter. Photo courtesy HUDSON'S BAY COMPANY

lated by the regional travels of Bay men like William Coats, Christopher Middleton, Joseph Robson and James Isham. For the new venture in 1754 the choice fell on Anthony Henday, a one-time smuggler from the Isle of Wight who had joined the company in 1750. With a party of Cree, Henday set out to follow Kelsey's old path across the top of Lake Winnipeg, along the Carrot River, then he crossed the South Saskatchewan in the vicinity of today's Saskatoon. He came to the North Saskatchewan near The Elbow and held a direction to the south of that river until he entered the fringe of the foothills country of the Rocky Mountains. He wintered with the Blackfeet somewhere close to the site of the present-day Red Deer.

When Henday returned to York Fort on Hudson Bay on June 20, 1755, he brought back a convoy of seventy canoes come to trade, and the first reports of the great mountain chain that towered against the western horizon. It was a giant step in the exploration of Canada, but it brought little comfort to his employers; Henday also reported that the French were firmly established as far west as the Saskatchewan and that the tribes of the deep hinterland could not be persuaded to make the long and arduous journey to the Hudson's Bay depots still clinging to the western rim of James Bay and Hudson Bay.

The spearhead from the St Lawrence had been thrust beyond the lakes into the middle west by Radisson and Groseilliers, who had made their first journey into that territory as early as 1659. The virtual extermination of the Hurons by the Iroquois forced the French traders to go into the beaver grounds themselves to bring the pelts out. In 1661, the renowned pair of *coureurs de bois* – known to all Canadian school children as Radishes and Gooseberries – were again in the Superior country and, this time, it is suggested they broke trail north to James Bay. Treated shabbily at Quebec, they defected to England and the authorities on the St Lawrence did nothing to exploit their advantage for nearly seventy years.

In the intervening period, the main French exploring initiative was into the kinder lands of the south-west. Passing through Father Allouez's mission at Green Bay, Father Jacques Marquette and Louis Jolliet, son of a Quebec blacksmith, reached the Mississippi in 1673. As it has come down to us, it was one of the great idylls of exploration: their two canoes were swept steadily southwards down the wide stream, past the entry of the muddy Missouri from the west and the Ohio from the east. Brilliantly coloured parrots flitted above them and sturgeon and catfish rose like logs to investigate their passing. Uneasy about entering Spanish territories, they turned back near the border of modern Arkansas. They had gone far enough, Jolliet reckoned, for him to report to Governor Frontenac that the river continued south – it was not the long-sought waterway to California and the Pacific Ocean.

They called it Colbert River, after Louis XIV's influential controller-general; the name Mississippi (at first spelled 'Messipi') was not in European use for some years. On the return journey, the French came up the Illinois and Des Plaines rivers, thus crossing the height of land where Chicago now stands.

The full exploration of the Mississippi, and the extension of the new French empire to the Gulf of Mexico, had to await the arrival of that challenging and controversial figure, René-Robert Cavelier, Sieur de La Salle. Fame can turn on mere rumour or chance remark but historians usually demand a written record – at times, it seems that just about *any* document will do. The Jolliet-Marquette achievement rests almost totally on Father Claude Dablon's later writing in the Jesuit *Relations*. Marquette was, of course, a Jesuit priest, and Jolliet was a graduate of the Jesuit Seminary at Quebec, but neither left us any personal journal or diary of the expedition. On the other hand, La Salle's explorations within the entire central rivers system were either discounted or disbelieved by the scribes of the era, most of them clerics, and his personal character slandered. La Salle was, of course, a bitter opponent of the Jesuits during his entire Canadian career and his patron, Frontenac, was in eternal quarrel with Bishop Laval.

The discovery of the Ohio down to Louisville is claimed for La Salle, probably during 1669-70, although no 'acceptable' documents exist in any archives to prove the matter. Like the Mississippi, the existence of the Ohio was reasonably well known from Indian reports before any white man had actually seen it. Both names mean 'beautiful river' in different Indian languages and, of course, they can be seen as merely two of the many connected waterways that drain the American heartland.

In any event, La Salle had set out from Montreal in the company of the Sulpicians François Dollier de Casson and René de Bréhant de Galinée with the intention of reaching the Ohio through the Iroquois country south of Lake Ontario. They split up in Burlington Bay when Adrien Jolliet, the brother of Louis, happened along and described the route he had taken across Lake Erie on his return from the higher lakes in search of copper mines. At least, so the priests later said (Adrien himself never reached Montreal). The priests turned to the west but travelled that year only as far as today's Port Dover on Lake Erie, and they eventually returned to Montreal via the Ottawa River.

The autocratic La Salle, never unhappy in his own company, either proceeded to try to do exactly what he had set out to do or, from the sceptics' point of view, he 'vanished from the record' until the summer of 1671. To study his whole tempestuous life, until his assassination in the Texas country at age forty-three, is to become convinced that the brilliant, mercurial La Salle was neither procrastinator nor liar.

There is no dispute, of course, that the Sun King granted him the territory about the mouth of the Cataraqui River, where Kingston now stands, and that he had royal permission to explore the territory between New France, Florida and Mexico. He built the *Griffon*, a ship of forty-five tons mounting seven cannon, in the Niagara River above the falls and sailed her with thirty men to Green Bay, arriving in the early fall of 1679. Surmounting troubles that would have broken just about any other man's heart (he gave his first fort, near Peoria, Illinois, the name of *Crèvecoeur*), he was finally able to begin his descent of the Mississippi in February 1682.

A month later, the La Salle party – of twenty-three Frenchmen and eighteen Indians – passed the point reached by Marquette and Jolliet nine years earlier: seven hundred miles of the river still lay before them. On the delta, on April 9, La Salle in costume of scarlet and gold took formal possession of the country, naming it Louisiana. It was the biggest acquisition for France in the New World since Jacques Cartier had planted his cross at the Gaspé 148 years earlier. Today the territory La Salle claimed for Canada numbers thirty-one states of the USA.

It was the Canadian-born La Vérendryes – father and four sons – who staked out the French claims along the rivers of the western plains. Like all their predecessors they were dreaming of finding a route to the Pacific, then thought to bite deeply into the western lands as did Hudson Bay from the north. From 1731 to 1744 when La Vérendrye Senior was Commandant of the Western Posts, the family (with a solid assist from relative Christophe la Jemeraye) built a chain of fur-trading and supply posts from Rainy Lake, to Lake of the Woods, to the junction of the Red and Assiniboine rivers (where Winnipeg stands today). Second son Pierre followed the Saskatchewan to its exit into Cedar Lake and built Fort Bourbon there. Two long journeys were made into Dakota territory, to seek trade among the Mandan Indians. At the site of modern Portage la Prairie, they built Fort la Reine across the route used by the western tribes then trading with the British on Hudson Bay. Daniel Greysolon, the Sieur du Lhut, who had already been to the head-waters of the Mississippi, had begun that interdiction with his pioneering post on Thunder Bay back in 1679.

In 1748, Louis-Joseph, the youngest of the La Vérendryes, was at the forks of the Saskatchewan – the deepest penetration of the prairies since Kelsey's day. When the Hudson's Bay Company responded belatedly, Henday found the French well established at The Pas; they exchanged courtesies but when canoes came down the Saskatchewan bound for the British posts, the French traders seduced the braves with brandy and the bales of beaver stopped right there. The Bay sent William Pink, Joseph Smith and Joseph Waggoner into the territory around Lakes Winnipeg, Manitoba and Winnepegosis, and Mathew Cocking into central Saskatchewan – and knowledge

of the western interior widened dramatically.

The developing struggle between the British and the French for the furs of the hinterland – and then between the Hudson's Bay Company and the independents who combined to form the North West Company – was to swiftly complete the overland penetration of the country. Jacques le Gardeur, Sieur de Saint-Pierre, had succeeded La Vérendrye as Commandant of the Western Posts. A tough-minded Montrealer who was to win fame in the Seven Years' War, he continued to drive a French wedge across the prairies. It was once claimed that his Fort la Jonquière stood on Alberta's Bow River, in the foothills of the Rockies, but a site near Saskatchewan's Prince Albert seems more likely. As the threatening war moved closer, Governor Vaudreuil called his captains back to defend Quebec, and the posts in the west were shuttered, one by one.

The giants of the Nor'West, both the Baymen and the 'pedlars from Montreal,' now took the wilderness stage. The Bay produced explorers like Hearne, Philip Turnor and Peter Fidler; the Nor'Westers great names like Pond, Mackenzie and Fraser. Some others – notably Edward Umfreville, and David Thompson of the Columbia – worked at different times for both of the trading companies. It was first the Englishman Hearne and then the Scot Mackenzie who reached Canada's other oceans by land.

A former 'middie' in the Royal Navy, Samuel Hearne was originally hired by the Bay as a seaman and sent to Fort Prince of Wales, at the mouth of the Churchill River. After two preliminary forays, he crossed the entire Barren Lands to the west and north with a party of Indians, emerging in July 1771 at the mouth of the Coppermine River, on Coronation Gulf, an arm of the Arctic Ocean. His journal, first published in 1795, is one of the world's classic tales of adventure and endurance. The expedition took nineteen months. It was Hearne's achievement, without doubt, but – as was the case with so much of Canadian exploration – he could never have survived or succeeded without the wilderness knowledge of his Indian companions. First among these was the Chipewyan chief Matonabee. The terrain was so forbidding that half a century would pass before the next Europeans – Franklin and George Back – would pass on their expedition overland to survey the Arctic coast.

Peter Pond blazed the trail for the Nor'Westers into the Athabaska Country in 1778 and, a decade later, Alexander Mackenzie joined him there. Once Fort Chipewyan was established, Mackenzie made his first attempt to reach the Pacific – but his 'River of Disappointment,' as he called it, led him north to the Beaufort Sea. His magnificent consolation prize was, of course, the mighty waterway that bears his name today. By 1793 he was ready to try again; this time he jumped off with a party of ten from the forks of the Peace and the Smoky – close to the modern town of Peace River – and paddled up the Peace and the Parsnip, down a stretch of the upper Fraser within a trench of the Rockies, then overland for fifteen days to the dazzling Pacific.

In his famous *Voyages from Montreal through the Continent of North America*, the explorer described his triumph: 'I now mixed up some vermilion in melted grease and inscribed, in large characters, on the South-East face of the rock on which we had slept last night, this brief memorial – 'Alexander Mackenzie, from Canada, by land, the twenty-second of July, one thousand seven hundred and ninety-three.' He then immediately moved camp to a hidden cove three miles away, fearing attack by the natives.

The rains soon erased the laconic message but, in a later day, the words on that rock in Dean Channel, near Bella Coola, were cut deep by chisel to mark forever the first crossing of the continent. There were still some sizable blanks on the map but Canada had been broken to the yoke.

A North West Company fur trader, Alexander Mackenzie was the first explorer to find an overland route to the Pacific as is proudly recorded on this rock in Dean Channel. Photo by HÄLLE FLYGARE

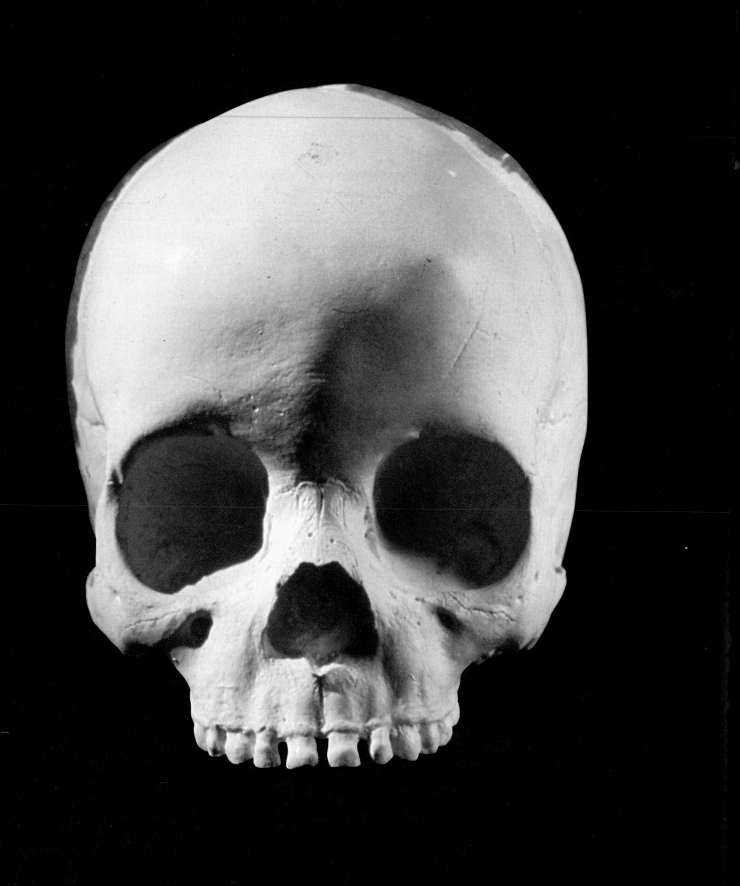

PART II

The entry of man

How the land shaped the people

The lands now called Canada were unchanged when they came into recorded history. The whole continent was a vast arena for the world of nature without man. No race originated here and no remains of man have been found that date further back than about forty thousand years. In Canada, very little is known of man beyond the last Ice Age which ended only about ten thousand years ago. Man is still a newcomer. How, then, did he enter this natural amphitheatre, seemingly isolated between three of the earth's greatest oceans?

On a globe, the Americas may be viewed as either islands, or as a huge peninsula of Asia running crookedly down the curve of the earth towards Antarctica. The Arctic Ocean and its ice and islands form a world of their own which is bounded by the continents of Europe, Asia and America. Men who could live and travel in the Arctic could readily move along the edges of the polar sea from Asia to America, as undoubtedly the Eskimo did.

The skull of a child which was discovered near Taber, Alberta, in 1961, is tentatively dated at 30,000 years or more, and is quite possibly the oldest human fossil in North America. Photo courtesy ROYAL ONTARIO MUSEUM

For people not accustomed to life on the ice, the nearness of America to Asia offered an even more obvious route of entrance. The Bering Strait between Siberia and Alaska is only fifty miles across and one can see the far side from either shore on a clear day. The open-water distance is halved by Big and Little Diomede islands in the strait. This is now believed beyond reasonable doubt to be the way by which the ancestors of the Indians came to the American continent. Two days' paddling in fair summer weather would have made the trip easy enough, in flight from enemies, or in quest of food.

Bering Strait is in many places no deeper than one hundred and fifty feet and, during the Ice Ages when the seas were lower, it is possible man walked from Asia to America, dry-footed. If the sea was down two hundred feet, there would be a land corridor two hundred miles wide. Some may have come by the long string of the Aleutian Islands, or even drifted across the northern Pacific on the warm Japanese currents. Eskimos still live on the facing coasts of both continents and there is nothing in those latitudes to hinder a crossing.

To come from Europe across the northern Atlantic, however, required better shipping than the skin-covered *umiak* of the Innuit. None was available for nine thousand years until the Norse with their sturdy cargo boats proved that Canada could be attained by the seabridge of the islands: from the Faroes to Iceland, to Greenland to Newfoundland.

Even better ships, ships that could sail the ocean by compass, were needed to use another island chain, that of Madeira and the Azores. Not until such ships had been evolved five hundred years ago did British, French, Italian and Portuguese mariners reach the present Maritime provinces.

It is evident that the lands which became Canada were found and settled by the northern routes, and that Canada, open to three oceans, was never capable of isolation from the influences of both Asia and Europe.

Man's history in Canada did not, however, begin in terms of the imposition of his crafts and will on nature. Much indeed of the heart of the story is how European man forced that change upon the first men to live in Canada – the Indians and Eskimos. These Mongoloid peoples lived not so much by defying as by conforming with nature. They were shaped by the land. They were, as Europeans recognized, natural men.

Perhaps the best example of such adaptation of man to the conditions nature imposed on him was that of the traditional Eskimo way of life. The Eskimo probably came later to Canada than the Indian but he was an outstanding example of how man could fit himself to live in and by harsh natural conditions. Certainly, few environments exact more of man than does the Canadian Arctic. Yet the Eskimo succeeded, while still a Stone Age man in knowledge and culture, in living on the rim of the polar world. It is true that his numbers were no more than perhaps twenty thousand at their peak. He survived and developed by using the human intelligence to exploit the narrow, but definite, margin of survival that Arctic conditions afforded.

The Eskimo used the opportunities the world of ice and snow gave to the hunter. Game animals, unless submerged in sea or snow, and even if coloured white, were readily visible to the trained hunter's eye. And the centre line of Eskimo life, the edge of the sea-ice, always afforded seals, walrus, whales, bears. These fed on the abundant marine life of the Arctic and were rich in fat and blubber, as well as the protein to sustain the hunter's muscles.

A wide range was necessary to a people who lived wholly on the results of the hunt. The means of the movement were the *umiak* for open water and the dogsled for ice and snow. The *umiak* carried the women and children, and the few household goods along shore, while the men hunted on land and fished at the river mouths. The sled, built of treasured driftwood, was long and narrow, well adapted to surmount ice-ridges and choppy drift. The dogs were fierce, powerful and impervious to Arctic cold with their long hair, and bushy tails to cover their noses when asleep. In a blizzard, they could lie for days covered deeply by snowdrift, without food.

The influence of the environment can also be discerned in the social patterns of the traditional Eskimo life. In the months' long winter 'night', boredom and the loneliness engendered by the long distance separating the settlements were dissipated by a high level of simple, spirited activity. As soon as the heavy frosts return to make icy highways of every lake inlet and sea strait, the visiting begins. Cached meats from summer hunting are brought in, the pot bubbles, tales are spun, elaborate jokes are perpetrated, the dance-drums throb, and families bundle together on the sleeping platforms. The killing edge of the Arctic wind is against every wanderer and no man who comes in peace is turned away without

food and a physical and mental recharging of human warmth.

Even the sexual mores – the wife-swapping that provided the usual dash of spice in the travellers' tales – were subtly shaped by the need of desperately isolated people to infuse new blood into narrow family circles. And a woman's greatest value was, sad for the romanticists, her ability with her needle – even an unmended tear in a skin parka, could, in a storm, tip the precarious balance of safety.

Restricted and penalized by nature in his physical existence, the Eskimo reacted by creating a free society, much less shackled than that of the European who seeks, however sincerely, to instruct him. There was literally no 'government,' or elected leader – only an outstanding hunter whose advice was generally, but not always, taken. There were no set hours for eating or sleeping and no time compulsion at all. There were no wars – an army was impossible when there was no 'organization' greater than scattered bands related by blood or marriage.

An astonishing skill and ingenuity went into making, from stone, horn, ivory, wood and malleable copper, the Eskimo's hunting weapons and his tools. The harpoon, with its detachable head and its floating bladder, and its throwing stick, was his chief weapon. Used from the kayak, the hunting canoe, it gave the hunter speed, range and power to secure the quick and elusive seal from the water. The fish spear and the bow drill were scarcely less striking examples of the practical use of the materials available and of the principles of leverage and elasticity, uncomprehended in theory but used with consummate skill.

Something more than skill appeared in the carvings of soapstone and other rocks of that desolation of ice and stone. The lamps, with their seal oil and moss wicks, were simple enough. But the ingenuity, patience and vivid eye of the Eskimo went much further in carving simple but potent representations of seal and bear, and strange figures of the evil spirits that plagued his life and had to be frightened or propitiated. His carving knife and his seeing eye had brought the Eskimo over the borders of magic and art.

Until the past century, these wandering families, coalescing in small bands when the food supply permitted, lived scattered over four thousand miles of mingled sea and coast in isolation from one another. They called themselves *Innuit*, 'the people' – they knew no others, except where at the mouths of the Mackenzie and Coppermine rivers, or in southern Labrador, northern Indians came into brief contact. 'Eaters of raw flesh,' the Indians called them; the Norse sagas speak of *Skraelings*, 'earth dwarfs.'

The Eskimo isolated themselves, or were isolated by their Arctic culture, from the other Asian and Stone Age people who had probably reached Canada before them. These were the people – actually a number of peoples of

The Eskimos were a people shaped by the restrictive land. Their clothes, weapons, food and shelter were all products of their immediate environment. Photo by R. HARRINGTON

significant differences – whom popular usage and history called Indians. They were so called by Christopher Columbus, who had sailed from Spain in the confident belief he would reach China by striking westward across the Atlantic. The first people he found on discovering his islands in the Caribbean were obviously not Chinese so he assumed he had reached the Indies, islands off the coast of Asia. Thus he referred to the people as 'Indians' and the mistaken name remained fixed for all the native peoples of the Americas. For themselves as a whole they had no name.

Those scattered through the forests and mountains, and over the prairies of Canada, were aware of themselves as tribes speaking sometimes related, sometimes different dialects – Cree was to become something of a *lingua franca*, an international language. Except for a few hostile contacts with the Eskimos, and a prophecy of god-like white men who would come over the sea from the rising sun – was this some memory of Norse seamen, Irish monks, or Portuguese mariners? – they had no notion of people who were not 'Indian.' They had neither metal, nor the wheel – nor the horse, until the early eighteenth century, for that animal had not survived in North America. They , too, lived in an isolated, self-sufficient world of their own, helped out for some tribes by simple agriculture. For all Canada, it is estimated they numbered at the time of undisputed European discovery (about 1500 A.D.) only 220,000 – all that could be supported by a hunting culture, even in a land with abundant game.

The distribution of Indian tribes over Canada seems to have occurred as a slow trickle from Asia and Alaska fanning out over the country, and from two back-eddies from the south. Perhaps the first in time, and the main stream, was that of the Algonkian peoples which flowed south-eastward by the northern forest to the Great Lakes, and on to the Atlantic coast, as far south as Virginia. In the St Lawrence Valley, possibly not long before the discovery of the river by Cartier in 1535, an eddy from the continental centre pushed a different kind of Indian, the Iroquoian, north-eastward down the St Lawrence to the gulf itself, where Cartier met some of them fishing at Gaspé. A similar eddy of kindred people, the Siouan, pushed north and westward up the Mississippi Valley and on to the prairies of western Canada.

Behind the northern forest stream, other tribes, the Athapascan, followed into the Mackenzie Valley, the northern fringe of the forest, and interior of British Columbia. There they found themselves pressing on the Rocky Mountain tribes which had moved down from Alaska by the coastal waters and the interior valleys. No single name covers these mountain and coastal tribes but, from the Haida of the Queen Charlotte Islands to the Interior and Coast Salish, they shared aspects of a rich and diverse culture.

The matter of first significance in Indian society in Canada was its mobility – the movement of individual parties for war or trade and of the bands from place to place through the seasons. As the land shaped their needs, they had developed the canoe, and in summer could move hundreds of miles by lakes and rivers. For winter, they had invented the toboggan and the snowshoe. The moccasin, the deerskin footwear so apt for use in canoe and on snowshoe, must be mentioned also. And the wigwam, pointed or domed, and covered with birch bark, rush mats, or skins, was easily moved, and easily repaired from the ever-present forest or the unceasing hunt.

It was this mobile, migratory culture of the Indian that lent itself so readily to the development of the fur trade, which in turn was to carry European traders inland until all of Canada had been explored and claimed.

The fullness of the Indians' conformity with nature was revealed, not only by his way of living, but even more by his way of life. He believed that all that moved and grew had its spirit, its *manitou*, and this made him a complete believer in the oneness of life, in all its forms, both material and spiritual. This perhaps explains his extraordinary tenderness to children and his invariable hospitality to strangers. All who lived, wherever they came from in peace, had a claim equal to any to food, shelter and human care.

It was the openness of Indian society that made the survival of the European immigrants, at first so few, possible at all. The smallness of the Indian population made it seem that there was room for all; the Indian used land, he did not have property rights in it. Only the right of bands to the acknowledged hunting grounds at all suggested the kind of claim Europeans were to make to the land.

To the Indian and the Eskimo, therefore, the first Europeans with whom they had steady contact – the fishermen and the fur traders – were welcome and fascinating visitors, who supplied the natives' wants for tools, weapons and clothing better than they could themselves. The white man's desire for beaver and fox fitted perfectly, at first, into the aboriginal way of life, and gave rise to that unique partnership that was the fur trade.

It was also a truth, which some could learn and some could not, that the European who could adapt to and come to terms with the demanding Canadian environment was the man most likely to succeed. He had the best chance, at least, of developing a sense of identity with his chosen land. He could find his place by natural laws. Those who insisted on attempting the transportation of European attitudes and habits, even political and social ideas and relationships, were often destined to collide with the uncompromising rocks of the Shield, or feel thin ice cracking underfoot. In the country of the mind, they still do.

The mobile home of the Plains Indian enabled him to travel lightly. The poles and skins of the tepee would later become the frame and coverings of the travois dragged by dogs or horses. Photo by KRYN TACONIS

PART II

Chapter Three
The kingdom of ice

When an Eskimo child is born in some parts of the Canadian Arctic, the mother ties a raven's claw about the neck as an amulet. She hopes that just as the raven can stay alive on next to nothing, so in adversity will her child survive in the world's harshest land where the margin between life and death can still be perilously narrow. At the beginning of written history, the dependence on what could be won from the icy sea and the frozen land was total.

No man ever lived more in harmony with his environment, more responsive to its demands, more submissive to its authority. When the ice-sheet drew reluctantly back into the high Arctic – where it merely waits with an awful patience to descend again – the Eskimo came into the Canadian North and, as the millennia slipped by uncounted, he developed superlative skills as a hunter and a provider. Where the seal took the fish, and the bear the seal, he mastered and ate the bear and kept its pelt for a robe. More than that, he came to an intuitive philosphical contentment, a oneness with his land in which death, his own or any other, was but an incident, a return to the place from whence one came; he also rose to an untaught creative expression, in sculpted soapstone and subtle folktale, that, considering his small numbers, ranks him among the world's artistic peoples.

Summon your imagination, stand behind a pressure ridge of ice on the sea near Bylot Island – now watch an Eskimo hunter take a sleeping ringed seal across a flat and open expanse, without benefit of stalking screen or modern rifle. Carrying only his harpoon with its walrus-ivory point and barb, its sealskin rope, the hunter creeps forward, using every ice hummock as cover. About a thousand feet from the animal, he slips to the ground and begins to edge onwards. The seal sleeps in short naps, a few seconds only, then lifts its head, on the *qui vive* for any enemy. A rhythmic schedule develops of slumber and alertness, and the hunter adapts his progress to this, anticipating the seal's movements to the split-second.

When the seal first spots him, a new object on the flat ice, it rises on its flippers to take a good look. The hunter is ready: arms pressed to his sides, knees together and feet raised, his head lifted, he imitates the action of a seal, adding even the barking cough. When the quarry accepts his outline and drops back to nap beside the open lead in the ice, the hunter scrambles forward a few yards. The charade is repeated endlessly, until the hunter is a mere ten paces away. A swift rush with upraised harpoon and the seal is speared. One smashing blow with the balled fist crushes its skull. The carcass is opened and the liver eaten, hot and raw.

The Eskimo hunter is still so much the master of his domain that a prolonged absence during a snowstorm is no cause for anxiety. In fact, it is bad form to raise even the possibility that he might not be able to overcome any difficulty the most violent blizzard brings. Stories of suffering that would get headlines in southern newspapers are regarded as amusing entertainment.

The environment that seemed so implacable to the first explorers and the traders, which still chills even the imagination of the average city-dweller (in Canada, as elsewhere), provided the Eskimo with weapons, shelter, transport, heat, light and superb clothing.

For three hundred years the igloo has been the very trademark of the Arctic. Yet it is not, as some may still imagine, the permanent home of the Innuit. Away from the European settlements, the Eskimo lives in a stone-and-sod hut in winter and a skin tent in the short summer. The igloo, a domed house about twelve feet in diameter and nine feet high, built from blocks of frozen snow in about an hour, was usually meant to serve only as overnight or temporary accommodation while on the trek.

In the rigidly apportioned work of the Eskimo family, this was a man's job. He cut out the wedge-shaped blocks with his snow knife, a heavy-bladed affair like a machete, about eighteen inches long. Fifteen large blocks made up the circular base and, as the sloping walls rose, the blocks were cut smaller. The builder placed them in position from inside the ring, using five blocks to complete the final layer. The remaining hole in the dome was filled neatly with a keystone block, bored to provide an escape hole for stale air and excess heat. The hole is called the *qinqag*, 'the nose.' It was stuffed with a handful of dried grass that could be moved about as a regulator. Without the 'nose' the igloo would drip melt-water from the combined heat of the seal-oil lamp and the closely packed bodies. If not enough fresh air was entering, the lamp would flicker to warn of the shortage of oxygen.

When the whole family was on the move, the Eskimo wife and the children mortared the chinks between the blocks with snow as the dome was rising. The father cut a low arched entrance and the mother entered to set up bedding and to get water boiling for fish or meat, and for the black tea without which no Eskimo is happy. A crawl tunnel was swiftly added beyond the entrance to keep the cutting wind from the doorway; it might include some side chambers to provide storage for items that could not be left on the sled with the dogs. Soon the wall surface inside glazed into ice and was so snug that heavy clothing could be shed.

In a well-made igloo the Eskimo could laugh at the worst blizzard. If he wanted the structure to stand for some time, he built a fire until the walls inside were running with melt-water which was soaked up by the blocks of porous snow. Then he snuffed the fire and opened the entrance wide to admit the freezing wind. In minutes, the entire five-inch-thick walls turned to solid ice and the whole house was welded to the ice-floor below.

The igloo could only be built where the snow had drifted deep and hard enough to provide the blocks – and there is much less snow above the Arctic Circle than below it. The precipitation in the far north is of desert dimensions – 5 inches annually, for example, in the Parry Islands and only 1.6 inches on Ellesmere. A general figure for the entire Canadian Arctic zone – above the tree line – would be about 10 inches; by comparison, the Pacific coast region gets 100 inches, and the Atlantic provinces up to 50 inches.

The animals of the Arctic, before the advent of the trading post, provided the entire Eskimo wardrobe, and the craft skill is not yet entirely lost. Without a single item from European technology, the patient cheerful women could design, prepare and produce garments of fur and skin ideally suited to the conditions. The hide of *tuktu*, the caribou, surprisingly light, provided the usual outer garments: two parkas, one worn inside with the trimmed hair towards the body, the other with the long winter coat outside, and knee-length trousers. The parka hood was often trimmed with luxurious white fox or ermine. Some bands wore shirts of birdskins, feathers to the inside. Two pairs of long skin stockings were pulled above the knee and sometimes topped with a foxtail tie. Inner stockings were made from hare fur.

Women's stockings rose to the upper thigh, fringed on the top with the mane of a male bear; they wore briefs of soft foxskin. Mitts and boots were of sealskin, the latter with extra soles of bear skin for use on rough ice.

Three sealskins were needed for a pair of men's trousers. The skins were first scraped to remove all particles of fat, then washed thoroughly and staked out to dry in the early summer. They were finely sewn with a bone needle, the fibula of a bird, using narwhal sinew as thread. Sealskin has been mostly superseded now by store textiles; wet sealskin hardens on drying and has to be softened by either chewing or scraping before it can be reshaped for wear. Where bears were plentiful, their skins provided handsome trousers – as many as three pairs from a single animal. Some lucky children whose mothers could afford the time were dressed in pretty outfits of ground-squirrel fur, with duck and loon feathers used for decoration.

The cardinal need in the Arctic is to stay dry. Dried grasses are still used between stockings and boots and inside mitts to absorb moisture condensing from feet and hands. Skin clothing is worn loosely on the body to allow some air to circulate underneath; if belted tightly, the body's perspiration would work through the skin clothing and the freezing temperature would turn the garments into armour. All snow is beaten from Arctic clothing before it is brought inside – there is a special utensil for this, the *tilugtut*.

The Eskimo hunter invented the skin-covered kayak, the most manoeuvrable boat ever made, for his pursuit of the seal and walrus in open water, and the sled with its runners of whalebone, the *komatik*, for overland haulage behind his 'huskies.' There is really no such breed as the 'Eskimo husky' – the dogs of the high north are mongrels of the most complicated lineage, and, to quote an expert, are 'of every conceivable size and appearance.' But they are all bred to one impulse – to pull, and to pull till they drop. The sled was held together with sealskin thongs – the nails of the Iron Age would not allow the sled flexibility to 'work' as it ran through soft snow and rough ice, at times hurtling downhill dragging its dogs and planing over steep unsuspected drops. The Eskimo rises grinning from any such mishap, and presses on with the never-ending hunt.

These black-haired, broad-faced people came into Canada from the coasts of Siberia and spread from Alaska, into the Mackenzie Delta, over the Coppermine to Boothia Peninsula and onto the Keewatin coast of Hudson Bay. The migration swarms, sparked by unknown famines or quarrels, branched up over the ice into the islands we know as Victoria, Prince of Wales, Somerset and Baffin. In times lost to us they went on into Greenland, and down into Ungava and Labrador. They brought with them an unwritten language, totally unlike any other, yet so rich it supplies, for instance, a hundred expressions for ice.

As the Wisconsin glacier receded, baring the scraped earth we know, the migrants moved generally east and south. There appear to have been several waves over a long period. They may have met and mingled with another Stone Age race, either originating in the West or strongly marked with European characteristics. These may have been the *Skraelings* of the Viking sagas, the primitive warriors who effectively prevented Norse settlements from taking root on Canadian soil, and who may eventually have conquered and absorbed the colony founded on Greenland by Erik the Red – its total disappearance is regarded as an historical mystery. This intriguing proposition is squashed, it seems, by the main body of Arctic archaeologists who insist that Thule culture, broadly representing the surviving Eskimo peoples, emerged following population drift from the Alaska-Bering Strait area.

The debate has flared and fizzled in academic halls for generations. Fuel was added by the discovery in 1908 by Vilhjalmur Stefansson of the fair-haired, blue-eyed Eskimos of Dolphin and Union Strait, below Victoria Island leading to the Beaufort Sea. Many European travellers in the Canadian Arctic have commented on an apparent racial mixture. Sir Martin Frobisher, in 1577, reported a white-skinned Eskimo, and nearly four hundred years later, Douglas Wilkinson, an experienced Canadian writer and photographer, described his first Eskimo this way: ' ... He resembled a tall tanned Scot; thin ascetic features, blue eyes, strong mouth, small black moustache. He might have been the trader or the policeman but for his dress, his deep colour, and his jetblack hair, cut bowl fashion.'

The Eskimo took for his own the lands that no other man coveted – although they have now been officially Canadian for nearly a century. Where he hunts, the cold of the sea can kill in five minutes, or less, and the cold of the wind can freeze the very cornea of the eyes. Death can be swift punishment for any deviation from the established tolerances: when the auk known as the murre cannot find open water he must eventually come down on the land, from which he cannot again become airborne. The ubiquitous raven arrives and merely waits until the murre's feet freeze to the ground and his struggles weaken before beginning to devour him. Only the profits from sleek furs, and more recently the lure of underground oil and minerals – and the requirements of continental defence – pull Europeans into these latitudes, and the *kabloona* usually stays only the minimum time required by his service contract. It is noteworthy that the handful of white men who do make a permanent life in the Arctic – some missionaries, traders and, yes, misanthropes – tend to quickly adopt much of the Eskimo way of life.

The coldest spot in Canada is not in the high Arctic – it seldom drops under 30° below

Fahrenheit at the North Pole, while Snag, in south-west Yukon, holds the Canadian record at 81° below. But the wind across the polar sea ice and the flat northern plains is strong and almost constant, and it can throw snow crystals as sharp as splintered glass into your face. The long winter darkness can be infinitely oppressing, and the summer achingly short. Generally speaking, in the areas that are inhabited – Canada has currently about 17,500 Eskimos – there are only fifty days without frost in the year, and the mean July temperatures are less than 50° F.

When the long halcyon days of summer do come to the Arctic – when the low sun stays in the sky through the twenty-four-hour 'days' – birds in the billions are hatched and fed by their wheeling, screaming parents. The huge colonies are drawn to the Arctic by the explosive development of certain algae upon the return of sunlight, providing inexhaustible food for the birds, fish and sea mammals such as whale, seal and walrus. The activity at the rookeries is ceaseless and the noise resembles that of a major waterfall. Murres have been known to fly thirty miles to bring shellfish for their young. The kittiwakes and terns fly swallowed fish into the nests, sometimes being forced to regurgitate in midair by the piractical jaegers. Snowy owls are gorging on those strange Arctic mice, the lemmings. The ptarmigan chicks try to fly from harm at ten days old but are caught by the thousands, to be eaten bones and all.

The sea-trout we know as Arctic char, fat from feeding in the bays, now crowd the rivers as they run up into the fresh-water lakes to breed, and they are taken in traps, by nets, by the spear – and they can even be caught by hand as they rest while trying to run against the rapids. The young loons are launched from their lakeside nests on the tundra, eiderdown is gathered, and, as the ice begins to work out of the fiords and bays, and the glaciers calve icebergs into the upper waters of Baffin Bay, endless streams of ducks and geese wing overhead. While the drakes and the immature birds moult they are easy victims to the Eskimo food gatherer.

Summer is the time of the kayak. In this marvellous one-man canoe the Eskimo hunter pursued the walrus, basking on floes of old ice, some thirty or forty of them crowded on the one chunk, their combined weight pressing it below the surface. An entire band would move to the summer campsites, pitching their tents on a gravel beach well-drained against the ever-increasing water run-off as the heat of the sun intensified. Streams of melt-water can flow so deeply and strongly on the ice that sleds have to be converted into rafts. The hunt continued as long as the hunters could stay awake, as food for dog and man had to be cached for winter use under the rocks and in the coastal caves left high up the cliff-faces in a land still rebounding from the tremendous weight of the ice-sheet.

The walrus can run to two thousand pounds. He has fed mostly on clams and other molluscs scraped from the ocean floor with his tusks at depths of up to 250 feet, staying under as long as ten minutes at a time. Before modern firearms were available the hunter faced by a roaring walrus had to thrust his harpoon into the beast's heavy upper lip – a blow on the thick skull was useless. When opened, the walrus provides a ready-cooked meal – the shelled clams in his middle stomach are partly digested and, according to Arctic gourmets, taste as though they have been sluiced in a sharp and tasty dressing. Conservation laws attempt today to prevent the slaughtering of walrus for their tusks, which are carved for the tourist souvenir market.

As August wanes, the musk ox in the archipelago and the caribou on the Barren Lands are fat, and innumerable hares leap about. The fox is not yet dressed in his fine white coat but his stomach is bulging with eggs, young birds and lemmings. Before the entry of woven cloth, the numbers of caribou determined how warm the Eskimo would be – it takes eight caribou skins to make a full winter costume for one man. The skins can provide bed and sled robes, tent coverings, as well as clothing. The skins are often holed by the larvae of the warble fly parasite which lives under the caribou hide; as he skinned the beast, the Eskimo hunter of earlier times would crack the insect's shell with his teeth and suck the body juices. But the great caribou herds that once took ten days to pass a given point are dwindling – perhaps only two hundred thousand survive in the Canadian North today.

The walrus weighing up to 2000 pounds, feeds on Arctic marine life, and is rich in fat and blubber, as well as protein needed to sustain the Arctic hunter's muscles.
Photo by LEONARD LEE RUE III

The frost returns to the Arctic. The biting insects vanish. The birds that short days ago filled the sky are gone – some will fly thirteen thousand miles to the other end of the earth. Away from the trading posts, the meat of the whistling white whale and the sworded narwhal has been dried on the rocks and stored as 'pemmican' for winter treks around the traplines. The thin ice forms on the sea, cementing the floes, then breaks to the tides and winds, thickens, then holds. All the mountains of the eastern islands will stay white now, the quickening winds whipping plumes of snow from the peaks.

Late in October, or early November – it depends on how far north he lives – the Eskimo watches the sun hang closer and yet closer to the horizon; then one day it does not rise at all, although for a while its rays can be seen against the upper flanks of any mountains within view. It will now be dark over much of the Arctic world until early February, although the aurora, the fascinating 'northern lights,' will arch and flicker across the heavens and, when the sky is clear, moon and stars will shine and refraction will bring some light from the south – the Arctic night is very seldom jet black.

With the sea now frozen over, the seals must come to the breathing holes. There the Eskimo hunter would stay, sometimes on a three-legged stool, his harpoon raised for the kill. Without the seal, the isolated Eskimo of the Canadian eastern Arctic could not maintain any independent existence. The man making the kill keeps the skin but the meat and the blubber are shared amongst all. Many seals will come to the same hole and it is not unusual for a hunter to take twenty or more on a good day. But, at other times, he will wait, near paralyzed by cold, for nothing. Only the nose of the seal comes out for air at the blowhole and the hunter must enlarge the gap to drag the animal out; when the bear makes a kill at the blowhole, he digs in one mighty claw and pulls his prey out by sheer strength, breaking all its ribs in the process. If a hunter secures a seal and cannot take it home immediately he will stand it upright, packing wet snow around the hind flippers. It freezes there – a signpost for the returning hunter.

Although the Eskimo prefers his meat boiled, on the hunt he will take it raw – sometimes eating directly from the steaming carcass of seal or caribou. A small knob of fat is eaten with a mouthful of meat. The heart and liver are still tidbits. The contents of the caribou's stomach – half-digested lichens – was often the only vegetable consumed (it has been likened to haggis). A sealskin full of birds caught in summer and frozen provided a change of diet: the feathers were rubbed off with the fingers and the birds eaten entirely. Frozen meat is thawed only to the point where it is crunchy. There is no waste – the dogs bolt anything that is thrown to them (except the liver of the polar bear, over-rich in vitamins), and the raven eats the droppings of the dog.

In the depth of the Arctic winter, only the walrus and the seals, ringed and bearded, remain in the far north as practically the only live source of food – and the walrus hide can freeze so hard that it will turn a harpoon. They tend to gather where the ice is thin, where cracks or open leads are caused by tides or currents, sometimes many miles from the land. Some narwhals and white whales, the *beluga*, may winter in the polar seas but they are usually far out to sea where the pack ice is more open. Where the sea ice is deeply covered with snow, the seals will hollow out dens near their blowholes – here the pups will be born. The hungry bear, the ever-roving king of the ice, scents out the den and will dig through to the sleeping seal before it wakes to slither to safety. Of the sea birds, only the incredibly hardy black guillemot always remains in the high Arctic.

The fox is trapped across the Arctic at this period, although the value of the prime pelt has plummeted since the mid-1950s when it was still bringing about $13. In the 1920s the natural silver fox could bring $500 a skin. The white fox thrives predominantly in areas where the lemming is plentiful, while his 'blue' cousin feeds around the tidal areas and particularly on birds he has cached in the summer – but the colour variation may be solely a matter of natural camouflage since the white fox is found almost exclusively in areas of heavy snowfall. The 'blue' is very rare in Canada, but the 'whites' have litters of up to twenty. When the wolf or wolverine pulls down a caribou, the fox is usually somewhere around to share in the feast.

The relentless, intelligent wolverine is the most-hated animal of the North; he can find and force open any cache and will note the tracks of a hunter at his trapline and simply check the traps himself when he is hungry. Some men have lost more than a hundred fox to a wolverine in a single season.

The impact of Europe on the Eskimo way of life, beginning with the first expeditions in the sixteenth century seeking the North-West Passage, is counted by most to be disastrous. Frobisher kidnapped a man, woman and child and fired on others – after five of his men had vanished during a foray ashore. But the Eskimo has traditionally welcomed the European, eagerly accepting the very real benefits of sophisticated technology – though the price has been high. Much of what is written in this chapter inevitably refers to an Eskimo ethos that is past, or fast fading. The rifle, the store-bought clothing, the canned foods, the outboard motor, the primus stove – each was a boon to people never far from the brink of starvation, but each moved the Eskimo a long step further away from his natural life.

Most of the seventeen thousand Innuit who now live in the Canadian Arctic have become dependent on the Hudson's Bay Company store, on family allowance cheques and welfare payments. Yet they cannot, in this current century at least, become assimilated into the European societies and, what is more, they do not want to. When the boy is taken from the hut and sent south to be educated he is often a misfit, a stranger, when he returns; he is not attracted to the unsociable competitive life of his white-skinned Canadian fellow-citizens yet is disturbed in his natural role of preparing to take his father's place.

But there is another side to the story. Peter Freuchen, a Danish explorer and trader who married an Eskimo and spent three-quarters of a century in the Arctic, wrote in his *Book of the Eskimos*: 'It has been maintained over and over again that the native man was far better and happier before he met the white man with his inventions and tools ... I know from personal experience that this picture is entirely wrong...Their existence was hazardous and insecure before the arrival of the white man. Any unexpected event, the least change in their routine, might lead to disaster.' The Eskimo has shown a marked mechanical ability in the maintenance of the simpler engines; he has been known to carve a replacement part from walrus ivory to keep an outboard motor running.

Freuchen recalled, in his youth, meeting Eskimos still using stone knives; it took them days to flense and cut up a single walrus. Others were stalking caribou on the snow-covered tundra with bow and arrow. While on Ellesmere Island, he had joined in the laborious making of fire from 'rubbing two sticks together.' He had come upon villages where the inhabitants had died of starvation, their last act being to kill and eat their dogs. He told of one woman who had personally described to him how she had been forced by circumstances to eat her husband and her three children.

The Hudson's Bay Company, with its chain of trading posts across the Canadian Arctic zone, was highly praised by the bluntly spoken Dane. In 1960 he wrote it 'has meant salvation for a great many villages, perhaps for the greater part of the population in the northernmost part of the world ... ' While an accurate census is still difficult in the Arctic, there is no doubt the Eskimo population – like the Indian – is on the increase in Canada.

Perhaps one other word. 'I am glad I do not have to live as my father and my grandfather did' – the Baffin Island hunter Idlouk is talking to author Doug Wilkinson. 'Today we might go hungry but we know that we can always get food from the white man to help us over the bad times, where before we would have starved to death.' Wilkinson has made many journeys into the eastern Arctic in the past quarter-century, once living strictly as a member of an Eskimo family for more than a year. In his book, *Land of the Long Day*, he adds: 'I have often heard the opinion expressed that the solution to the problems of the Eskimo was to remove all white men from the area and get the Eskimo back to his old way of life. I do not hold with this view, and I have yet to meet the Eskimo who does.'

Chapter four
The realm of the river

The engrossing saga of the fifty Indian tribes of Canada across the many thousands of their years is too often dominated by the few decades of violence arising from the French attacks upon the Iroquois. The total picture has been distorted by this, and by the endless speculation on whether the alliance between the *Ancien régime* and the Algonquins and Hurons against the Confederacy of the Five Nations prevented the French from assuming control of the entire continent. This is a pipedream – but strictly a white man's pipedream.

The Indian had no written language of his own – no native Chaucer or Shakespeare could arise, no Racine or Voltaire. The accounts of his way of life, his aspirations and dreams, religions and folklore, are those written by Europeans who, however sympathetic, inevitably applied European cultural and philosophical standards and instinctive reactions to the strange, and often unsettling, life of *les sauvages*. It is only in recent times – and not everywhere yet – that white Canadian academics and administrators are beginning to properly weigh the critical differences created by the Indians' Asian heritage.

No pitched battle was ever fought in the 'War of the St Lawrence' and, although sizable forces for the times marched to crush the Mohawk and the Seneca – Louis XIV ordered the Marquis de Tracy to 'exterminate them' – the main sufferers were undoubtedly the Hurons of southern Ontario and the hapless *habitants* of Lachine and other outposts. There was almost continuous hostility between the major tribal or langage groups (and sometimes within them) but before the introduction of European tensions and firearms, the clashes were often more noisy than bloody, tests of manhood with actual casualty rates that at times did not reach double figures.

In almost all entries in the darker record of violence, the Indian was present as an ally, or a pawn, of the opposing European powers. The Hurons campaigning with Champlain in 1615, the warriors with Montcalm at Lake George, Pontiac and his uneasy alliance, the Iroquois with the Butlers during the U.S. War of Independence, Tecumseh defending Upper Canada against the Americans – all were thrust into warfare not really of Indian making. In one of the very few direct encounters between European and Indian on our soil – at Cut Knife Creek in 1885 – it was the whites who retreated.

Important as the Iroquois certainly were, doubly armed in their knowledge of simple agriculture and in their fierce warrior spirit, they never numbered more than 15,000 in the total Canadian Indian population of about 220,000 – and despite their vaunted organization, seldom did all the tribes of the Confederacy act together. Vital as they were in the first century of the struggle for furs, the Iroquois should not overshadow in the national story, for instance, the 50,000 members of the tribes on the Pacific coast. These were the richest, most accomplished, most 'civilized' native peoples in all of what is now Canada and the United States; the fact that they are less well known to most Canadians is, again, a result of the European chronicling – the documented history began with Cartier on the St Lawrence.

As the ancestors of all the native peoples of the Americas spread during a period of fifteen thousand years from the Alaskan gateway to the Atlantic shores, and on to the very tip of Tierra del Fuego, thirteen thousand miles to the southwards, they took up unoccupied lands bounded by natural frontiers of wide river or high mountain, forest edge or sea coast. No doubt, later and stronger arrivals sometimes usurped territories already staked, and depleted hunting grounds or population 'explosions' forced one tribal group into seizure of adjoining ranges – this flux was still in progress at the time of the arrival of the first Europeans.

When the tribes, or more truly, clan groups of related peoples, became settled in their highly varied areas, as they began to adopt something of the form of nations, their cultures started to take

A Stoney Indian of 1890 with horse, and travois. His tribe, once numbering 10,000, depended on the buffalo for all its basic needs. Photo courtesy GLENBOW-ALBERTA INSTITUTE

differing shape and style, complex depths and subtleties. Nearly always, these patterns of life and spiritual systems were related to the chosen environment – the land shaping the people in the classic Canadian manner – and, more dimly, responsive to hereditary folk-memory of a Siberian or Chinese past.

While the millennia slipped by, the centuries which saw in Europe the Sumerians, Egyptians, Carthaginians, Greeks and Romans flower and fade, the Indian nations developed societies, languages and even physical looks as different one from the other as were those of Italians, Scots and Poles. Those who came later in the migration waves brought new influences with them. Nowhere did Canada offer the lotus life but where good soils, good hunting or good fishing provided a safe margin of survival, and therefore some leisure, distinctive patterns arose in art and artifact, in social custom and spirituality. This then was the first Canadian culture.

The inexhaustible harvest of the sea supported the fascinating peoples of the Pacific coast. These six nations came later into the knowledge of the European but they had found their way down through the mountain passes and ocean channels in the earliest times after the retreat of the glaciers. The roaring rivers like the Stikine, Skeena, the Bella Coola and the Fraser raced melt-water through gorges in the Coast Range and offered routes to the fruitful edge of the sea. The Coast Salish ('Salish' means, simply, 'People') inhabited the territory on both sides of the Gulf of Georgia, including the site of modern Vancouver. They were flanked to the west, on Vancouver Island, by the Nootka, and to the north by the Kwakiutl. Beyond were the almost landlocked Bella Coolas – the mercurial tribe discovered by Alexander Mackenzie when he reached salt water from the east on Cascade Inlet in 1793. The Tsimshian nation lay to the north again, across the valleys of the Nass and Skeena. The tattooed Haida (another term for 'People') held the beautiful but bracing Queen Charlotte Islands. A seventh nation, the Tlinkit, now lives almost entirely in Alaska, although a few merge with the interior Kutchin, in the southern valleys of the Yukon.

The way of life of the Coast tribes was the strongest and most distinctive of all Canadian Indians. They were, in the first place, rich by primitive standards. The unfailing salmon rivers, the abundant marine life from whale to clams, ensured their food supply. They smoked and dried fish for the winter and pressed edible seaweeds and berries into food that could be stored for long periods. For furs they could draw on both sea and land, and in the prolific cedar they had a strong yet workable material that supplied planks for houses, trunks for dugout canoes, poles for carving, the last a craft which, when steel tools were acquired, was perfected into the compelling art of the totem pole.

These people, secure in their great square houses with the carved fronts, free to range the coastal waters, rich in furs taken from the sea or traded from the inland for the oil of oolakan fish, had means for leisure and consumption such as no other Indians of the continent had. Hence the lavishness of their culture in economic display, in the arts of carving and of weaving, in myth and in ritual, in fraternal societies and in elaboration of the religious notions of all Indians. They even invented a form of badminton and the spinning top.

The most striking features of this remarkable society were its class system from nobles to slaves, the ceremony known to Europeans as the potlatch, and the carvings – both of dance masks and of totem poles. The latter are well known and, like the war-bonnets of the Plains tribes, have been misunderstood. Both really are records: the pole a clan history; the war-bonnet, a warrior's achievements. Perhaps one-third of the people in some tribes were slaves, to be prostituted, sold or killed without thought; then came a 'middle class' of commoners, and a thin crust of nobility. Slaves were seized in the coastal raids, made possible by the dugout canoes up to sixty feet long that were the particular pride of the Haida and Nootka.

The potlatch seems strange indeed, until we see that it is only a version of the lavish expenditure to advertise and display status that occurs in all human societies – not least in our own. The potlatch was at bottom a feast on some ceremonial occasion, the commonest being the marriage of a daughter. The feast had to be of such abundance and variety as would honour both the status

Totem poles of Pacific Coast Indians portray, in their own language, family legends for a people who never developed a writing script. Photo by PETER VARLEY

of the host and of the guests. It might have, but not necessarily, the strange mask dances of the culture. But it was accompanied by gifts, again such as would do honour both to him who gave and to them who received. The lavishness of the potlatch in all its aspects was not, however, limited by the immediate means of the giver of the potlatch. For such a purpose he could properly borrow. Indeed, the quality of the potlatch came to be conditioned by the extent of the borrowing which went into it. And the debts became debts of honour, hereditary in families descending from generation to generation. The potlatch thus became a competition in indebtedness, and social status was measured by the extent and age of hereditary debt.

The carving of mask and house pole, of horn spoons and ornaments, was a unique art in this land, the equal of anything from Aztec Mexico or Incan Peru. No native nation in Canada before the white man came had metal tools – there was some soft natural copper but smelting was unknown – and the cutting tools were adzes of stone and chisels of jade (from the gravels of the Fraser, near Lytton); sharkskin was used as sandpaper. Charcoal, ochre and clays provided colours for painting and decoration.

The Coast peoples did not weaken under leisure, as many highly civilized Caucasian societies have done. They hunted the porpoise, the sea otter, the deer, elk, bear and moose. In eight-man teams they pursued the whale out of sight of land, harpooning animals three times the size of their hunting canoes, inventing flotation bladders and other technological aids to get the prize back to the beach. While bringing in the dead whale, they lashed his lips together to prevent the carcass from shipping tons of water. If a whale split a cedar dugout with his threshing tail, the Indians had a practised technique by which they trod water while a specialist lashed the craft together again and temporarily caulked the split; then they reembarked and proceeded to tow the kill ashore. The waiting villagers drummed a welcome on the roofs of the houses with sticks.

When Captain James Cook, with his ships *Resolution* and *Discovery*, spent a month in Nootka Sound in 1778 he was fascinated by this staccato welcome, and his journal describes his Indian hosts sympathetically and minutely. He found them 'a docile, courteous, good-natured people.'

The advanced Coastal nations maintained a trading liaison with the tribes of the British Columbian interior plateau – the Kootenay, Chilcotin, Carrier, Tsetaut and Tahltan – and with some of the more westerly of the peoples inhabiting the difficult terrains of the Mackenzie Valley and beyond, including the Kutchin, Nahani, Hare, Dogrib, Beaver and Chipewyan.

The tribes in the great trough that lies between the Coast Range and the Rockies all shared a similar existence but came from three different language-groups. The Kootenays had once lived on the prairie foothills but had been chased into the mountains by the aggressive Blackfoot; until the bison were shot from the plains in the late nineteenth century, the Kootenays still made annual forays to get meat and skins. The Interior Salish traded berries, twine, goat wool and tanned hides with their cousins on the coast around Burrard Inlet and the lower Fraser.

The nine tribes in the North-West Territories, between Alaska and Hudson Bay, were all members of the Athapascan language group and considered by anthropologists to have been the last major migrant group to enter. Here the tundra was at its most forbidding but it could still offer a homeland to men who adapted to its harsh demands. They wintered in the spruce forests and emerged on to the Barrens to hunt. It was often said that an Athapascan of the Mackenzie could go alone into the forest in October with only a bone knife and walk out the following spring both well clothed and well fed. These people were probably still moving south when Europeans found them, and some groups – the Apache and Navaho are examples – penetrated far into the present United States.

When early travellers' tales included stories of 'men with tails,' creatures half-animal, half-man, in the Canadian North, they were echoing reports of the Chipewyans, the most populous of the Athapascans. Their name means 'Pointed Skins' and described their caribou-skin tunics which flaunted a dangling tail behind, and sometimes in front as well. To safeguard their hunting ground they fought with their neighbours, the Cree to the south, and with the Eskimo to the north.

44

They feared the Eskimo as sorcerers, and killed them whenever possible. Samuel Hearne, on his overland journey from Hudson Bay to the mouth of the Coppermine River on Coronation Gulf in 1771, witnessed such a massacre at Bloody Falls when his guide, the Chipewyan chief Matonabee, led his party of war-painted braves in an attack on a small Eskimo camp. The Eskimos were caught asleep and ran naked out of their huts where the Indians speared them like fish. One girl of about eighteen transfixed by a spear, grabbed Hearne's legs and as he pleaded for her life, the Chipewyans 'paid not the smallest regard to the shrieks and agony of the poor wretch who was still twining around their spears like an eel.'

The Chipewyans and the Crees were major suppliers, and middlemen, to the Hudson's Bay Company after it became established in the late seventeenth century. The milder-mannered people on their western borders were called in Cree, *Awokanak*, 'Slaves,' and the English translation has stuck to both tribe and to the huge lake of the territory. The Hare Indians, so timid they hid from any strangers, were as elusive as the animals they snared for food and clothing. The Athapascan lands made up about one-quarter of the total land area of Canada and, at its peak, the population was never much above one person to every 200 square miles – perhaps the world's lowest. It is much the same today.

Some of the Beaver and Sekani, the most southerly of the Athapascans in Canada, had obtained horses by trading with the Sarcee or other tribes of the upper plains. Eight nations speaking four languages held the Canadian plains – the Assiniboine, Blackfoot, Blood, Cree, Gros Ventre, Piegan, Sarcee and Sioux – and they once numbered about 35,000. The Algonkian Gros Ventres ('Big Bellies') moved south into the United States in the late eighteenth century. It was the *Siksika*, the 'Blackfeet,' who were to become in the world's eye the epitome of that mythical creature, the tall, slim hawkish 'Red Indian' of the Wild West. On their home range encompassing the sites of modern Edmonton and Calgary, they sprang into power and prominence when the horse finally reached the prairies sometime before 1750.

In earlier times the Plainsmen had to hunt the bison on foot, stalking him under a camouflage of skins or surrounding an isolated bunch with a ring of hunters, moving inexorably inwards. When the horse filtered up the middle of America from escaped or stolen Spanish stock in Mexico, the Canadian prairie was waiting, a pasture without equal in the world. Soon a band of five hundred Indians might have two thousand mounts. Now each buffalo hunt was no longer strictly a matter of survival; the speedy sure-footed ponies would run down the heavy beasts, herd them swiftly into killing pounds or, at times, stampede them over cliffs. The mounted hunter could cover up to sixty miles in a day, yet, until the repeating rifle appeared, the vast herds – sometimes twenty-five miles long and two or three miles wide – showed no sign of diminishing. It has been calculated that the tolerable depletion of the herds by the Indians – say 10 per cent per year – would give fifteen pounds of meat and fat per day to every man, woman and child.

This plenty with its accompanying leisure gave rise to another remarkable Canadian culture. The riders of the wide plains assumed the dashing manner of the Mongol horsemen who were, quite possibly, among their Asian ancestors. Their mastery of the horse astounded the first Europeans to visit them, and they turned the talent to war. As frontier cavalry, they were superb, one hundred mounted men changing direction as one to an almost imperceptible hand signal. They could discharge first an arrow, and later a bullet, a full gallop, with the greater part of their bodies shielded by their own mounts. A racing brave could pick up a feather by hand from the ground.

Military societies grew up within the Plains tribes, demanding strict and elaborate initiations – it was the beginnings of an aristocracy. The purpose of war was seldom annihilation of the enemy, rather a warning-off, or even close to a perilous game. It became more honourable for a warrior to take high risk to humiliate an enemy than to kill him; thus the coup-stick, a light wand adorned with feathers, was introduced. The fiercest braves would dash into a fight, bent on touching as many enemy with the coup-stick as possible – counting *coup*, in the French term – while dodging the enemy's clubs and arrows. When anyone could shoot a man from a distance, to touch him with

the muzzle of the gun was a feat; to touch an enemy with the flat of the hand was the peak.

The Blackfeet were the most daring and accomplished horse-thieves; this, too, was a way for a warrior to win honour. To raid a band's horses was to steal their prestige. A young and buxom girl was worth twenty horses, a rifle the same number, and some Blackfeet could count private herds of up to three hundred head. With banner streaming from his lance, ribbons in the mane and tail of his pinto, his eagle-feather headdress high and proud, a chief of the Plainsmen at full gallop was a magnificent and romantic sight, reminding some of the earliest Europeans of the mediaeval knights of chivalry. The full headdress of countless movies was originally the property of the Sioux alone. No camp was safe from the depredations of these horsemen – they raided as far south as the plains of Texas.

Whenever a national group acquired guns in the fur trade, they would fall upon their ancient enemies who might fight bravely with the old weapons but would soon have to give way, until they, in turn, became armed and fought back on more equal terms to re-establish the balances. Thus the Cree had driven the Assiniboine away from Lake Manitoba until the coveted firearms filtered farther west. Then the Assiniboine, the Cree and even the Ojibway from around Lake Superior, with muskets and hatchets supplied by both French and English traders, began to press the prairie tribes.

The Assiniboines – more latterly referred to as the Stonies – once numbered about ten thousand. They hunted the wolf, antelope, deer and elk once thick at the sloughs. After a buffalo kill, their women moved in to butcher the meat, to dry it for pemmican, to dress the hides for sleeping robes and *tipi* (teepee) coverings, or into buckskin for clothing. The buffalo was the supermart of all the Plains tribes. The horns were made into cups and spoons, the tail into a whip or a flywhisk. The tongues and the humps were the gourmet's delights, and the bladders were storage for everything from war-paint to medicines.

Pemmican became the iron ration of the Canadian West and it sustained not only the Indian hunter on the trail but also the European trader during his lonely wintering and the Métis canoemen on the long hauls to Thunder Bay, or even to the St Lawrence. Without pemmican there would not have been the fur trade as we know it; a piece the size of a man's fist would sustain him all day. The meat was usually air-dried in strips on racks of sticks, then shredded and pounded to a coarse powder. Rendered tallow was lightly mixed and the whole packed tightly into a buffalo stomach. Sometimes saskatoon berries, and even leaves of peppermint, were added for extra flavour.

Among the many unique ceremonies developed within the first Canadian culture, the Sun Dance of the Plains tribes and the Feast of the Dead among the Iroquoians probably hold most interest. Much has been written about the curious backwardness of the Canadian aborigine – in some aspects he was, at the time of Cabot and Cartier, not as far advanced technically as were the woaded Britons of Caesar's day – but in his ceremonials he reached a richly storied complexity and elaboration, the equal of ritual anywhere.

The Sun Dance, with its sensational self-immolation, dominates the prairie legends and it was still practised, secretly, until outlawed by a worried Canadian government in 1885 during the Northwest Rebellion. Staged when the sun was baking the plains, regenerating life, the Sun Dance had roots in a mythology of heavenly bodies – the Morning Star was the son of the Mother Moon and the Father Sun – and it became an occasion for the young braves to establish their worthiness to enter the warrior class. To show how they could withstand pain, a prime virtue among all Indians, they slit their pectoral muscles and threaded rawhide thongs on pegs through the holes and then on to a central pole in the dance lodge. At the climax of three days of feasting, dancing and purification ceremonies, they danced against the thongs until they pulled them through the ridges of muscle and skin, usually fainting with pain or exhaustion. They often then took a new name for their maturity and sought also a personal vision, or a hallucination in their hysteria, to guide them in later life.

The bizarre Feast of the Dead, as celebrated by all the Iroquoian peoples living on both sides of

A Blood Indian brave shows how well he bears pain by dancing against the thongs threaded through his pectoral muscles in the Sun Dance ceremony, 1880. Photo courtesy GLENBOW-ALBERTA INSTITUTE

Lake Ontario and the upper St Lawrence, was carefully documented by the Récollet and Jesuit mission priests. Every ten or twelve years among the Hurons a certain village group would be chosen to act as collective host for the ceremony and great stocks of food, venison, berries, corn meal mixed with fish or meat, would be laid in.

The women of all villages would now disinter the remains of all their relatives who had died since the last ceremony. The bones would be scraped, washed (sometimes painted red) and wrapped in beaver skins. All believed that the spirits of the departed travelled along the Path of Souls – identified as the Milky Way – but part of the spirit had remained in the bones and must be honoured.

For ten summer days, feasting and dancing with processional ritual was the order. Valuable robes, tools, dishes, even belts of wampum bead money, were placed in a large grave and then the assembled chiefs reverently laid in the assembled bones, covering them with bark and earth. Some of these pits have been found, containing many thousands of bones. It seems obvious that some kind of life-after-death was envisaged.

These were the only agricultural peoples in pre-history Canada, and in some ways they were the most advanced, especially in social and tribal organization. Classicists like to refer to them as 'the Greeks of America.' When Cartier and Champlain penetrated, the eight nations of the Iroquoian language-group held what was probably as attractive and fertile a stretch of land as existed on the continent. It should perhaps be remembered here that the digging, weeding and cultivating were done by the women, and thus the aversion of the present-day Indian male to steady farm-work or any repetitive chore, is deeply rooted.

The Hurons – the best farmers of all with their fertilized crops of maize, pumpkins, beans and squash – lived mostly in the Lake Simcoe-Georgian Bay area, their water routes to Montreal and the west giving them a strategic position in the developing fur trade. About fifty miles below them, including the Guelph-Kitchener area, were the villages of the Petun, often called the Tobacco nation; they grew more of that weed of the deadly nightshade family than they could use and traded it to other tribes. Along the shores of Lake Erie and across the isthmus of Niagara were the Neutrals. Their name told the story of their neutrality in the bitter inter-family enmity that had developed between the Hurons and the remainder of the Iroquoians, the Confederacy of the Five Nations. The territory along the northern and western shore of Lake Ontario – from Toronto to Kingston – was virtually a no-man's land, used by all at their peril, although a Seneca village, Teiaiagon (meaning 'The Crossing'), once stood near the mouth of the Humber River.

The main hunting ground of the Seneca abutted the Neutral territory and the rest of the federated nations – the Cayuga, Onondaga, Oneida and Mohawk – spread around the southern and eastern shore of the lake and down the St Lawrence, in that order, from west to east. In the rafters of the multi-family longhouses in their palisaded villages hung the drying corn that would feed them when game was difficult or impossible to find. A mere handful of corn would sustain a brave on the warpath, or a trader in the winter forests, and thus made mobility possible. The domestication of maize was a major feat of Indian husbandry – it is the only cereal which cannot survive except under cultivation – but no animal of the Canadian wild, except the dog, was ever raised or tamed to human use.

It is around the Five Nations that the most widely known Indian legends are spun. As comparative latecomers on the scene, they were beset by enemies on all sides but they developed in the crucible of crisis a near-mystical power that gave their warriors a fierceness, an endurance and, above all, a fearsome reputation far beyond their weight of numbers. Their governmental organization gave them tremendous advantage over the quarreling war parties of their opponents; every disciplined Iroquois warrior was worth ten of the enemy. They had no exclusive patent on cruelty, yet in their wholesale torture of prisoners, including women and children (and notably non-combatant priests), they showed an appalling imagination and persistence.

Their binding spiritual *Orenda* was inspired by the prophet Deganawida, possibly not until late

This Indian deerhide knife sheath with its fine geometric design and porcupine quill decoration comes from the central plains. Note the European thimbles attached to the thongs. From an HBC COLLECTION, LOWER FORT GARRY NATIONAL HISTORIC PARK

in the fifteenth century, and propagated by his apostle, the storied Hiawatha (whom Longfellow mistakenly characterized as an Ojibway). The sentimentalized concept of the 'noble savage' in the writing of Jean Jacques Rousseau, François-René de Chateaubriand and James Fenimore Cooper arose to clash with the equally over-played accounts of the bloodthirsty barbarian.

When the Council of the Five Fires was established among the Iroquois – it was, in effect, the first parliament on this continent – a trading alliance within a series of self-governing federations was offered to all tribes, from the Micmac and Malecite of the east, to the Algonquins on the north, the Ojibway of the west, the Susquehannah and the Erie to the south. As late as 1633, the pipe of peace was offered to the blood-brothers, the Hurons, sitting astride the Iroquois' trading lifeline into the hinterland.

It was a clear and cold choice that was offered: co-operate or die. But the swelling volume of the wondrous European trade goods was there to seduce the reason of any man still imprisoned in the Stone Age. No sophisticated concept of sensible shares for everyone could withstand the simple doctrine of winner-take-all. And, of course, in the collision of cultures that was just beginning, there was never a chance of an Indian winner.

Yet such a conclusion is too simple. Canadian history, during more than half its length, was made by a partnership, however ill-defined, of Indians and Europeans. A more serious and sympathetic attempt should be made to assess the Indian contribution.

Some hint of what the contribution was may be found by looking at the 'heroes' the Europeans found among the tribes as the traders made their way across the continent. They were not, on the whole, warriors opposing the advance of settlement. There was Joseph Brant fighting the American frontiersmen in the last stand of the Iroquois in the War of Independence. There was Big Bear, refusing to accept the coming of Canadian settlement and fighting against the Canadian militia in 1885. But they were really players in the multi-faceted drama of the Canadian fur trade, a joint enterprise between Indian and European. Not only did the Indian furnish the canoe, the toboggan, the deadfall, the snowshoe, corn, maple sugar and pemmican. He gave other and personal help.

It is among such men that myth-hungry Canadians should look for heroes. Well known is Matonabee, who guided Samuel Hearne to the Coppermine River in 1771. Less well known but more important is Ochagach, the Cree chief who told La Vérendrye in 1728 of the route from Lake Superior to the 'Sea of the West,' Lake Winnipeg, thus helping the trader penetrate the Winnipeg basin. Ochagach even drew a map, an Indian map, and puzzling, until one realizes that it is drawn not by measured miles but by daily canoe journeys.

Even more illustrative of Indian-European co-operation was the welcome the Saulteux chief Peguis gave to the Selkirk settlers on the Red River, helping not the fur trade but settlement itself. The Saulteux had always tried, after the custom of the shattered Hurons, to add to the results of the hunt the more reliable and keepable fruits of the garden. Thus, our maps show from the region of Sault Ste Marie, from which they derived their name as a branch of the Ojibway tribe, to the Lake of the Woods, the place name of 'Garden Island.' These were places where corn might be planted in the spring and be safe untended until fall.

When Peguis came with his band to the mouth of the Red River, they began the planting of corn at Netley Creek, the beginning of agriculture in the West. It gave them a base for the hunt, and some food against the privation of winter. The wise and patient Peguis saw in the settlers those who, with a greater knowledge of farming, might help his people increase their food supply. He therefore aided the settlers in the struggle with the fur traders of the North West Company. Out of that lonely instance of friendship and co-operation between Indian and European came the Indian farming settlement and parish of St. Peters, an integral part of the Red River colony.

Indians are more numerous in Canada today than they ever were, and have still to find and be admitted to a just and accepted place in Canadian life. To such a place they are entitled, for the Indian was one of the chief shapers, however unintentionally, of modern Canada.

The tomb of Joseph Brant, principal chief of the Six Nations Indians who, with the help of his sister Molly, kept the tribes loyal to Great Britain and led the Mohawks to Ontario in 1784. Photo courtesy ONTARIO GOVERNMENT TRAVEL BUREAU

PART II

Chapter five
For fish and fur

A great range of snow-capped mountains once towered along the Atlantic marches of Canada, running out of present-day Maine into New Brunswick, branching left into the Gaspé and right to Cape Breton, and on to Newfoundland. It was as high as the Rockies, maybe higher. Millions of years ago, as the earth began to assume its present form, the ranges – we know them as the Appalachians – started to crumble and subside, and the waiting ocean hungrily invaded the land, creating the thousands of bays, gulfs, inlets and estuaries that distinguish the Maritimes coast today. Some sizable mountains remained, of course – from the Shickshocks of the Gaspé which reach 4160 feet at the peak of Mount Jacques Cartier, to the Long Range in northern Newfoundland with heights like Gros Morne, at 2651 feet. But others sank completely beneath the sea, remaining in our times as great plateaux just a few feet in places under the restless surface. In one of the strangest paradoxes of the Canadian story, it was the lure of this hidden world that was responsible for the opening of Canada by the men of Renaissance Europe, rather than any attraction of the looming land beyond. While the likable industrious beaver gets star billing as the first symbol of Canada, he is in truth stealing the limelight from *Gadus callarias*, the humble codfish.

A century before De Chaste, Pontgravé, De Monts and Champlain began to establish the fur trade on a permanent basis, the courageous fishermen of Portugal, Spain, France, England, and even Italy, were crossing the Atlantic in their small but sturdy boats to harvest the teeming fishing grounds found by John Cabot on his discovery voyage of 1497. He had sailed into one of the world's great unknown treasures, the shallow waters east and south of his 'Newe Founde Launde.' One oft-quoted report of his discovery noted that the surface of the sea was literally shimmering with fish 'which can be caught not only with the net but in baskets let down with a stone.'

It may be, however, that some unsung heroes were making regular journeys there years before Cabot left Bristol on his first voyage and, like fishermen everywhere, saying nothing of their incredible luck. The map drawn by Andrea Bianco in 1436 has the legend *Stokfis* printed on the western sea beyond Greenland – and 'stockfish' is the common north European word for the cod. *Isla Stokafixa*, Codfish Island, is marked in the approximate position of Newfoundland. João Corte-Real had been rewarded by the King of Portugal for his discovery of the Terra de Bacalhão – again, Land of the Cod – before either Columbus or Cabot sailed. All Europe was then Roman Catholic, without any knowledge of refrigeration in summer or an unfailing food supply over winter, and the market for the nourishing, imperishable salt cod was boundless. It was the pork and beans of its day, the 'beef of the sea,' and, in some parts of the world, it has never been superseded.

Certainly, from 1500 onwards, fishing fleets were setting out from a dozen European ports for Canadian waters as soon as winter storms moderated. By 1510, from one record, we know that cod cured with salt from the evaporation pans of Brouage was being sent up the river highways of France by the merchants of Rouen; from another document we learn that, by 1530, one hundred and fifty English ships were crossing the Atlantic yearly. As the fishermen ran into harbours along the Canadian littoral, either for shelter in a storm, to dry the plump split fish or to forage for fresh water and firewood, they encountered the Algonquins of the eastern woodlands and swapped their simple gutting knives for soft beaver robes.

Back in France, particularly, the fishermen found that the furriers would pay keen prices for fur to supply the felting industry which had recently made brilliant technological strides. The broad fur hat for gentlemen was the height of fashion. In this way, the fishermen began to make 'some-

*The humble codfish of the Maritimes should get star billing as Canada's first symbol in preference to the beaver. Well before furs became the rage in Europe, the cod was the most popular export of the New World.
Photo by JOHN DE VISSER*

thing on the side' for themselves above their share of the codfish haul. When Cartier came on his epochal voyage into the Gulf of St Lawrence in 1534 he went into the wide Chaleur Bay of today's New Brunswick and reported: 'When we were half a league from a point [it was Paspebiac], we caught sight of two fleets of Indian canoes that were crossing the bay, in total about forty or fifty canoes. When one of the fleets reached this point, a large number of Indians sprang out on the beach and set up a great noise, waving to us to come ashore, and holding up furs on poles ...'

The fishermen who thus pried open the door of Canada probably had only the slimmest idea, if any, of why 'the banks' off Newfoundland provided such amazing catches. One Cabot reference reported that the ship had trouble making way through the shoals of fish; even today, after nearly five hundred years of exploitation, fish can swarm so thickly that they are forced above the waves by the legions beneath. It is a zone of icebergs, frequent storms, where fog rolls down for a hundred days a year, yet nowhere else in the world does life explode with such awe-inspiring fecundity. It is another of the paradoxes of the Canadian saga.

There are five 'banks' – wide areas of the flattened sunken hills – off the coast of Newfoundland and Nova Scotia, but the greatest of them is the so-called Grand Banks, lying about fifty miles off Cape Race. Three hundred and fifty miles long by two hundred miles wide, it lies in a north-east to south-west direction, seldom more than five hundred feet deep and usually closer to one hundred. Most of these waters are within the photic zone where enough sunlight penetrates to ensure the growth of plankton, the microscopic plant and animal life upon which all fish ultimately live. As readers of Rudyard Kipling's *Captains Courageous* will recall, at least one upthrust breaks the surface in stormy weather. Sable Island, 180 miles east of Halifax, is merely the peak of another bank, one hundred miles long. The island of St Pierre is all that is visible of a large bank which runs beneath much of Cabot Strait.

Across these submarine tablelands, there is a continuous collision of two giant rivers – the icy Labrador Current sweeping down from Baffin Bay, through Davis Strait, around the Avalon Peninsula, and the Gulf Stream surging north from the Caribbean and the Gulf of Mexico. Piled up by the trade winds, the tropical waters pour through the narrow Strait of Florida and flow up the American seaboard, fourteen cubic miles of warm water per hour. Where the breezes from the south hit the cutting breath of the Arctic, dense fogs form and sometimes hold for days, sending modern ships creeping along courses of radar blips. Where the waters collide, a mighty swirling is set up in the shallows, mixing and bringing to the surface all the minerals and chemicals required to ensure a planktonic 'bloom' of unimaginable luxuriance. The nutrients are never exhausted, as in other seas, because the Arctic flow brings down ice that, as glacier, has scraped mineral debris from the land; this melts in the spring and early summer over the Banks at the tepid touch of the stream from the south. The Gulf Stream, too, adds an extra dash of salt and other elements to the combination.

The result is an inexhaustible larder for uncountable marine animals. In the eternal cycle, the first seasonal warmth triggers the cell-division of the phytoplankton in their fantastic shapes, so small and so dense that perhaps two millions would drift in a single pint of water. They bring a faint blush of colour even to the grey Atlantic. All the waters of the Banks burst into life as the larvae and young of a hundred species, from shrimp like grains of rice to tiny herring and mackerel rise to feed on the plankton. Each fingerling is prey to a predator who, in his turn, is taken by another swifter and stronger. The scale of the marine life rises from the capelin to the swift porpoise and the humpback whale that gulps down thousands of herring daily.

No fish is more voracious than the cod; normally a bottom-feeder, it rises into the lush summer plenty of the smelt and squid shoals, quickly adding firm flesh that can produce giants of up to two hundred pounds. The family includes most of the commercial species that today find their way as 'fish fillets' into the freezer cabinets of the supermarts – the smaller tomcod, the haddock, hake, cusk, pollock and whiting. The cod would snap at anything – even the bare hook – and the earliest fishermen took them on handlines, and then developed nets and gear strong enough to raise heavy wriggling hauls.

After the defeat of the Spanish Armada in 1588, the rivalry on the Banks was concentrated between the French and English. It was, however, not national aspiration but the differing fishing techniques employed by these two that was to set the course of history on Newfoundland, always the main base for the fishery. The Bretons and Gascons had the advantage of a homeland climate that allowed plenty of salt to be produced by solar evaporation, especially along the wide tidal flats of ancient Saintonge; France also boasted an efficient transport system to get the fish cargoes swiftly inland via the Seine, the Loire and Garonne. Thus the French on the Banks fished 'green' or 'wet' – that is, they salted each day's catch aboard and when the hold was full they ran for home. Some of their vessels made many voyages without once landing on Newfoundland.

The whitest and firmest fish fetched high prices in Europe, and the 'seconds' were sold to army quartermasters; slave-holders in the Indies took anything that was left. Whale-oil (they called it 'train') and seal-oil were valuable secondary products from Newfoundland and Labrador waters. The cod livers were later saved for their vitamin-rich oil.

England's cloudy skies allowed only minor production of solar salt and her West Country captains had to go ashore into the harbours of Avalon to dry and cure their catches. The salted, split fish were spread on racks, known as flakes, and turned frequently; the process took six weeks. This led to the establishment of shore facilities, with the necessary labour, and, in the course of time, to settlement. Sir Humphrey Gilbert had already claimed the territory in 1583, but for two hundred years English fishing interests, with Royal Navy collusion, tried to prevent colonization, to retain Newfoundland only as a moored seasonal base for the cod fleets and as a training ground for future jacktars.

From 1662, the French garrisoned Placentia and dominated the southern shore, raiding the English settlements until the Treaty of Utrecht in 1713 confirmed English sovereignty over the island. After the loss of all Canada in 1760, France was given the islands of St Pierre and Miquelon, off the Burin Peninsula, as havens for her fishermen.

In the wrangling over the Treaty of Paris, finally signed in 1763, the French negotiator, the Duc de Choiseul, declared he would choose to be stoned by the Paris mob rather than give up France's fishing rights entirely. Whatever the potential value of the huge land beyond the gulf that had now changed hands, the statesmen rated the cod banks as vital to their food supply, and for the seamen trained in the fishery. They still do. The fourteen-nation International Commission for the Northwest Atlantic Fisheries now regulates the cod fishery, specifying the size of net mesh to allow young fish to mature, but total yearly hauls of over a billion pounds with modern stern trawlers brought even the teeming cod to danger point. To maintain control of a resource once thought inexhaustible, Canada has now extended its territorial waters to two hundred miles offshore.

As the cod drew more and more Europeans to Canada's north-eastern coasts in the sixteenth century, the beaver had already begun to pull the more adventurous among them deeper into Grande Baye, as the Gulf of St Lawrence was once known. Other fishermen-traders coasted the Bay of Fundy, and ran their twenty-ton ships into the fiord-like harbours and wide river estuaries. By Cartier's time, the Beothuks, Micmacs and Malecites, the Montagnais, the seal-hunting Naskapi of Labrador were obviously acquainted with European goods and aware of the sailors' unaccountable willingness to accept their sweat-stained fur clothing and bed-robes as fair exchange. Some of them came forward making the sign of the cross. Cartier wrote, in 1534, of the Indians of Chaleur Bay: 'They bartered all they had to such an extent that all went back naked, and they made signs to us that they would return on the morrow with more furs.'

The beaver, that forty-pound rodent with the thick soft coat which science would name *Castor canadensis*, provided the woodlands tribes with their commonest single garment. Once widespread in all provinces that offered its favoured watercourses, marshland, willow, birch and alder, the diligent beaver possesses a curiously appealing image. Canadians accepted it (long before the maple leaf) as the national emblem; when Sir William Alexander of Nova Scotia was

created Earl of Stirling and Viscount Canada in 1633, he included a beaver in his coat-of-arms. The first Canadian postage stamp was the 'three-penny beaver' of 1851. The name is kept alive honourably on the excellent magazine published by the Hudson's Bay Company.

Modern man tends to applaud the beaver's putative monogamy and sociable family life, its cleanly grooming habits, its engineering ability in the construction of dams and dens, complete with separate living room and nursery, with entrances cleverly below water level to frustrate predators. Where a log is required for a dam to raise the water level, the beaver will patiently fell a sizable tree with its protruding incisor teeth, then tow the trunk to the desired site. When man finally realized he had all but exterminated the creature, he turned protector and, through enlightened conservation, the beaver has made a comeback in the last quarter century with half-a-million pelts a year now available in controlled trapping.

The colder northern territories produced the finest pelts, from brown to black – with the occasional albino. The Indian women scraped the inner side of the pelts, and rubbed them with marrow or brains. This loosened the long guard hairs which fell out with usage, leaving the shorter dense fur. Up to eight skins were needed for the long tunic garment, worn with the downy fur to the body. These robes, well greased with body oils, pliable and soft, became the main target of the traders. Each fibre of fur was serrated with barbs, making perfect material for the matting process of the feltmakers.

To the Indian, the trade appeared miraculous – and soon essential. 'The beaver does everything to perfection,' a Gaspé native laughed to Father Chréstien le Clercq. 'He makes for us kettles, axes, swords, knives, and gives us drink and food without the trouble of cultivating the ground.'

As the Europeans came into the countryside – the sensible men bending to the will of the land and accepting its gifts in return – they found the beaver good to eat among the natives' exotic meats of moose, bear and porcupine. The broad tail was a delicacy. As the fur trails led westward, the Europeans would sample and enjoy wild rice, corn, maple syrup – but a certain time had to elapse before they would follow the *tabagie* custom of actually taking choking smoke from burning weeds into the lungs and expelling it from the nostrils. The explorers could never have believed their heirs would raise tobacco to godhood. The Indians also shared their condiments – a mayonnaise from the oil of walnuts and hickory nuts, bear-grease used like butter, a sauce of sunflower-seed extract.

Venturing from the first frail settlements clinging to the wilderness coasts of Newfoundland and Nova Scotia, the traders marvelled at nomads who would run down a moose on their snowshoes in winter and then move their family wigwam to the carcass rather than attempt to transport the meat. In summer, they would hope to catch the massive beast in water, browsing off its favourite lily roots.

Their earliest journals describe the moose-calls made from a cone of birch bark, with which an expert could seduce any animal in the vicinity, and the respect the Indians paid to the remains of the bear or beaver they had eaten. The cleaned skulls were placed on poles out of the reach of the dogs. There was a spirit in everything, all Canadian Indians believed, and the bear *manitou* would accept that his body had been taken, not in anger or greed, but because the hunter must feed and clothe his family.

In his 1615 journey through southern Ontario to the Bay of Quinte, Champlain described how deer were herded to the hunters. Long fences were sometimes constructed of sharpened saplings, converging at a corral where killing squads waited. Gaps were left in the fences occasionally, with snares and deadfalls awaiting any animal that came through. Pounds of a similar kind were built on the plains to catch antelope and buffalo.

The requirements of hide and fur for clothing of a scattered population were adequately satisfied by these larger animals and the many other fur-bearers – muskrat, marten, fisher, otter, raccoon, badger, wolverine, wolf and fox – but hunting soon deteriorated when the white traders offered metal trade goods (and later brandy and muskets) for all the fur that could be gathered. It

The fur of the beaver which provided the woodland Indians with their long tunics was the prime target of the early traders. Photo by LEONARD LEE RUE III

had quickly become unthinkable for a tribe to deny itself the advantages of the European goods – both for warlike and peaceful purposes – and relentless pressures built up between the nations. Nicolas Denys reported in 1672: 'Above everything, the kettle has always seemed to them the most valuable article they can obtain from us.' The simple iron or copper cooking pot allowed the nomadic tribes much more mobility; previously most of them had to transport their cumbersome wooden tubs in which water was boiled by the addition of heated stones.

On the far prairies and in the foothills of the Rockies, where the roaming buffalo herds provided plenty of food, the Indian could turn his mind to other pursuits. It was the brief halcyon period for the Plainsman after the arrival of the horse and before the arrival of the white man. Eagle feathers were coveted as war decorations and the savage birds were taken by a method illustrating the complete harmony between the Indian and his natural environment. The hunter dug a pit on a rise, carefully spreading the excavated dirt some distance away. He roofed it with sticks and grass and set out a large piece of raw meat as bait, carefully installing himself in the hole. The bait was tied to a length of *babiche*, rawhide thong. Now the hunter had to compose himself, to lie motionless for a day if necessary. An eagle might circle for hours, suspicious of danger, before swooping down. If the hunter was properly concealed, the bird would attempt to seize and fly off with the bait. In a flash, the man would sweep aside the camouflage and grab the eagle by the legs. Before he could subdue it, he could expect to be ravaged by beak or claw.

Voyages to Canada for furs alone had begun some time in the second half of the sixteenth century and the fur trade soon became independent of the fishing. It ceased to be casual barter, as the tribes began to collect furs farther and farther inland by hunting or by trade, and to bring them down to 'fairs' at some agreed rendezvous, or forward them through 'middle-man' tribes who jealously guarded their direct contact. By the end of the century, Tadoussac, where the Saguenay River enters the St Lawrence, had become the major trading point.

It was to Tadoussac that Champlain came on his first voyage to Canada in 1603, and here that the Sieur de Tonnetuit, Pierre Chauvin, attempted to establish the first permanent trading post. Later, Quebec, Trois-Rivières and Montreal all tapped the furs coming out of the hinterland on the western rivers. The traders increasingly had to move their forward bases, even though this steadily increased their overhead costs, and the *coureurs de bois* ranged ever more deeply.

It was private men and free enterprise, then, that kept the northern sea route in use and developed trading ties with the new land. Yet the great commercial and imperial designs were only delayed, not dropped; state energies were absorbed by religious wars in France, the need to preserve the Reformation in England, the bitter struggle of the Dutch for independence from Spain. Businessmen, seamen, patriots of all kinds, still hoped to find a northern passage to Asia, and in northern America, mines to equal the wealth of the Spanish Indies. As the kings and queens, the governments of those days, had not enough money to pay for their costly courts and their wars, they had none for exploration. There arose, therefore, a partnership of businessmen, seamen and governments in which the first provided money, the second the skill, the third political sanction and diplomatic defence. In a phrase, exploration had to pay its own way. This is why from Champlain to La Vérendrye, Henday to Fraser and Mackenzie, the fur trade and explorations were inseparable. Furs financed the search for the route to Asia; the search opened new territories to the trader: in this joint venture, Canada was made.

As the French from the St Lawrence and the English from Hudson Bay, in their different styles, sought ever more furs in those far territories, the Indians began to learn the values of the competitive system – they tried to bargain where the price was best. But for some there had not been free choice. In 1634, seven hundred Hurons brought 140 canoes loaded with pelts to Champlain's warehouse, and there was glee in New France. A decade later, the Iroquois who were trading with the Dutch, and then the English, from Albany and New York, decided on the elimination of the Hurons who barred their way to the fur lands of the Canadian Shield, and New France was brought close to utter failure.

Kettles such as this 8-quart copper vessel were brought out in nesting sets of 5 or 6 and represent a standard HBC trade item for over 150 years. Photo from an HBC COLLECTION, LOWER FORT GARRY NATIONAL HISTORIC PARK

The Iroquois had depleted their own hunting grounds and those of the Mohicans on their eastern flank. The Iroquois 'approach like foxes, attack like lions, and disappear like birds,' wrote a despairing Jesuit in Quebec. Louis XIV eventually had to send 1200 musketeers and pikemen of the Carignan-Salières Regiment to enforce a twenty-year truce on the St Lawrence.

French trader-explorers opened routes west into the Lake Superior country and beyond, and south into the Ohio and Mississippi valleys – where again they found the Seneca, strongest of the Iroquoian federation, opposing them. From the regional stronghold of Chartres, near modern Kaskaskia, Illinois, the French tried for a generation to eliminate the Fox Indians who would not permit them to trade with the Sioux through Wisconsin. They campaigned against the Chickasaw who persisted in trading with the colonists in Virginia who offered better prices for the pelts. Eventually, Chartres became a four-acre, stone-walled fortress with a garrison of three hundred.

The 'fur wars' were never wholly quenched. The Chevalier de Troyes and Pierre le Moyne (the fabulous Iberville) had raided most of the British posts on Hudson Bay, and Louis Coulon de Villiers tried to stem the American colonial traders and speculators pushing into the Ohio country.

Even after the fall of New France in 1760, the struggle was kept simmering in the Northwest between the Hudson's Bay Company based on the Churchill and Nelson river systems and the Nor'Westers, that lusty bunch of frontier capitalists in Montreal who took over and expanded the routes pioneered by the departed French. It lasted, with more than a little bloodshed, until 1821 when the two outfits merged, flourished mightily and ruled the Canadian West clear to the Arctic and Pacific coasts until 1858. Another decade passed before all of the vast fur kingdom of Rupert's Land was vested in the poor but promising Confederation of Canada.

This lonely cenotaph in the Arctic commemorates Sir John Franklin who disappeared while searching for the Northwest Passage. The marble tablet was commissioned by Lady Franklin. Photo courtesy PANARCTIC OILS LTD

PART III

The settlement years

INTERLUDE:
How the people used the land

Consider the land before it acknowledged a white master. Cartier's great enterprise, to seek the fabled kingdom of the Saguenay and find another route to the riches of the Orient, had foundered. The banks of the St Lawrence yielded neither gold nor diamonds. And the sixteenth century was to see two more such failures. One was by the English who sought to use Newfoundland, which they claimed in right of Cabot's discovery. There, Sir Humphrey Gilbert planted a colony, as a halfway base to Asia, but Gilbert himself was lost at sea, and the colonists were taken back to England. From 1578 to 1599, a persistent French nobleman, the Marquis de la Roche, attempted no fewer than three times to establish colonies on the coasts of New France, only to fail in all cases. No one, English or French, could yet achieve what the Northmen had done in Greenland, and the Spanish in the West Indies and Mexico: plant a colony of Europeans that could establish itself among the Indians and in the conditions of America. The fail-

ures in Canada were indeed particularly severe – although none as dramatic as Walter Raleigh's lost colony in Virginia. The truth was that the business of colonization was a difficult one and had to be learned.

It was, of course, Samuel Champlain who launched upon the endeavour that was to colonize Canada, but that was certainly not his purpose or intention. He was a man committed to a dream – to explore New France and make it a base for the crossing to the western sea that must lie somewhere beyond the headwaters of the St Lawrence.

At the heart of this endeavour lay a contradiction on which much of the early history of Canada turns. The fur trade was risky, and the traders had no wish to have added to their costs that of bringing settlers and aiding them to establish themselves. Settlers were little or no help to the fur trade. This was not because they would drive the animals or the Indians away. The early comers were too few to do that. The danger was that in the long winters they would become fur traders themselves – as, in fact, many were to do. Thus the fur trade was, as both the founding of New France and later the Red River colony were to show, a most unstable base for the beginning of settlements. Yet there was no other means.

The fisheries were an equally unsuitable foundation. There was small reason for settlement in the fishery as there was little that needed to be done during the winter on the bleak shores of Newfoundland or Nova Scotia – *Acadie*, as it was called by the French.

Yet in all these places – Newfoundland, Acadia and Canada – settlement did take place. How?

The island of *Terre-Neuve* had already long been used as a landfall, a place for wood and water, a many-harboured shore for drying fish. Even in the southern Avalon Peninsula, the island offered little good soil or weather for farming. The rocky land broke in cliffs and coves to the sea, while inland there was mostly barren scrub land, swept by cold wind and fog. The island was suited to the purposes for which the fishermen had put

On the rugged and desolate shores of Newfoundland only the hardiest settlers overcame the winters. But the reward for survival was freedom from laws difficult to enforce in such a vast and inhospitable terrain. Photo by JOHN DE VISSER

it: an adjunct of the fishery of the great submarine banks off its eastern shore.

Yet in the seventeenth century men did begin to live in the many harbours of the east coast, chiefly in the Avalon Peninsula. They were English fishermen from West Country ports, men from Dorset, Devon and Cornwall, and as the century wore on they were joined by men from southern Ireland, Waterford, Cork and Kerry. Some were 'planters' – settlers who served the fishery, of whom some became substantial merchants. It was they who waged the long war of planter against fisherman that was the core of Newfoundland's history. Some men were left to 'winter' – to guard the boats and the drying flakes and to do repairs on boats and tackle. Some stayed, not to remain in Newfoundland, but in hope of getting passage to the New England colonies. Others shipped for 'two summers and a winter' were left by masters who wished them to tend the flakes, or to avoid the cost of taking them home. They were 'beached.'

How did they live, when colonies so readily failed, on that inhospitable coast? What shelters did they make? What was their food – leftover salt cod and, perhaps, for the Irish, potatoes? And how did these scattered beachcombers slowly come to form communities? The answer to that seems to lie in the fact that some of the work in 'making' the fish was done by women shipped as part of the crews. Thus, women entered Canadian history in the role of fishermen's or peasants' wives. It was a humble role, but it was also indispensable, for without women there could be no lasting settlement. Island families were begun, and permanent housing was required. In this lowly way was laid the foundation on which their daughters in later centuries were to raise new roles for women in Canadian life.

In these enforced circumstances on the St Lawrence and on the Atlantic shores, European man first began to make permanent use of the Canadian land. And not only were the circumstances harsh: settlement was against the actual policy of the governments. All men shipped to the fisheries, for instance, were to return home to be there for the 'press' to take them into the Royal Navy in time of war. It was therefore forbidden for any to remain in Newfoundland. No one was allowed to have property, no law existed, no government was formed, except for the 'fishing admirals,' until a naval officer was sent each summer. Louis Hébert, Canada's first true settler, was harshly treated by the French authorities who sought only furs. Yet all these men persisted.

Here was the first instance of a practice as old as the European migration to the Americas, that was to have deep and continuing significance in the western continent – the defiance of a law that could not be enforced in the vast spaces and little travelled areas of the long coasts and deep woods of the new land. During colonial times, Europeans of every race coming to America

could, for their own purposes, defy those who claimed to govern them. Here were the seeds of freedom and independence.

In Nova Scotia, the story was both the same and very different. Here too was a great fishery with submarine banks and countless coves for shelter and for drying fish, both on the Atlantic side and along the shores of the gulfs of Fundy and St Lawrence. (There was, of course, no New Brunswick then.) But it also had a fur trade, long considerable, and it did come to have settlers. Nova Scotia was always pulled two ways – south to New England and north to Canada – with the result that for over a century and a half its history was one of war and conquest.

Several definite characteristics may be seen, now that it is possible to look back. The first is that many people, particularly the New Englanders, wanted to treat Nova Scotia as though it were Newfoundland, and keep the beaches open and the lands unclaimed for the use solely of fishermen. Another was that in Acadia in the French period a monopoly of the fur trade was impossible. The many harbours, the multitude of little valleys, the great sea arms of Fundy and the Chaleur, made it quite impossible to prevent anyone from trading freely in furs. The third was that Nova Scotia had, unlike Newfoundland, much good land, which unlike that of the Canadian interior, did not have to be cleared of forest. This was the land of the Annapolis Valley and the tidal marshes of the Minas Basin.

Here, a handful of peasants, men and women, presumably from the tidal marshes of the Bay of Biscay where the same sea-farming was practised, began to build on the river shores the dykes of clay and timber that kept back the tides while letting the inland water out at low tide. Here, suddenly, on the west shore of the Atlantic was a rich farming countryside, made by an enduring peasantry. A few hundred only of such quiet, unrecorded people came to Acadia's Fundy shore, the ancestors of the many thousands of Acadian French today. Still tidal, still dependent on the sea, this was yet the first real land community in Canada.

The founding of Acadia had been the work of the Sieur de Monts and Champlain, when they attempted to establish a monopoly of the fur trade in 1604. They had chosen Acadia rather than the known St Lawrence because the winters were less harsh. When they found, however, that a monopoly was quite impossible to enforce in Acadia, they returned to the great river and founded Quebec in 1608. Quebec was a seaport; Montreal could be reached by small boats, and the heartland, like Newfoundland and Nova Scotia, was reached and exploited by sea. But with settlement the French at once began to become part of a continental pattern, and to be drawn farther inland.

Down the corridors of the lakes and the Ottawa, they held open the entry to the continent. They founded Louisiana in the Mississippi Valley and, with La Véren-

Quebec stands majestically overlooking the St. Lawrence from Cape Diamond, named in 1535 by Cartier who hoped to find wealth in the New World. Photo by JOHN DE VISSER

drye and his sons, advanced to the Red River and the Saskatchewan.

The degree of the commitment of New France to the wilderness has to be examined to be understood. It had not been the intention of the founders that New France should be 'Indianized.' Champlain and the Jesuit fathers and, later, Louis XIV and Colbert hoped to 'Francize' the Indians. But the fur trade and the Jesuit missions were a binding tie to the country as it was, unimproved by man, and to the Indian way of life. And it was not only that the colony, and the missions to some degree, depended on the furs for livelihood, or at least currency. It was also that to carry on the trade, particularly after 1650, and to reach the Indian, both traders and missionaries had to immerse themselves in the wilderness, and live, outwardly at least, as Indians.

This meant, in the first place, learning how to sit in a canoe all day without movement and without panic in the white water of the rapids. For the *coureurs de bois* it meant learning how to paddle the canoe with the quick Indian thrust and turn. Going upstream into the country, trader and priest had to carry their possessions over the portages. They had to learn to suppress the calls of nature while on the water. They had to eat the two meals a day, boiled corn and fish, from the common pot swung over the campfire. They had to sleep as they could, on rock, sand, fir boughs or under the canoes. They could not be tired, ill or late, for the travelling Indian moved without pause except for sleep, or bad weather. And always there were the mosquitoes, the biting flies, the strange scent and language of the Indians.

When the journey was over, the French reached the confusion, noise, filth, dogs, vermin, children of the Indian village, dirty and untidy like any encampment not under soldierly discipline. Here, there was neither quiet nor privacy. To the Indians all doors were open, all affairs were communal affairs. And whites, especially the priests with their black robes and magical rites, were the objects of the insatiable curiosity of people who knew no strangers and to whom the white men literally came from another world.

The trader, the simple *coureur de bois*, was drawn far more deeply into the Indian way of life. He shared his feasts, he drank with them, he slept with the women – for most tribes were completely hospitable in this as in other respects. He learned that to live in the forest as an Indian, an Indian wife was indispensable, to cook the meals, to carry the camp utensils, to make the soon-worn-out moccasins, to dress the furs. Soon there were half-blood children. Soon it was difficult to leave a way

of life become so completely one's own, and which was so free of all restraints and compulsions, other than those of nature, and even of time itself. Many a *coureur de bois* became completely Indian.

The same thing might have happened to the early Dutch or the English – indeed it did sometimes, in the fur trade of New York, as the career of the Flemish Bastard, a famous Mohawk half-breed reveals, or all along the English frontier, as the tales of Daniel Boone indicate. But the English frontier was only the breaking surf of the forward thrusting tide of settlement. The English remained committed to farming settlement and thus, basically hostile to the nomadic Indian way of life.

From New Orleans to Detroit, from the headwaters of the Ottawa to the middle Saskatchewan, the French traded against the English, carrying their goods to the tribes, living among them, aiming to carry off the light and valuable furs and leaving the heavy to the English. But however outdone, however repelled, the English advanced as irresistibly as an incoming tide. When the war cut the supplies of French goods, the English traders advanced with their pack trains, their cheap strong goods, their gunsmiths to mend the Indian weapons, and the diplomacy of the Irish William Johnson, as adept as any *voyageur* at winning the confidence of the Indians.

The advance of the British meant that at long last the trial of strength for the control of the continent had come. If the Ohio country were lost, the Illinois and Wisconsin country would be also, and with them the inland connection between Canada and Louisiana. The trade and empire of the interior would be French no more.

From this point on, moreover, a third party offered competition to the fur traders. This was the land speculator. He would be British because the French were not yet interested in land west of Montreal. He might be a simple pioneer squatter, moving ahead of settlement to take up free land, and sell the improvements he made to the genuine farmers who would not be long behind him. Or he might be a Virginian planter buying years ahead of the advance of the soil-exhausting tobacco plantations, or a London capitalist acting in concert with Americans. Land speculation was, of course, the dawn of agriculture. With speculation, the struggle in the interior ceased to be one for trade only – it became one for the land itself. And agriculture meant the end of the fur trade, and the Indian way of life.

Nature was now to be conquered and bent to human purpose.

The coureur de bois learned to travel in the woods Indian style, carrying heavy supplies so that the weight on the hips was held in place by the tumpline at the brow. Photo by CHARLES STEPHEN

Chapter Six
Seigneur and soldier

The flow of people into New France was seldom more than a trickle and at Champlain's death in 1635 the population was still below one hundred. At this time the population of France was fourteen millions, three times that of England and Wales. The first official census in Canada, by Intendant Jean Talon in 1665, counted 3215 heads. The first struggling century listed fewer than 16,000 people, while the English colonies in New England and down the Atlantic seaboard already numbered more than 250,000. There were spurts of French immigration, a few hundreds at a time, including some important boatloads of marriageable girls, but there were also long periods when the stream dried up entirely. According to one oft-quoted comment, Canada was commonly regarded in France as 'the last resort of the ruined.'

Colonization was, of course, discouraged by the fur trading monopolies who, rightly, saw every established settler as a potential competitor. The population increase came mostly from one of the world's highest birthrates; girls married at fifteen and families of a dozen healthy children were common. Only about four hundred, men and women, ever emigrated, for instance, to Acadia, the Maritimes of today, where the first settlements were planted. By 1710 they had swelled to 1500, and by 1755 to 14,000. Although Protestants – including Roberval, De Monts, the Caens, La Tours and possibly Cartier himself – played significant roles in the founding of New France, they had been barred from the country by Cardinal Richelieu in 1632. By 1760, at the Conquest, the entire population was only something over 60,000 – approximately the size of modern Victoria or Sherbrooke. From this hardy and fruitful core has sprung nearly one-third of the present nation.

New France saw little of the glories of the Sun King. Canada was never to raise even a single château to rival those that were lining the banks of the Loire at the time. It could not benefit, like New England, from a flow of strong-minded dissenters seeking a refuge from religious persecution at home – with Protestants refused entry, it could not absorb any of the 400,000 Huguenots who fled France after the revocation of the Edict of Nantes. Neither did France have, like Spain, a great interior of hazardous climate like Castile, to furnish hundreds of eager soldiers and colonists ready to leave a harsh and fickle motherland. When the Company of One Hundred Associates did despatch a colonizing fleet of eighteen ships, war broke out and the expedition was captured by Sir David Kirke in the name of England's Charles I.

From where, then, did the first settlers, the *habitants*, come? The records are few and scattered. We know of men from Normandy, Brittany, Anjou, Poitou, Aunis, Ile de France. We know an average passage cost 40 *livres*, plus the cost of any meals provided, and that a death rate of only 10 per cent during a voyage was considered good. There were those who came to do definite jobs – hired workmen, called *engagés*, to work in the fur trade and missions and build the towns and churches. There were soldiers to defend them – and some of these at the end of their term of service or enlistment, chose to remain in the colony. Eventually, many soldiers did, the most famous example being that of the Carignan-Salières Regiment, which settled the Richelieu Valley after 1666. There were, too, the few family men – like Louis Hébert and Robert Giffard – who were persuaded to come and take up grants of land. But the pace of agricultural development can be measured by the fact that only one-and-a-half acres of land was cleared in the first twenty-two years of the colony.

If there were to be farmers, though, a system of land granting was essential. In a traditional society like that of France, still feudal in structure, direct grants to the farmers themselves were impossible. A simplified version of French feudal land holding was therefore introduced. These were large grants of lands made as *seigneuries* to retired army officers, leading citizens, officials,

The building of Canada began with the axe. After the land was cleared and the house built, attention could be paid to the furnishings which made it finally a home. Photo by P. GAUDARD

and also to the religious orders that had the means to attract and assist settlers. These domains, resembling the mediaeval English manors, were at least twelve square miles in extent, and some ran up to one hundred. The new *seigneur*, or squire, joined the *petite noblesse* of Canada after taking an oath of loyalty. He was expected to divide his land into farms and to let them for small rentals to peasants who would swiftly clear the land. The habitant also had to provide some labour to the seigneur – only about three days a year – and to have his grain ground in the mill at the big house. He was supposed to deliver to the rustic 'lord of the manor' his *droit de pêche*, one in eleven of any fish caught in the streams on the property. He was expected to serve in the militia, and to accept the seigneur's justice in any legal dispute. There were 250 of these manors created by the mid-eighteenth century.

The *habitants* have been wildly romanticized in much Canadian literature but, within the tight limits of a society ruled at a distance by a despotic king and a small coterie of often-debauched aristocrats, and close at hand by governors of varied quality and iron-willed ultramontane priests, they were a simple, sturdy, cheerful people, immeasurably better off than were the peasant class in their homeland, or elsewhere in Europe. They were, by comparison, free men. Although governed by edict, often harshly – the records show sixty-nine men hanged for theft and six broken on the wheel – public assemblies were for some years held annually at Quebec at which important issues affecting the colony were discussed. Any man could be heard.

The seigneurial system itself was probably of little effect, and its pattern of land-holding conceals rather than explains the way the land was actually taken up and improved. For instance, many of the squires worked right alongside their tenants and lived in much the same way, and not one in ten of them were authentic members of the nobility (which could only be attained by inheritance or through letters patent issued by the King). What the system did do was to create a situation in New France where the land, being held, not owned, could not be mortgaged or used in commerce. Free and well-off as he came to be, the *habitant* was bound to a distinctive, non-commercial way of life as long as he remained on the farm.

In a very real way, then, New France was old France taking root on new soil. This transplantation was strengthened when the Jesuit missions became parishes as settlements thickened, and as Canada became a bishopric in 1659. Still more did it become so four years later when New France became a royal province and the old governors – really the local managers of the fur-trade colony – were replaced with a royal governor, a royal intendant, and a council, which with the bishop governed the colony under the direct supervision of the king's minister.

Yet the land *was* new and strange and had to be broken to European needs. At the beginning the *habitant* had to learn from the Indian and from the first *coureurs de bois* to use the immediate resources of the country, the hunt, the fisheries of the river – particularly the eel fishery – the sugar of the maple, the berries of the meadows and forests. The same natural meadows gave pasture to his livestock in summer and hay in winter. Then, taking tenacious hold, he began to plough the land, introducing North America to the many uses of agriculture, which would end the reign of nature and the Indian way of life.

Slowly, in the course of a century, the wooden plough of northern France, with its two great wheels, its iron share and wooden mouldboard, came to the fields, now widened and cleared of stumps. Oxen or horses drew the ploughs. It was an epic, an unrecorded battle. First the meadow sod was turned with hoe and mattock. Then to fight the forest, the *habitant* had two weapons, axe and fire. After the meadows came the *brûlés*, the burnt-over land, the results of accidental forest fires or of deliberate firing. Then the axe began the slow task of chopping, stroke on echoing stroke, the scorched logs and stumps to complete the clearing. Next, perhaps after some years to let the charred stumps rot, the heavy mattock and the wooden plough began to turn the soil for the broadcast sowing of wheat, the main crop of New France. This was the process of *défrichement*, of clearing and breaking the land for farming.

There grew up on both banks of the St Lawrence between Quebec and Montreal, and on the

Richelieu, a farming countryside of villages and houses along the river edge. Forests lots ragged with stumps and rough green fields struggled on either side of the parish church. The houses were log, squared logs between uprights, but on the older farms, stone houses in Norman style reared their flared eaves and dormer-windowed roofs. On the fields running up from the river grew a hardy Swedish wheat and peas, on the meadows deep with hay the fodder for the cattle. And in the simple but comfortable houses were reared the mothers of the exploding generations, one son for the farm, others for new land, for war or the fur trade.

The farmlands and the fur trade were the twin pillars of the colony. In all its fierce growth, and in the violent issues in which the little community was to be involved, there was a certain harmony. The government was autocratic and could be stern. But at its best, and usually, it was benevolent, careful of its people and their welfare. King Louis ordered his Intendants – the 'business managers' of New France – that they must first ensure the inhabitants 'enjoy complete tranquility among themselves,' and feel security for their possessions. The vicious system by which public office, and thus power, could be purchased was prevented from taking root in Canada and the rich were taxed to take care of the deserving poor. The merely indolent were put to work.

Certainly, with its paternalism, its insistence on tradition and a definite pomp, the colony was Catholic and Latin, very much a projection of France into the wilderness. The *fleur de lis* floating over the Château St Louis, the trumpet proclaiming the coming of the Governor down the Grand-Allée, the clamour of housewives in Bonsecours market, and the drill orders barked in the Place d'Armes at Montreal, made New France very much provincial France, the France of Rouen, St Malo, Brest and Brouage. And the society so governed was the same: vigorously commercial, for all its feudal form; dynamic, for all its tradition. Everywhere there was a freedom, even an insubordination, an indocility, that shocked most administrators fresh from France or visitors from elsewhere in Europe.

The Swedish traveller and scientist Peter Kalm noted the new egalitarianism, a generation before proletarian revolution wracked Europe: 'When one comes into the house of a Canadian peasant or farmer, he gets up, takes off his hat to the stranger, invites him to sit down, puts his hat on, and sits down again. The gentlemen and ladies, as well as the poorest peasants and wives are called *Monsieur* and *Madame*.' Kalm was shocked by the short skirts worn by the Canadian women; he noted in his journal that the garment 'hardly reaches half-way down the leg.'

There was always an extra measure of isolation in the Acadian settlements, with the ships from France sailing directly into the Gulf of St Lawrence, usually by the high northern route through the Strait of Belle Isle. It was safer that way in the on-again off-again wars. Intendant Talon planned a road from Quebec to Acadia, but it was never built.

Jean de Biencourt, the Sieur de Poutrincourt, tried desperately from 1606 to establish his family on his seigneury of Port Royal, in Annapolis Basin, given him two years earlier by Governor de Monts. He took produce from his fertile lands back to France to show King Henri IV, seeking support for his settlement, the first to be permanently established on the continent above Florida. It was at Port Royal that Hébert, a former Paris druggist, first turned to farming, and where Champlain tended the garden he wrote about so lyrically. They raised wheat and corn, beans, cabbage and turnip, and gathered nuts and berries. They hunted moose, bear, deer and raccoon. The sheltered inlet provided plenty of fish, crabs and *moules*. Here, for the first time, Europeans tried to master the Algonkian bark canoe, and staged the first play written in North America – Marc Lescarbot's *Le Théâtre de Neptune*.

The raid by Samuel Argall out of Virginia in 1613 crushed Poutrincourt's hopes but his son, known as Biencourt, and young Charles de la Tour remained in Acadia. Several colonists, a mere handful, survived in the forest, aided by friendly Indians. This remnant was solidly reinforced by about three hundred settlers between 1632 and 1636, mostly sturdy peasants who put down roots in the tidal marshlands at the head of the Bay of Fundy. Here they would stay, surviving all pressures and crises, rebounding even from the tragedy of the Expulsion of 1755.

On the shores of Minas Basin, at Chignecto and in the valley of the Petitcodiac River, they began the dyke-farming some of them had known in Europe. Across the upper flats inundated by the farthest rushes of Fundy's fifty-foot tides they built embankments and dams that would shut out the sea but allow the marshes to drain. After a few years' rains, the salt was washed from the new soil, and thousands of acres of rich land thus rescued. It was certainly easier than clearing forest. Cattle and crops thrived, and imperial plans were laid to have *Acadie* become a larder for the French possessions in the West Indies. But the Acadians, too long forgotten and ignored by the outside world, turned inwards to rely upon their own simple faith and crafts, and resisted nearly all efforts – either French or British – to use them. One governor at Quebec railed that they behaved like republicans, accepting neither royal authority nor the courts of law.

There was a more worldly air about the colony along the St Lawrence. Quebec, a capital from its inception, was terminal port for the voyages from France, and more responsive to some – but not all – of the new ideas, styles and manners yeasting out of Europe. Quebec rose at the exact point where the continent took hold of the sea entry. It was the key to Canada. A humble trading port, a crumbling fortress, these were lowly beginnings – but of the fundamental strength of the position, of its majesty of riverscape, and far mountain horizons, there was never any question. And the sheer loft of Cape Diamond above the river opposite the heights of Lévis confirmed as time went by the sense of gathered elements, of a conjunction of land and water, prepared from ancient eras.

About fifty ships called at Quebec each navigating season, and as many as twenty or thirty sail could at times be seen in the basin. The arrival noted the long narrow green fields on the Ile d'Orleans, the whitewashed stone houses, the spaced exclamation marks of the church spires. Then came the striking sight of Fort St Louis on the crown of the steep rock – at this moment the veteran crews demanded a *pourboire* from all who were seeing Quebec for the first time (backed up with a threat of a ducking in a water barrel).

At the docks were the homes and warehouses of the main merchants, while the bureaucrats lived in Upper Town, reached by a steep roadway. Their houses were of stone, or of timber frame filled with stone, usually long and narrow with a central chimney; steep roofs were of cedar shingles. To protect the mortar from winter storms, the houses were often plastered, and windows were kept small. Like any provincial French capital, the streets of the partially walled town were narrow and, to modern eyes, filthy with refuse and open drains. Along them dashed the fine horses so admired by the *Canadiens*, bearing their owners in *calèche* or *carriole* to tavern, picnic or party.

Rarely in law, and never in fact, has Quebec ceased to be a capital since its foundation. Government, cathedral, garrison, university: all the institutions of a capital city it had from its first century. Fur trade and timber trade, shipyards and shipping, imports from Europe and exports to the Maritimes and the Indies, kept it a commercial city also, an equal rival of Montreal until steam and the deepening of the river channel carried the hulls of trade past it to its inland rival. Eventually and fittingly, the ancient capital proud on its rocky perch, was the site of the conference at which the union of all British North America was planned. There could have been no better site for the shaping of large and far-ranging plans. From the days of Champlain and Frontenac, men could not but think grandly in Quebec.

Sophisticated visitors during the *Ancien régime* were often astonished at the level of gaiety and good living. The Conte de Frontenac was a friend of Molière's and he encouraged the theatre, with amateur performances of Racine and Corneille by army thespians. Sometimes newcomers wrote home censoriously of the *habitant*'s pursuit of simple pleasures, of dancing, card-playing and singing.

It took some time for a European, especially a townsman or a courtier, to adjust to the altered social conditions, to the near-total cessation of farming for five months of the year, and to the sense of isolation creeping out of the vast wilderness. Jean Bochart de Champigny, Intendant for

The French heritage of the earliest St. Lawrence settlers is evident in the traditional architecture of this St. Joachim house with whitewashed fieldstone walls and flared eaves. Photo by JOHN DE VISSER

sixteen years, wrote: 'The men are all strong and vigorous but have no liking for work of any duration; the women love display and are excessively lazy, those of the country districts just as much as the towns' people.' Once he had food and clothing and shelter adequately provided for, the habitant could seldom be persuaded to continue to work hard to improve his lot. This attitude can perhaps be traced to the influence of the untrammeled Indian way of life, so patently enjoyed and remembered by the several hundred *coureurs de bois* who returned to Quebec, Trois-Rivières or Montreal after ranging far into the depths of the continent.

One officer complained that the girls of the country were being ruined by too much education in the schools run by the nuns of Notre Dame – they no longer were content to be housemaids but sought to marry into the merchant class. A priest was dismayed to note that the *habitant* cow girls wore hoop skirts and lace on Sunday, just like ladies of fashion in France. Intendant Talon noted reprovingly that a mere 7500 colonists were spending 100,000 *livres* a year (something near $200,000 in modern values) on wine and brandy, and he ordered the number of taverns reduced and a brewery built to provide a milder drink. Clandestine brothels flourished in the port, and periodic efforts would be made to banish the harlots to the countryside, especially when some notable was due to arrive; here, as everywhere else across the globe, the *filles de joie* were soon back in business.

The young Baron de Lahontan, a spirited officer who served in Canada between 1683 and 1693 and in later life wrote a three-volume bestseller on his experiences, offered this impression: 'The Canadians are well-built, sturdy, tall, strong, vigorous, enterprising, brave and indefatigable. They lack only the knowledge of literature. They are presumptuous and full of themselves, putting themselves ahead of all the nations on the earth; and unfortunately they do not have the respect that they might for their relatives ... '

His views can be matched with the remarks of Pierre Boucher, who came to Canada at age twelve and rose to be Governor of Trois-Rivières, the first Canadian to write a history of his own land: 'Good people may live here very contentedly; but not bad people, because they will be under close watch. Therefore I do not advise any of the latter to come as they might be compelled to leave, as many have done already. It is these who loudly decry the country, not having found in it what they expected.'

Boucher also was the first Canadian to be granted letters patent of nobility from the French Crown. He had been sent by the Governor, Baron d'Avaugour, to report personally to Louis XIV on the state of the colony. He took the seigneury of Boucherville, opposite the island of Montreal, and founded a family famous in Canadian annals. As the first aristocrat created in New France, his story should be more widely known. He spent four years with the Jesuits in Huronia and his first marriage was with an Indian girl, Marie. Then at thirty-two he wed Jeanne Crèvier, this marriage producing fifteen children. Pierre Gaultier, Sieur de La Vérendrye, was his grandson, and Marie d'Youville, the founder of the Grey Nuns, was a grand-daughter. The eighteenth-century guerrilla leader and explorer, Joseph Claude Boucher, Chevalier de Niverville, and the nineteenth-century Premier of Quebec, Sir Charles Eugène Boucherville, were others in this distinctly Canadian line.

The seigneury system did not, as popular idea persists, originate with Cardinal Richelieu; it began, in fact, when Richelieu was but a thirteen-year-old army cadet in Paris. The Marquis de la Roche, whose colonization plans were wrecked on Sable Island, was authorized in 1598 'to grant lands to gentlemen in the forms of *fiefs* and *seigneuries*.' Any man who had the funds or position to suggest he might aid in developing the wilderness could qualify for *la petite noblesse*. He was asked for no initiation fee and no annual rents. He could sell his seigneury but then he had to make a payment known as the *quint* to the Crown; it represented, as the word implies, a fifth of the value of the land.

Louis Hébert was granted a seigneury at Quebec in 1623, Guillaume de Caen took Cap Tourmente the following year, and Robert Giffard was given the lands about Beauport in 1634 – and

74

the modern city of Giffard, a residential suburb of Quebec City, recalls the good doctor. The grants were basically intended for men who could help colonize the land, but one absentee director of the Company of New France was given the whole of the Ile d'Orléans. Of sixty seigneuries granted between 1632 and 1663, fewer than a dozen went to *bona fide* farming squires – speculators held the rest – and in the first fifty years of New France not more than four thousand acres of land had been cleared. Eventually one in every six of the grants was rescinded, but the system was not formally abolished until 1854.

The best-known landed family of early Canada was that founded by the son of a Dieppe tavernkeeper who reached Quebec as a boy of fourteen in 1641. Charles le Moyne had an uncle Simon, already in Huronia with the Jesuits, and he joined him there, quickly learning the Iroquoian language and customs. He settled at Montreal, taking the seigneury of Longueuil across the river on the eastern bank, becoming one of the bravest of the band who supported the Sieur de Maisonneuve in holding Ville-Marie against the Five Nations. He went with the Marquis de Tracy to quell the Iroquois in 1666. He had married a *Canadienne* heroine, Cathérine Thierry, and they fulfilled at least one part of the seigneurial obligation by contributing eleven sons and two daughters to the colony.

These sons, each given the added name of some place familiar to the family, were a truly amazing bunch. Nearly every one of them is worth a movie, and one, Iberville, has already provided a television series. He was the Cid of New France. Iberville (Pierre, that is) first trained as a cadet in the French Navy, then returned to become the most famous warrior of New France. He was the scourge of the British in Hudson Bay. Seizing the isolated forts was no real feat but, in 1697, with his single ship *Pelican* he defeated three British ships, sinking one and capturing another. His other exploits ranged from establishing Biloxi on the Gulf of Mexico to destroying St John's. He died at Havana, Cuba, just short of his forty-fifth birthday, from yellow fever contracted during his attacks on the British West Indian islands of Nevis and St Christopher.

Iberville had taken three of his brothers on raids to Hudson Bay: Chateauguay (Louis le Moyne), Ste Hélène (Jacques) and Maricourt (Paul). Chateauguay was killed in the attack on the Hudsons Bay Company's Fort Nelson, and Ste Hélène died of wounds while defending Quebec against Sir William Phips. Bienville (Jean Baptiste) founded Mobile, Alabama, in 1702 – the first capital of Louisiana – and then, in 1718, he began the settlement on Lake Pontchartrain that grew into the great city of New Orleans. Charles, the eldest son, was Governor of Detroit and Trois-Rivières before being appointed Governor of Montreal; in 1700 the seigneury of Longueuil was raised to a barony by Louis XIV and Charles created the first baron. When the British dismantled the whole structure of French titles in Canada, the Longueuil peerage was allowed the only exception.

The incoming British found much to admire in *Canadien* society. The first two British Governors, Murray and Carleton, openly preferred their erstwhile enemies to the get-rich-quick merchants who swarmed into postwar Canada. James Murray, a dour little Scot who had been seriously wounded as a brigadier on the Plains of Abraham, once declared: 'I glory in having been accused of warmth and firmness in protecting the King's Canadian subjects, and of doing the utmost in my power to gain to my royal master the affection of that brave, hardy people whose emigration, if it shall ever happen, will be an irreparable loss to this Empire.'

Sir Guy Carleton, also scarred in the taking of Quebec, wrote: 'This country must, to the end of time, be peopled by the Canadian race.' He brought about the passing of the Quebec Act, ensuring the continuance of French civil law, language and the Roman Catholic faith, and extending the official boundaries to include the lands won by the French explorers on the Ohio and Mississippi. When the rebelling American colonists struck north in 1775 to add Canada to their infant republic, they were defeated before they crossed the border: with some few exceptions, the people did not rise to support them and, in fact, five hundred of them, under Colonel Noël Voyer, stood waiting on the walls of Quebec to defend their capital.

Chapter Seven
The British vanguard

All Europe was suddenly stirring to colonial ambitions. New France was established on the St Lawrence, exploiting the discoveries of Cartier. New England had been formed out of the northern reaches of the original Virginia territories. The ex-Sheriff of Bristol was trying to plant Newfoundland's first formal colony at Cupids, on Conception Bay. New Netherlands was taking shape along the Hudson. Now a Scottish patriot began to dream of a New Scotland in the Americas.

William Alexander was perhaps the most ill-starred and unlikely of all the colonizers of Canada. In a pursuit that broke many men of deep purse and worldly experience, he was born poor but proud – and he was a poet and a scholar. Given a huge royal grant of lands – *Nova Scotia* , in the court Latin of the time – based on the claims of Cabot and Gilbert, he found the plaguy French already climbing to some footholds there. He sent out two ships in succeeding years, without managing to plant a single colonist. When his son and heir finally did establish about seventy Scots on the Fundy mainland, half of them died from scurvy and the rest were shipped home within three years when King Charles I handed back Canada to the French.

Although he once held title on paper to all of present-day New Brunswick, Prince Edward Island, Nova Scotia and the Gaspé, plus a ribbon of land 150 miles wide on *both* sides of the full length of the St Lawrence River, Alexander, Senior, died at seventy-three so much in debt that his creditors surrounded his bed like a circle of vultures. For what it was worth, though, he had by then the dignity of a belted earl.

There are few areas of the world that can offer a more confusing history than that of the Canadian Maritimes. Closest to Europe, that sea-splashed shore concealed the mysterious Vinland of the Norse voyagers, while the palisaded villages of the early colonizers were mere specks of civilization hidden and often forgotten among the wilderness of river and upland sparsely inhabited by the Algonkian peoples who called themselves *Meeg-a-maage*, a name soon reduced to Micmac. Eight times in a single century the territory the French called Acadia and the British called Nova Scotia changed flags under invasion and counter-attack and as the European rulers swapped it back and forth, became a pawn in their imperial chess games.

A further minor confusion – not all that minor in some Nova Scotian minds – arises from the casual application of the adjective 'English' to all endeavours from the British islands until, at least, Wolfe's victory at Quebec. Thus the Scots from Kirkcudbright, Ayr, Renfrew and Clackmannan who came into the Canadian mainland in the early seventeenth century are almost invariably said to comprise the first 'English' settlement attempt, although their ventures discussed here occurred eighty years before the uneasy union between England and Scotland in 1707. And no Scotsman or Irishman was ever assimilated merely by act of king or parliament. Even by Confederation in 1867, there were still many more Scots and Irish in Canada than there were English.

From the district where Robert the Bruce was raised, no man was more Scottish than William Alexander, the man who gave Nova Scotia its name, its arms and its flag. He was born at Alva, near Bannockburn, in 1567, into a sept of the Campbells and was fortunate to be given a classical education at the grammar school in Stirling by a nephew of the famous Buchanan who had been tutor to the boy-king, James VI of Scotland. Alexander studied at Edinburgh University and at Leyden, in Holland. Himself chosen tutor to his relative, the seventh Earl of Argyll, he was introduced to the English court under the patronage of the powerful Campbells. Scotland's James had, of course, become James I of England in 1603, and he immediately installed Alexander as a court favourite, first helping his fortunes by appointing him Crown agent to collect debts owed the

*The Micmac house in its quiet setting suggests the
pre-European mood of the Maritimes. This Algonkian
group remained loyal to the French throughout their
struggle for the continent. Photo by* MALAK

Sovereign in Scotland (the rate of commission was 50 per cent), and then raising him into the knightage in 1609.

Alexander had published in 1603 his first major poem, a lengthy tragedy about Darius, the emperor who lost Persia to Alexander the Great, and in the following decade he issued a string of similar works, including a twelve-part tome on *The Great Day of the Lord's Judgement*. In his mid-forties he was one of the major literary lights of the kingdom. He had further ensured the King's approval by marrying a daughter of Sir William Erskine, brother of the Earl of Mar – both Erskine and Mar had been in charge of the education and training of the son of Mary Queen of Scots.

James was an accomplished writer himself and sponsored what is quite probably the most beautifully written book ever published, the King James Version of the Bible (1611). He chose Alexander as his collaborator in translating the Psalms of David. He also appointed the new knight, first, Master of Requests for Scotland, and, second, to the Privy Council of Scotland.

Alexander was now rising fast, showing a most unpoetical ambition, and he struck out for lasting fame by persuading the King to grant him a portion of the American lands as a satrapy of his own. Jamestown had been planted in Virginia in 1607, the Plymouth Colony was finally successful at Cape Cod in 1620, and now New Scotland would occupy the Atlantic lands north of the St Croix – the river that serves as border today between the United States and Canada.

This was, they knew, the same territory where De Monts, Champlain and the Poutrincourts had once established Port Royal for France – but Captain Samuel Argall, from Virginia, had swept the French out during 1613 and 1614. Or so they all complacently assumed. On September 10, 1621, Alexander became overlord and hereditary Lieutenant-General of the new domain of Nova Scotia. His charter gave him 'free and absolute power for arranging and securing peace, alliance, friendship, mutual conferences, assistance, intercourse, etc.,' to build forts, establish garrisons, and 'to do all things ... as the King might do if present in person.'

Sir William's first colonizing ship sailed from Scotland the following year, after recruiting settlers from the lands of Sir Robert Gordon of Lochinvar. He had transferred to Gordon, with the King's permission, the island of Cape Breton, now styled the barony of New Galloway. There was no rush to emigrate: only those who purchased land would have any permanent rights to the soil and, under the leases offered, farmers had to pay one-thirteenth of all revenue to the Lieutenant-General. The settlers mentioned in the scanty records were all penniless, illiterate labourers, save one blacksmith. After a long and rough crossing, the ship ran into another storm as it approached Cape Breton and the captain turned into St John's harbour for shelter. There, he decided to disembark all his passengers and return to London to pick up more supplies.

Alexander sent another ship, the *St Luke*, the following season – he had now committed himself to the large expenditure of £6000 – to pick up the stranded colonists and get them to the mainland. This captain learned at St John's that some of the Scots had died during the winter, others were out fishing on the Banks, and only ten could be located to proceed to Nova Scotia. He contented himself with sailing down the coast, looking for possible settlement sites; they are known to have examined Port Mouton, the harbour on the south-western shore named by the Sieur de Monts twenty years earlier. Returning to Newfoundland, the *St Luke* dumped the luckless immigrants and took in a profitable cargo of dried cod for the return journey. Some of the Scots found passage home with the West Country fishing fleet and others merged into the shore population of Newfoundland.

Alexander was fifty-seven, heavily in debt, but he was dazzled by the glittering promise of his private realm in Canada and he now proposed to his royal patron that the colony be financed by the sale of titles. King James had raised the sum of £225,000 for his private treasury by creating the Order of Knights Baronet in 1611 and selling the hereditary titles to English landowners who were prepared to pay one thousand guineas cash and to each maintain thirty soldiers for three years in the always troublous province of Ulster. Now he agreed to create a baronetage of Nova

Scotia, with the coveted title of 'Sir' going to the first 150 worthy Scots (and to their heirs in perpetuity), who would send six armed settlers to New Scotland and support them with food and equipment for two years. The applicants had also to pay Alexander 'ane thousand markis Scottis money towards his past charges and endeavouris.' They would each receive a land grant, a manor three miles long on the seacoast and six miles deep, and the right to wear around their necks an armorial badge with a tawny orange ribbon. It was not suggested these gentlemen should go to the trouble of sailing the Atlantic to gain their honours; the patents would be distributed at Edinburgh Castle.

Alexander gave his literary talents full rein and put out a booklet extolling the 'very delecate meadowes' of his lands and including a map complete with rivers shrewdly named for Scotland's Tweed, Forth and Clyde (the latter the St John River of modern New Brunswick). But business was terrible with no takers in the first six months; Alexander then offered to supply the settlers himself, with the titles being sold for straight cash on the barrelhead. Even after two years, only twenty-eight Scots had risen to the bait and Alexander, who was preparing more colonist ships, slid deeper into bankruptcy.

Charles I had succeeded his father, and he pushed Nova Scotia's interests even more energetically. Sixty-four baronets were on the official roll when Sir William Alexander's eldest son – who was also Sir William in his own right – set out from Dumbarton in March 1628 with two ships full of settlers and supplies. The Alexanders and the Kirke brothers had joined forces in the Company of Merchant Adventurers to seize Quebec and a monopoly of all Canadian trade, while Britain was in a state of war with France in support of the persecuted Huguenots. Three of the swashbuckling Kirkes captured Cardinal Richelieu's fleet sent to strengthen the starving Champlain at Quebec, and the frail capital of New France fell to Louis Kirke in July 1629. The younger Alexander who may well have taken part in the capture of Richelieu's ships, then sailed across the Gulf of St Lawrence with Lord Ochiltree, one of the Stewarts from Clackmannan, to establish, at last, the first Scottish settlement in New Scotland.

The site chosen was at Port-aux-Baleines, already a popular fisherman's haven, close by the site of the future Louisbourg, on Cape Breton. Ochiltree named the settlement Rosemar, disembarked his fifty subjects and immediately levied a duty of 10 per cent of their catch on all fisherman in the vicinity.

But the tide of Alexander's fortune was still out. A French captain, Charles Daniel, arriving tardily to assist Champlain, put in at Cape Breton where the angry fishermen told him that Quebec had fallen and that the Scots were digging in at Port-aux-Baleines. Daniel turned his two armed ships on Rosemar on September 8, captured the settlers and their supplies, and pulled down their buildings. Daniel used the materials and labour of his prisoners to build his own fort at Grand Cibou – today's St Ann's Harbour – where he left a small garrison before returning to France.

Meanwhile, Alexander had proceeded with his ships and the remainder of his emigrants – about seventy in all – completely around the Nova Scotian coast to the site of the earlier French Port Royal, in the landlocked Annapolis Basin. He was guided by Claude de la Tour, the French trader and frontiersman, who, with his son Charles, had escaped Argall's attack in 1613 and had since remained in Acadia, with his headquarters at Fort Pentagoet, at the mouth of the Penobscot River. Charles had established himself in Fort Loméron, at Cape Sable.

The La Tours were the stuff of legend. Claude had been captured by David Kirke and taken to England where he had met Sir William Alexander, Senior. Alexander had persuaded him to assist the Scottish settlements – since the British were now holding Quebec – and La Tour helped the younger Alexander to set up Charlesfort, six miles from the original Port Royal. His knowledge of the Canadian wilderness, and of the Indians, must have been invaluable. Charles de la Tour visited his father in that autumn of 1629 and both Frenchmen approved an agreement recognizing British sovereignty and the rights of the Alexanders. Before winter set in, Alexander sent his two

ships home for fresh supplies, and also sent Claude de la Tour with a draft agreement for Sir William, Senior, to sign; this document conferred on the La Tours a baronial fief stretching from modern Lunenberg around the toe of the peninsula to Yarmouth.

In England, the spirited Claude, now sixty, married a Scotswoman at the Court of King Charles, and accepted baronetcies for himself and for his son Charles. It was now admitted, though, that Louis Kirke had taken Quebec ten weeks *after* the signing of the Treaty of Susa, which terminated that round of hostilities between England and France, and that the seizure was therefore technically illegal. The doughty Samuel Champlain was battering at every door for the return of his beloved Canada. Charles de la Tour now refused to confirm his allegiance to Britain, baronet or not, and the diplomatic battle for Nova Scotia/Acadia lasted a full two years.

Finally, King Charles, in desperate financial straits with his recalcitrant Parliament, agreed to sacrifice the Scottish colony in return for the payment of the balance of the dowry of 800,000 crowns still owing from his marriage to Henrietta Maria, sister of Louis XIII. The Treaty of St Germain-en-Laye confirmed the deal.

The Scots were withdrawn, although some of them who had married local girls chose to remain, adding the French-speaking MacDonalds and MacNeills who still can be found among the indestructible *Acadiens*. Sir William Alexander was given a royal warrant for £10,000 as compensation – and Parliament, of course, refused to honour it. King Charles also added a portfolio of titles – they did not cost him, or the country, a penny. Alexander became Viscount Stirling, Lord of Tullibody, and then leapt into the Earldom of Stirling in 1633 with the subsidiary Viscountcy of Canada, and to yet a second Earldom (of Devon, the pretty tributary of the River Forth). His son predeceased him and all of these handles fell upon a single grandson.

The Alexander home is a mecca today for those who would seek the very beginnings of British settlement of Canada. The stone walls display the coat-of-arms of 107 of the baronets of Nova Scotia. All the honours were later confirmed as baronetcies of the United Kingdom and several are still being happily enjoyed today by lairds such as Sir Michael Bruce, Bt, and Sir Norman Dugald Campbell, Bt. One man who made good use of his title was the same Charles de la Tour who once haughtily rejected the bauble. When the British next seized Acadia – in 1654 – La Tour was shipped to London as a prisoner. There, he grandly flourished his patent as a Nova Scotian baronet and so convinced Oliver Cromwell of his good intentions that he was sent back as Governor for the conquerors.

That mid-century British foray had been mounted from Boston, by Major-General Robert Sedgwick, and, even though the respective homelands in Europe had been again technically at peace at the time, it was sixteen years before the French resumed control, after the Treaty of Breda. Again and again the British returned to reassert their control, almost at will against the neglected French outposts, and the fishermen and traders of New England came to regard most of Nova Scotia as their legitimate range. All the while, the Acadian farmers around the head of Fundy enlarged their families and their farmsteads, sold their produce and their spare labour to all comers, and struggled to stay aloof from the imperial wars.

All of 'ancient Acadia' – excluding, skilfully, Cape Breton and the lands across the Chignecto isthmus – were ceded by France in 1713 but it was not until the founding of the fortress city of Halifax thirty-six years later that the British presence was finally and forever established in New Scotland. A fortified post was maintained on the Gut of Canso, where fishermen had provisioned and sheltered since the early sixteenth century, and an attempt was made in 1728 to establish a new colony, to be called Georgia, on the northern bank of the Kennebec. This latter, forgotten, endeavour was aborted by New Englanders already pushing north who maintained they had inherited tracts there from dubious original purchases from the Indians of the Abenaki Confederacy. The French under Vaudreuil and Beauharnois at Quebec encouraged, bribed and bullied the Indians to oppose any and all English-speaking ventures while Louisbourg was under construction on Ile Royale (Cape Breton). Through those years, the one man more than any other who kept

Louisbourg on Cape Breton Island was the strongest and most costly fortress in North America. Begun in 1713 it was demolished by the British in 1758 and has since been partially reconstructed.
Photo by H. DURAND

the British fact alive on the northern mainland was, paradoxically, the French-born, Swiss-educated Major Paul Mascarene.

It was Mascarene's fate to spend nearly forty years as the unsung and mostly unrewarded commander-cum-administrator of Nova Scotia, living much of that time in the mouldering fort at Annapolis Royal. A choleric Welsh soldier, Richard Phillips, who had been at the Battle of the Boyne with King William, was the Governor of record for thirty years at a salary of £1000, but he spent only a total of five years in Canada. He settled one argument in his officers' mess by breaking a full wine bottle over his opponent's head. The man he appointed as his Lieutenant-Governor, Lieutenant-Colonel Lawrence Armstrong, was subject to fits of melancholia and eventually committed suicide by sword. Mascarene, the next senior officer in the garrison, then became the president of the Council of Nova Scotia, but the skinflint Phillips, from his seat in Britain, refused to grant him the £500 yearly that had been paid to Armstrong.

The regiment had taken over from the forces led by Nicholson and Samuel Vetch, who had captured Port Royal in 1710 (for the last time) and renamed it Annapolis Royal. Vetch of the Cameronians renewed the Alexander dream by becoming the Scottish Governor of Nova Scotia and ruling for seven years. Especially recruited under the colonelcy of the favoured Phillips, the regiment had companies stationed at St John's and Placentia in Newfoundland, and at Canso and Annapolis in Nova Scotia. During the span known as 'Walpole's Peace,' the garrison's morale and training slumped: the quartermaster went mad and the padre was living openly with another man's wife.

Mascarene patiently used his mother tongue of French, and his warm humanity, to try to resolve the unique problem of the *habitant* Acadians, the majority of whom refused equally the French orders to relocate as providers of food to Louisbourg, and the British orders to acknowledge full allegiance to the Crown under pain of expulsion. The French burned homes at Beaubassin in their attempts to force a full migration to Ile Royale or Ile St Jean (Prince Edward Island), and drew into their guerrilla bands some of the younger hotheads.

Twenty years a Frenchman before his arrival in England in 1706, Mascarene could understand and sympathize with the Acadians in their unshakable love for their patch of soil but he could not convince them of the inevitability of their fate unless they swore loyalty to George II; when the climactic war was joined for North America, the British policy-makers would never countenance several thousand uncommitted French – the only large permanent body of men in the Maritimes – in their rear, however professedly neutral. One loud American voice was accusing London of harbouring a guerrilla army that would cut British throats 'whenever the priests shall consecrate the knife.' But Mascarene stood almost alone against expulsion in 1745, when Governor William Shirley of Massachusetts sent General William Pepperrell to the surprisingly successful first siege of Louisbourg.

It was Mascarene, too, who had hired the Acadians to cut timber to strengthen his fort at Annapolis and thus stand off attacks by DuPont du Vivier and the Chevalier de Ramezay. He also had to cope with near-mutiny and lack of combat experience among his own men. Finally, to complete his humble duty, the sixty-five-year-old Mascarene stood shabbily on the scrubbed deck of *H.M.S. Beaufort* on July 13, 1749, to hand over all his official papers and his authority to the gorgeously attired thirty-six-year-old aristocrat Colonel Edward Cornwallis, newly arrived in the harbour of Chebucto as Governor and Captain-General of Nova Scotia.

His father a baron, his mother daughter of an earl, himself a former page to His Majesty, Cornwallis at once brought style, substance and the steely glint of power into the stepchild colony. He had influence everywhere – his twin brother became the Archbishop of Canterbury and, incidentally, the first owner of McNab's Island.

For reasons of empire, Louisburg had been returned to France under the Treaty of Aix-la-Chapelle but the British immediately moved to establish Halifax as an instant fortress, a counterweight on the lower shore. The site had been suggested a dozen times over the previous forty years and the grandiose plan called for two thousand houses on fifty streets. Cornwallis brought 2576 settlers with him in thirteen transports, losing only one child en route – a near-miracle for the times. He also brought a fire engine, a complete hospital, bricks, seeds, blooded horses, Bibles (in French and English), baubles for the natives, and plenty of powder for the fort he quickly built on Citadel Hill. He wrote back to the Duke of Bedford (after whom he named the inner harbour): 'The coasts are as rich as ever they have been represented – all the officers agree the harbour is the finest they have ever seen – the country is one continual wood, no clear spot to be seen.' The fishing was so good that 'a man may catch as much in two hours as will serve six or seven people for a week.'

This was, at last, the taking-up of Nova Scotia, 120 years after Sir William Alexander had been granted the territory by the first of England's Stuart kings. The Jesuit zealot, Father Jean-Louis le Loutre, promised *'une guerre éternelle'* from his headquarters with the Shubenacadie Indians but the Chevalier de la Corne drew the French behind the Missiquash River, on the Chignecto neck, where they built Fort Beauséjour to bar the way to the interior of New France. Soon, Fort Lawrence stood on the eastern bank – flint and touchwood for the Seven Years' War.

Elsewhere in the Maritime provinces, as that final contest loomed, the French still held Prince Edward Island with those *Acadiens* who had been persuaded or bullied into relocating and the remnant of the colonists brought out in 1720 by Daniel de Belleville. In Newfoundland, a British colony in name only since 1583, settlement was still rigorously opposed by the invincible combination of naval and mercantile interests; the Admiralty wanted young lads hardened and readied for the Navy by voyages to the Banks, and the West Country merchants clung tightly to a trade worth £600,000 a year. While Nova Scotia was advertising for immigrants, Newfoundland was still rounding up and deporting unwanted people.

Cornwallis had brought, in truth, a mixed bag. As bait to quality migrants, the British offered surplus senior officers six hundred free acres, with another thirty for each member of a family; each 'qualified settler' was offered fifty acres, plus ten for each child. One retired naval personage built a stone house staffed with sixteen Negro slaves. But the great majority of the arrivals were the ragged poor of Hogarth's London, drawn by the promise of a year's rations and watching for a chance to slip away to the American colonies where, they said, every man was a king. Many of the wretched grumbling Cockneys died of typhus in the first winter, their unworked plots in the thin sour soil taken up by thrifty and phlegmatic German and Swiss farmers squeezed out of Europe's crowded fields.

The reports of 'good rich land' that had reached England had all emanated from the Fundy side of the peninsula and, after an uneasy peace was concluded with the Indians in 1753, settlers soon pushed into the valleys of the Avon and Shubenacadie towards the orchard and crop land around the Minas and Annapolis basins. George II, who was ruler of Hanover as well as King of Great Britain, encouraged more German emigration and within five years Lunenburg was established, eighty miles down the coast, on the great bight of Mahone Bay. The transformation of these peasant farmers into the best schooner skippers on the Atlantic is one of the most engaging of Canadian tales.

After the wrenching tragedy of the deportation of the obdurate Acadians, and the total destruction of Louisbourg by Amherst and Wolfe, seven thousand New Englanders streamed into the Annapolis Valley and the Minas Basin lands, founding the settlements of Falmouth, Horton and Newport. On the south shore, cod fishermen established Yarmouth, Liverpool and Barrington. As discontent with distant autocratic government rumbled ever louder out of the Thirteen Colonies, a thousand Yorkshiremen settled Chignecto and the marshes, the family of William Owen took up the island of Campobello, and boatloads of Ulstermen and Scots arrived to thicken the British blood. The first representative assembly – the beginning of democratic government in Canada – met in Halifax in 1758.

Among his officers, Cornwallis had brought out Captain Horatio Gates, who was, as it hap-

pened, the illegitimate son of the Duke of Leeds. This Gates fought with Braddock in Ohio, remained in Virginia, became a patriot leader in the War of Independence, and won fame defeating 'Gentleman Johnny' Burgoyne's attack down the Champlain Pass from Canada. The battle at Saratoga signalled the end of the dream of a British continent in the Americas. In the long, heartbreaking struggle, the real victims were the thousands in the Thirteen Colonies who remained loyal to the British Crown and lost their hard-won farms, homes and businesses when the rebels, flushed with victory, refused to honour the terms of the Peace of Versailles.

In a hegira that dwarfed the movement of the Acadians, about one hundred thousand of these Loyalists left or were driven out of the new republic. One-third of them chose Nova Scotia, and their descendants remained to echo the opinion of Thomas Chandler Haliburton: 'I don't know what more you'd ask [said Sam Slick of Slickville]: almost an island, indented everywhere with harbours, surrounded with fisheries – the key to the St Lawrence, the Bay of Fundy, and the West Indies; prime land above one vast mineral bed beneath, and a climate over all temperate, pleasant and healthy. If that ain't enough for one place, it's a pity – that's all.'

PART III

Chapter Eight
Battles for the land

On December 6, 1757, across the river from Fort Anne at Annapolis Royal in Nova Scotia, a small party of British soldiers was resting at noon from cutting wood. The river flowed black and wide between them and the fort; the clearings along the banks were white with snow back to the woods. The men's axes stood struck in the logs they had cut; the three or four muskets they had brought, expecting no danger, were stacked out of reach while they ate dinner. Their voices rang loud and cheery around the fire and across the hush of winter.

Like a sheet ripped, the silence split with musket shots from the nearby forest. Grenadier John Miller pitched dead in the snow. His companions ran for the river but were captured on the shore. Marching their prisoners roughly back, the raiders tore off Miller's scalp and vanished into the woods.

The woodcutters had kept no guard because they had thought there was no danger. The French stronghold of Beauséjour on the Chignecto isthmus had been swept away by Colonel Robert Moncton more than two years earlier, and the grim deportation of about six thousand *Acadiens* – about half the regional population at the time – had followed when those sturdy but stubborn people refused to acknowledge the fact of British power. But there was still abundant, persistent, elusive danger. In the hills and forests, bands of refugees, men, women and children, were still in hiding.

Desperate men had to supplement their hunting with raids on their former farmhands for livestock and fruit. Desperate, they accepted military supplies and officers from New France and the help of Indian allies. Desperate, the embittered refugees became the danger the expulsion had been meant to end and some of them joined the guerrilla warfare on the frontier under leaders such as Charles de Boishébert and Boucher de Niverville. So Grenadier John Miller lay dead, his scalped head scarlet against snow, because he and his fellow Redcoats stood between the Acadians and the land their fathers had made.

The petty little raid, quickly forgotten among the great decisive events of those years, can be seen as the beginning of a new kind of warfare in Canada. Hitherto warfare had been for trade; now it was also to be for possession of the land. The story of the wars for trade and empire – the great epics of Louisbourg, Ticonderoga and Quebec – have been often told; that for the land itself has not, but is concealed within that for trade. Yet it lies nearer to what Canadians remember – that this is their country – as the memories of the great empires fade.

The hearth of Thomas Haliburton's home, called "Sam Slick's House," contains iron pots typical of those brought by the Loyalists to Canada. Photo courtesy INFORMATION CANADA

In Acadia there had been no war for possession of the land between Indians and French. There was no need. The French who settled there made their farms on the tidal marshes, unused by the Indians. But they could not escape the wars for trade. In 1713 Britain was ceded the old Nova Scotia of Sir William Alexander and Charles de la Tour and the neutrality of the Acadians came under pressure from two sides. On one, France hoped to recover Acadia, and saw in them an aid to doing so. On the other, the British, determined to hold the territory, believed it necessary to enforce the terms of the Treaty of Utrecht, by which the Fundy farmers were to swear allegiance to the Crown or to leave within two years. They in fact did neither, and the British failing to persuade them to take the oath, were loath to enforce the deportation. The Acadians, therefore, in the long peace from 1713 to 1744, thought they had made their point and were accepted as neutral.

They were not, in fact, so regarded by the French of Quebec, or by the British. Roman Catholic missionaries, in particular the Abbé le Loutre, kept them not only firm in the faith, but urged them to remember their ties with France. And when the French war parties came, the quiet folk could not deny them food and shelter, the constant need of guerrilla fighters living on the country, or prevent the more spirited young men from joining and guiding the parties.

The British took note and did not forget. To the feeble government and garrison of Annapolis Royal they added, immediately after the war's end in 1749, the strong imperial naval and military base of Halifax. Then they renewed in sterner terms the demand that the Acadians take the oath of allegiance. The peasants obstinately evaded the demand, hoping that the success of past evasions would recur.

They misread the times, and the temper of the British government, and of the New Englanders now interested in the lands as well as the fishing coves of Nova Scotia. In an act of preparation for war as deliberate as the founding of Halifax, the government of Nova Scotia organized the expulsion of the Acadians. It was an act of war as calculated, if not as brutal, as the devastation of the Palatinate in 1689 by the troops of Louis XIV.

Men, women and children were herded into the transports – forty-six vessels were used – and dispersed among the American colonies. The greatest number, 2182, were embarked at Grand Pré and other convoys left Pisiquid (now Windsor) and Cobequid Bay. Some escaped to French-held territory on the St John and the Petitcodiac. Others were simply missed or fled into the woods. These it was who fed, sheltered, and joined the French and Indian raiding parties such as that which had shot John Miller.

This aspect of the great war of seven years was not a war for empire; it was simply a war for the lands and homes from which the Acadian had been expelled, and which they never were to recover. After the siege and fall of the stone fortress of Louisbourg in 1758, further resistance by the Acadians was futile; deportation proceeded with some human cargoes sent directly to France from Ile St Jean and continued sporadically even after the capture of Montreal ended the war. Perhaps 11,000 from a total Acadian population of 15,500 were either deported or displaced and, although a considerable number eventually returned, thereafter they were a dispossessed people. In the parish of Ste Anne de Beaupré, overlooking the Ile d'Orléans, twenty miles below Quebec, all was quiet in August 1759. The sustained thunder of General James Wolfe's guns at Point Lévis, as they bombarded the Lower Town of Quebec across the river, could indeed be heard. But their rumble had become an accepted sound since the attack began on June 27 and in no way disturbed the cattle in the meadows or the men scything the wheat for harvest.

There were, of course, nearer sounds and evidences of war than the guns at Lévis. From the tented camp of the British along the Montmorency came the bugle calls at dawn and dusk, and on some days a crackle of musketry when the French Indians farther up the Montmorency crept too close to the British lines. The *habitants*, called into the militia, knew the Château Richer, the stone house of Father de Portneuf, *curé* of Ste Anne, as the headquarters for the men of the resistance the priest was leading. It was an open resistance openly proclaimed: the priest had once invited a British officer to dine with him and explained that both were soldiers and that he hoped he might

An ancient anchor in Nova Scotia conjures up pictures
of the ships which carried the early brave settlers to
Acadia, and later transported them away to exile.
Photo by JOHN DE VISSER

be 'excused in fighting for his poor parishioners, and defending his country.' So men of his large armed force came and went to the house, men carrying muskets and intent about their business.

Wolfe had been stung by his unsuccessful foray at the end of July on the Beauport position, held in the British view by 'militia and peasants,' and a scorched-earth policy went into effect along the St Lawrence. On August 23 a force of three hundred from the 43rd Regiment advanced on Ste Anne with a field gun. The soldiers concealed themselves and covered the Château Richer with their muskets. Then without warning the cannon fired round after round through the house.

De Portneuf with thirty men ran out to close with the attackers. On the dry grass of the lawn, on the dust of the village road, they were mowed down by the withering musketry. When all were killed, all were scalped in the barbarity that the war of raid and ambush had aroused, even in regular troops. Presbytery, church and the village houses were fired, the billowing smoke visible to the troops at Lévis, the French in Quebec, and the *habitants* down the river. Other raids, mostly mounted by the American Rangers with the British, took place at Baie St Paul, St Joachim, Murray Bay, Kamouraska and Ste Anne de la Pocatière.

The same script as in Acadia was now being enacted in different terms along the St Lawrence. The conquest of Canada was, like that of Acadia, being carried out for the sake of trade and empire. It was meant to end French power in America. The toast of the British messes in 1759 was, 'British colours on every French fort, port, and garrison in America.' But in the valley of the St Lawrence, as in the tidal estuaries of Fundy, there were French people living on and by the land, farmers not traders, and to them the wars had been wars for their lands and homes. What were they to do? Could they, like the Acadians, hope to be neutral?

In fact, they had no such choice. In New France government was strong, as it had never been in Acadia. The *habitants* were subject to *corvée*, obligatory labour, and men from 16 to 60 were liable for service in the militia. The *habitants* of New France toiled and fought in the great war for empire as did the Marquis de Montcalm's professional regiments from France. But the people fought for the land that was in contest, not just for imperial gain and grandeur. They were defending the fields in which their wives and daughters worked along the banks of the *fleuve St-Laurent* while husbands and sons were in the forests of the Allegheny, or at Ticonderoga, or working canoes up the rapids of the St Lawrence to Cataraqui and Oswego on Lake Ontario.

The *Canadiens* had a long tradition of defending their homes against Iroquois raids – and of making raids of their own, Indian fashion in *la petite guerre*, a swift and sanguine warfare of ambush and retreat. Under the Le Moynes, their grandfathers had struck at the English posts on James Bay; under the Hertels, at the New England border towns. They knew of Sir William Phips' failure at Quebec and of the wreck of the armada of Admiral Sir Hovenden Walker in the St Lawrence – the victories commemorated in the church of Notre-Dame-des-Victoires in Quebec. New France had been and could be defended; it did not lie entirely open to the sea like Acadia.

When Admiral Sir Charles Saunders and General Wolfe brought another British fleet up the St Lawrence to Quebec in 1759, the *habitants* therefore were dismayed, not dispirited. When Wolfe appealed to them to be neutral, they defied him. 'The King of Great Britain,' announced Wolfe, 'wages no war with the industrious peasant, the sacred orders of religion, or the defenceless women and children; to these, in their distressful circumstances, his royal clemency offers protection. The people may remain unmolested on their lands, inhabit their houses, and enjoy their religion in security; for these inestimable blessings, I expect the Canadians will take no part in the great contest between the two crowns.'

The people and the priests made no submission, no profession of neutrality. Such was apparently their choice, but had they decided otherwise then General Montcalm was ready to loose his Indians upon them, so grim was the temper of the times. They defended their homes, as their firing on the British boats at Baie St Paul, sounding the river for the advancing fleet in June, had shown them ready to do.

The same Indian allies of the French, some of them *Canadiens* disguised as Indians, harried the

A Quebec bake oven, symbol of the home and land
which the habitant would defend against all comers.
Photo by DON NEWLANDS

foraging parties of the British army, killed and scalped stragglers, and raided the rear of the British lines. 'We went out to make oars,' a Grenadier sergeant-major wrote, 'with a small party to cover us. Five were killed, of which four were scalped ... ' The American Rangers struck back, bringing in the scalps of those they killed. The French guerrillas could only have been sustained in the field by the *habitants* and, at the end of July, Wolfe had issued his second proclamation, warning that if the raiding did not cease retaliation would follow.

The men shot at Ste Anne had died that the Canada they knew might remain French. Nor was their hope wholly to be disappointed. For, as the great war lurched to its close, with the fall of Quebec in 1759 and of Montreal in 1760, the British conquerors were satisfied to have ended French power in America. They did not harry or penalize the *habitants* – like the Acadians, they were free to leave, or to take the oath of allegiance.

The Canadians, excepting their officials and bureaucrats, remained in the only fatherland they knew and, as the Treaty of Paris had the ring of finality, took the oath of allegiance. Unlike the Acadians, in the final battle for the land they had fought openly, then accepted the honourable hand of the conqueror. They kept the land that was theirs and affirmed that they were Canadians, rooted in the soil of Canada. They fought, and lost, and won.

On the early snow along the bank of West Canada Creek in the Adirondacks a few dark forms lay, not yet wholly still. The echoes of rifle fire hung in the sharp late autumn air. The Americans with their Oneida scouts passed the corpses swiftly, to be sure their living companions had gone. When they returned, they examined the dead. It was October 29, 1781.

One of them, as his gold-braided hat signified, was an officer. An Indian swiftly ripped off his scalp and emptied his purse. An American emptied his pockets, and then, as a companion across the river later reported, 'holding up a commission and waving it, said he had Butler's commission.' Captain Walter Butler, of Butler's Rangers, had died commanding the rearguard of the retreat into Canada of a last expedition from the St Lawrence to the Mohawk that had failed, as earlier ones had done, to free the lands of the Butlers and their fellow Loyalists from the rebels of the Thirteen Colonies.

Now, as the wheel of fate turned, it was men of British blood who were being expelled from the lands of their fathers. Like the Acadians before them, they must find new lands deeper in the wilderness, lands they would make Canadian. But some of them fought bitterly without quarter, in regular units and as guerrillas, for the ground their forebears had broken and made their own. They were, on the whole, poorly used by inferior British commanders.

In that fierce, even savage, civil war, which we call the American Revolution, perhaps as many of the two and a half million colonists stood originally for the King and a united empire as did for independence. Certainly, in the great province of New York more men came out in arms for the Crown than for the republic and the struggle was one not so much for independence or loyalty as for life and land. For it was clear that those who lost would forfeit their land.

Nowhere was the War of Independence more a civil war based on local feuds and neighbourhood resentments than in northern New York, the Mohawk Valley and the land south of Lake Ontario. This was first and foremost the land of the Iroquois Confederacy. Neutral between Britain and France from 1701, they remained except for the Oneidas, loyal to Britain in the revolution. Their warriors fought for the Loyalist cause, and on its defeat most of them found refuge in Canada on lands ceded them by the Mississaugas, lands where their descendants live to this day.

Famous then and now were certain important landed proprietors who brought tenants to their own lands in the Mohawk Valley. The chief of these was the Irishman Sir William Johnson, Bt, renowned for his influence on the Iroquois, holding the post of Superintendent of Indian Affairs. He was a great landowner, and from Johnson Hall at Johnstown ruled as baronial chieftain of many tenants, the latest of whom were Catholic Highlanders, innured to war. In the summer of 1755, Johnson had fielded three thousand men in the Champlain Pass and administered a bloody rebuff to the fresh army of French regulars brought to Canada by the new Commander-in-Chief, Baron Dieskau. When the revolution wracked New York, Johnson's only son, Sir John, was authorized by Governor-General Sir Guy Carleton to raise the King's Royal Regiment of New York, known as the 'Royal Greens' and the 'Royal Yorkers.'

Next in rank, wealth of land, and social influence were the Butlers of Butlersbury. When the Seven Years' War was over William Johnson and John Butler had returned from the battlefields to enjoy the peace that had confirmed their possession of their estates. Self-made men, they had created places of wealth and power on the borderland of New York. The French menace gone, time would consolidate the positions of their sons – no one then could foresee the skirmish at the ford on West Canada Creek twenty years later that would bring death to Walter Butler and presage the expulsion of the Johnsons from their spreading lands.

The warfare in northern New York was in the first place a British and Indian war against American settlers; next it was a social war, of tenant against landlord, of small-owner against great, made the more bitter as all titles and all status were so new. It was waged with a peculiar bitterness because the American patriots, striking first with the *élan* of rebellion, drove the Loyalist men north into Canada and imprisoned their families, sometimes using them as hostages. Finally, the Mohawk and the upper reaches of the Susquehanna and the Delaware were larders for General George Washington's armies in New Jersey and Pennsylvania.

After Burgoyne's failure in 1778, the Loyalist regiments – of which Butler's Rangers was one – raided deep into New York to terrorize the enemy, to free the captives, and to destroy the farms and food supplies that fed the rebel forces. The Dutch-born New York Loyalist, Major Arent de Peyster, organized bands of raiders from Detroit to draw strength away from the Continental armies. A young English major named John Graves Simcoe was leading the Queen's Rangers, made up of Loyalists from New York and Connecticut.

It was a fierce and bloody business, filled with names of massacres like Wyoming and Cherry Valley, and, in popular American folklore, with the names of border ruffians like Joseph Brant, Henry Hamilton, the Butlers, Alexander McKee and Simon Girty. Washington once offered $300 for the scalp of McKee, the Indian agent who encouraged loyal tribes to harry the inland frontiers. The legends contained some fearsome exaggeration, and there was no recognition that each side was fighting for what it could claim as rights.

It was a war that should never have been fought and which the King's men could never win. Independence for the swiftly maturing American provinces after a century and a half was surely inevitable and right. But to those Loyalists – the Americans now prefer to call them 'Tories' – who chose courageously to stand for the monarchy and constitutional government, it meant the loss of a homeland just as precious as any patriot's acre.

When the War of 1812 was nearing its close, Major George C. Salmon, of the 2nd Norfolk Militia, wrote to Lieutenant-Colonel Parry Jones of the 103rd Regiment at Burlington:

My dear Sir,

We have received the Communication from Widow Thomas's and will forward it to Burford – I am sorry to inform you Dickson's party have murdered old Capt. Francis, he slept in the new House and a family that works the Farm in the old House adjoining. They came in the Night to the old part and insisted on having Francis, they said he was in the next House, to which they proceeded, the old man said he would surrender himself a prisoner but begged them to spare his life which they declared they would not – he then looked out of the upper window if there was any way to escape and was shot through the head – The Family heard him fall – They then desired them to take out the Goods but would not suffer his remains to be removed which was burned with the House.

The brutal murder of Captain William Francis of the Norfolk Militia, though corroborated, remains unexplained in the surviving documents. Perhaps it is sufficiently explained, except for the peculiar atrocity of its circumstances, by the general character of the war in the Upper Canada peninsula. After the defeat of Major-General Henry Procter and Tecumseh, his Shawnee ally, at Moraviantown on October 5, 1813, the western peninsula, with the Niagara, lay open to American invasion. But the victorious General William Henry Harrison did not follow up his opportunity, and Burlington Heights remained the base of British operations. The two peninsulas lay open to the passage of the armies and to the appearance of raiding parties of American irregulars, some of them American settlers who had become British subjects.

The result was to reveal that the War of 1812 in Upper Canada was only in part a struggle over maritime rights and power in America between Great Britain and the United States. On the Niagara frontier and in the western peninsula it was a war for the land itself, a harsh war like that in northern New York during the American Revolution. In fact, it was a second chapter and continuation of that war. Thomas Butler, brother of Walter, and Lieutenant-Colonel of the 4th Lincoln Militia, had taken part in the victory on Queenston Heights in 1812.

The raids of rangers and irregulars, of bushwackers like Andrew Westbrook and of volunteers like Joseph Willcocks, late of the Upper Canadian Assembly and Lieutenant-Colonel of the Canadian Volunteers (U.S.), devastated the countryside, particularly the lower Thames Valley and the north coast of Lake Erie from the Niagara to Long Point. They were designed to destroy flour and livestock that would provision the British forces and to capture the officers of the militia, such as Captain Francis, to make that force useless. But local feuds and personal enmities, as in the Mohawk Valley before, had played their part in the devastation, with results like the shooting of Francis.

Underneath lay always the question: to whom should the land belong – to the Loyalists and their children, and those who would give at least passive allegiance to the Crown, or to citizens of the United States? In fact, the occupied lands of Upper Canada in 1812 belonged to both British subjects and Americans. Those who were Americans, whether they had taken the oath of allegiance or not, far outnumbered the British. Indeed, if it is remembered that the Loyalists were Americans, those of American descent made up the overwhelming majority of Upper Canadians. It was this fact which made the American expectation that the conquest was only a matter of marching not wholly unreasonable. Upper Canada at least seemed a plum ripe for the picking.

The successful defence of the province seemed unlikely. There was only one regular battalion in the province in 1812, the 43rd Regiment of Foot; the militia could not be relied on; and the Assembly would not at first grant the authority to suspend *habeas corpus* so that those suspected of American sympathies might be held without trial. The regular army of the United States was authorized at 35,000 men. It is easy to see why Major-General Isaac Brock, Commander-in-Chief and acting administrator of Upper Canada, said: 'I speak loud and look big.'

To win Indian support early successes were vital and these Brock gained by the capture of Michilimackinac and Detroit. As the familiar pattern of local border and Indian warfare developed, the remembered issues of 'loyalty' and 'treason' arose again after a long generation. It was the background of uncertain loyalty that led to the 'Bloody Assize' of Ancaster in May 1814.

At that now-forgotten trial, nineteen men who had been captured from two American raiding parties, all British subjects, were tried for high treason for which the penalty then was hanging, drawing and quartering. Four were acquitted, one pleaded guilty, fourteen were convicted; seven were reserved until the will of the Prince Regent should be known, eight were executed.

The particular raids had taken place in November and December of 1813. One was led by Benajah Mallory, a former member of the Upper Canadian Assembly. Their purpose was to capture militia officers and to destroy grain, livestock and flour mills that might furnish the British troops with provisions. (One of the raiders stole a greatcoat and blanket from the house of Captain Samuel Ryerse, uncle of the famous educator Egerton Ryerson.)

Members of the first party were surrounded and captured at night in the house of John Dunham, the 'ringleader' in Woodhouse, Norfolk County. Loyal members of the militia, having learned of the raid, held a meeting of thirty-six persons, twenty-one militia officers, at the house of Captain William Drake, and resolved to defend 'the persons and property' of the inhabitants and to attack the marauders. They made their move on the night of November 14, advancing in darkness through swamp and forest to surround Dunham's house. A brief brisk skirmish resulted in the killing or wounding of a few of the raiders; eighteen 'rebels' were captured.

In December a party of militia led by Lieutenant Henry Medcalf captured a similar party at McRae's house, near Chatham on the Thames River. Of the prisoners taken those who were American were prisoners of war, and treated as such; but those who had taken the oath of allegiance, nineteen in number, were British subjects, and liable to a charge of high treason.

The conflict of loyalties can be felt even yet; then they were far sharper. Loyalty had been an issue since the opening of the war. Mere passivity, a neutrality of farmer folk not unlike that of the Acadians, could be tolerated as long as supplies were furnished and the militia allowed to function. But when British subjects, even though of American birth and however war-weary, took action in concert with American forces to deny provisions to the defenders of the province and to destroy the militia by capturing its officers, the offenders had to face the due process of law.

The Governor-General, Sir George Prevost, issued a special commission for the trial for high treason of the nineteen prisoners, and of fifty others who had not been taken, sixty-nine persons in all. The place of trial was Ancaster as, alone of towns in the western part of the province, it was not in enemy hands, and offered enough accommodation. The Attorney-General of Upper Canada, the twenty-three-year-old John Beverley Robinson, a son of Loyalists, managed the prosecution with that calm wisdom and moderation of temper that marked him all his life. The judges were the members of the Court of King's Bench of Upper Canada; none of the three was a Loyalist, or Canadian-born. The members of the jury were men of the locality.

The trial was in every respect a formal, civil process, in no sense irregular, neither ordered in panic nor pursued in passion. The warm June weather emphasized the atmosphere of peace that bathed a town already the most beautiful in the province. Soldiers might guard the court, dispatch riders trot through the main street on their way to Burlington Heights, or to Norfolk County. Other raiders, with the Canadian volunteers led by Major Abraham Markle, a former member of the Assembly of Upper Canada, had landed at Dover and devastated the Norfolk shore as far as Turkey Point. The armies along the blackened Niagara frontier, with Newark, Lewiston and Buffalo in ashes, were manoevring, as the trials ended, for the battles of Chippawa and Lundy's Lane. In the court, day after day, the prisoners one by one stood trial.

When the court rose, fifteen stood condemned to die the death of traitors. The wave of horror and pity that came in from the countryside, expressed often by loyal subjects and public officers, can still be felt across the years. The plea of Polly Hopkins, eleven years married and with four children, that mercy might be granted to her husband is no less moving now than it was then.

The executive council of the provinces consulted the justices and the attorney-general and as a result seven of the fifteen were reprieved until the will of the Prince Regent should be known. They were sent to Quebec to await the further verdict, and pass from history, saved no doubt by the ending of the war. But eight men, Isaiah Brink, Adam Crysler, John Dunham, Noah Payne Hopkins (Polly's husband), Dayton Lindsey, George Peacock, Benjamin Simmons, Aaron Stevens, were taken to the gallows erected on Burlington Heights, where Hamilton cemetery now is, and hanged. One may hope that they were hanged until they were dead and without the further barbarities the law permitted. What happened is unknown; silence covers the sequel of the 'Bloody Assize.'

The stream of time has washed away the blood and cooled the passions resulting from the two generations of warfare from 1754 to 1814. Yet in the several 'bloody assizes' of those years, verdicts were also reached. The Acadian lands won from the tides of Fundy were no longer Acadian, but British. The seigneurial lands of the St Lawrence were French, those of northern New York American, those of Canada, Canadian. A boundary was drawn and fixed along the mountains and the rivers. The battles for the land were over.

PART III

Chapter Nine
All the King's men

The first parcel of those immigrants to Canada whom history remembers as the United Empire Loyalists reached Nova Scotia in March 1776 in some haste and disarray when General Sir William Howe decided to evacuate Boston amidst the menace of the rebels entrenched about the port. He had won the bloody affray of Bunker Hill but he then came under cannon-fire from the Dorchester heights. The passengers in his naval transports were the one thousand men and women, mostly of some position and status in New England, who so detested the 'levelling' democracy raging in the Thirteen Colonies that they were willing to forsake their native land to remain under the British flag.

Of course, they may, in that first episode of the revolution, have thought the move would be only temporary, until Britain's overwhelming sea power and its regiments of seasoned Redcoats could be brought into play. Some had mixed feelings. The grandmother of Sir Leonard Tilley (who became one of the Fathers of Confederation) once told him: 'I watched the sails disappearing in the distance, and such a feeling of loneliness came over me that, although I had not shed a tear through all the war, I sat down on the damp moss with my baby in my lap and cried.'

Eventually, as the War of Independence ran its incredible eight-year course – incredible in its conception, execution and fluctuations of fortune – about fifty thousand Loyalists opted for Canada, or were obliged to go. The failure of the Philadelphia Congress to head off this expulsion, or their covert encouragement of it, was within a generation to cost the United States control of the entire continent above the Rio Grande. It sacrificed, too, much of the leavening of civilizing culture just beginning to rise in the American mix. Even by 1800, Harvard could boast only three professors.

The floodtide of migration north came in the autumn of 1783 when General Sir Guy Carleton, now Commander-in-Chief of the shrinking British North America, finally evacuated New York. Manhattan and Long Island had been held for seven years, since the Howe brothers, army and navy, defeated Washington and Israel Putnam at Brooklyn and Kips Bay. As the grandiose plan for splitting the rebel states in two – Burgoyne down the Richelieu and Howe up the Hudson – came to nothing, and when Cornwallis surrendered his trapped army at Yorktown on Chesapeake Bay, the Loyalist families crowded into New York with what they had been able to salvage. For many, that amounted to the clothes they wore.

The peace treaty, signed in a small hotel in the Rue Jacob in Paris, indicated that Loyalists would be reinstated in their property, and that all debts owing at the outbreak of the rebellion would be honoured. On the contrary, the vindictive fury against 'the Tories' mounted and it was obvious the Congress was never going to act forcibly against the violations. There was, wrote one Loyalist woman, 'no other resource but to submit to the tyranny of exulting enemys or settle a new country.' The British government accepted the moral debt, carried the refugees to new lives in Britain, the West Indies, in Nova Scotia and in the huge inland colony then known only as Quebec. A few groups with fishing interests chose Newfoundland.

There had been some flurries of rebel support in Nova Scotia – a fumbling local invasion from

Maine petered out at Fort Cumberland – but, following the evacuation of Boston, Halifax became the base of British power on the Atlantic and the navy cleared the Bay of Fundy of all enemy activity. Fort Howe was built at the mouth of the St John River to replace the sacked Fort Frederick. At one 'town meeting,' Massachusetts-style, where support for the Yankees was being discussed, an old retired soldier suddenly marched into the hall. He was in full uniform, snowy head held high, musket loaded and bayonetted. At the speaker's table he turned, snapped to the 'on guard' and demanded in a steady voice that the man should rise who was plotting against Crown and Constitution. There was a rush for the door, and the meeting adjourned.

At New York, the Loyalists had formed associations, mainly of regional groups, and appointed agents to travel to Nova Scotia on preliminary surveys. As early as 1775 Governor Francis Legge had sent an official invitation to enter his province, and as the area of conflict widened, several shiploads arrived. The vanguard of the main body arrived in the fall of 1782, jamming an already crowded Halifax; tent towns were pitched at Point Pleasant and on Citadel Hill, dockside warehouses turned into dormitories, churches were commandeered. Three hundred Loyalists were taken directly to the Annapolis Valley.

John Adams, the New England lawyer who succeeded Washington as President of the new nation, figured the committed Loyalist as one-third of the population, with another third lukewarm, sitting on the fence ready to come to terms with either of the opposed factions. When the Declaration was adopted on July 4, Adams indicated the undercurrents when he stated gleefully that the 'patricians' could now 'stamp and foam and curse, but all in vain.'

In some ways, the revolution was more a civil war, with 'Cavalier' and 'Roundhead' factions. Families were split tragically. Benjamin Franklin's only son William, then the Governor of New Jersey, rejected his father's cause and eventually removed to England. John Jay's brother was a Loyalist, as were both the mother and brother of New York's Governor Morris. Of the fifty-six signers of the Declaration, in a religious era, only one was a clergyman and only one Roman Catholic.

When the die was cast, known Loyalists were treated as enemies of the state, some few were hanged by mobs, others were whipped, tarred and feathered, property worth millions was confiscated – including many of the largest estates in America. Slaves were confiscated, too, and one patriot general, Thomas Sumter, used them as pay for his troops; a private got one Negro for each enlistment of ten months. Thomas Jefferson's noble sentiment that 'all men are created equal' did not quite apply to all men.

Thousands of Loyalists fought back in recognized regiments like Simcoe's Queen's Rangers, Tarleton's British Legion, Thompson's American Dragoons and Johnson's Royal Yorkers, and in raiding parties such as those led by the Butlers from Niagara. Battles were fought at Oriskany in upper New York, at King's Mountain in the Carolinas, in the capture of Charleston in 1780 where five thousand rebel soldiers were taken; and bloody and bitter guerrilla clashes occurred at Paoli, Hancock's Bridge, Cooper River, Hanging Rock, Waxhaw Creek, and in the Mohawk and Schoharie valleys. But the Loyalist spirit, running fiercely in men fighting for a principle honestly held and for the homes and possessions of their families, was squandered by appallingly inept British generals and was never a deciding factor in the crucial battles. There was no Marlborough and no Wolfe in those campaigns.

The Loyalists, burning with outrage as they began from scratch again in the wilderness, quickly changed the character and stiffened the backbone of Canada, still at that time a mainly French-speaking sprawling state uncertain of its shape or strength. They created Upper Canada, the Ontario of today, and carved out New Brunswick as a Loyalist province on the flank of ancient Nova Scotia. It was a Loyalist from New York who took the first settlers to the Red River colony, the future Manitoba. For more than a century the Loyalist breed played a dominant, moulding role in Canadian politics and education, military and mercantile life, and the distinct influence of their descendants is far from negligible today. This nation is more truly 'American' than

Sir Isaac Brock's monument on Queenston Heights commemorates the place where he died defending the land against the Americans in the 1812 War. Photo courtesy ONTARIO MINISTRY OF INDUSTRY AND TOURISM

chauvinists think, and as north-south intercourse inevitably expands, it will likely become ever more so.

The Loyalist cause was never one of simple black-and-white dimensions. For instance, most of the Loyalists, or 'Tories' in the later U.S. folklore, were strongly in favour of resistance to the restrictive and intrusive colonial legislation rammed through the British House of Commons by the government of Lord North. While they did support the principle of constitutional monarchy, some regarded the Hanoverian George III as a usurper of the throne. The Loyalists were by no means all 'English' or even British – they included, for instance, Dutch, Germans and even some French.

The strength of the Loyalists in the American colonies in 1775 is seldom remembered today. Only a vocal and virile minority were for open rebellion. Weeks after Bunker Hill, the Continental Congress adopted a Pennsylvanian resolution seeking a reconciliation with Britain. The written rules of the 'Minute Men,' the Massachusetts militiamen who first actively resisted the redcoats, included, in the first place: 'To defend to the utmost of our power His Majesty King George III, his person, crown and dignity.' Although Thomas Paine's widely circulated booklet, *Common Sense*, pleaded political independence and called the King 'the Royal Brute,' although that King was hiring thirty thousand mercenaries, the so-called Hessians, in Europe to stamp out the revolt, the radicals in Congress had to resort to questionable high-pressure tactics to win approval of the Declaration of Independence on July 2, 1776. Six of the colonies – major ones like Pennsylvania and New York – were, at first, against the resolution. One delegate, Caesar Rodney of Delaware, rode eighty miles at the gallop to swing his state's vote for independence.

Governor John Parr hastened the establishment of new townsites – one at Port Roseway, formerly Rasoir, now renamed Shelburne in honour of the British Prime Minister; another on Passamaquoddy Bay; a third on both shores of the fine harbour at the outlet of the St John, under the protection of the guns of Fort Howe. The Loyalists of Penobscot, thriftily dismantling their houses and their brick coffee shop, moved north to the new border and founded St Andrews. More shiploads arrived in the spring of 1783 and the final New York convoys, with eight thousand people, came that autumn. On the day before Carleton handed over New York, the total number of Loyalists despatched to Nova Scotia was calculated at 35,010.

Not all of the settlements flourished. Two thousand were landed at Port Mouton where they shivered until lumber arrived from Halifax to build their new town, Guysborough. They subsisted on a ration of one pound of biscuit and one pound of salt pork a day. When all their labours went up in smoke the following spring, most moved away – some to a new Guysborough on Chedabucto Bay, others to found St Stephen on the St Croix. The scanty soils and bitter winters of the eastern coast soon discouraged the settlers at Shelburne. Hundreds of them moved to St John's Island – a separate province since 1769, soon to be renamed for Prince Edward, Duke of Kent – and to the better farmlands of the Annapolis Valley. For a brief hour of glory Shelburne boasted sixteen thousand residents and played host to Prince William Henry (afterwards King William IV); beflagged warships stood in the harbour and fine homes were raised in King and Queen Streets. But within a generation, the population had dwindled to three hundred.

On the Fundy shore a happier story was being written. In one convoy twenty ships crammed with Loyalists and their goods dropped anchor by Partridge Island, in the harbour at the mouth of the St John River where the twin towns had been named Carleton and Parrtown. Loyalist agents had previously scanned the fertile valley as far upstream as Oromocto and reported the river as being the equal of the Hudson or the Connecticut; they examined and admired the major tributaries, the Kennebecasis, Nerepis, Belleisle, Jemseg, and noted particularly the ice-free harbour and the plentiful fishing. They asked for mill stones, materials to build saw mills, shovels, hoes, axes, plough shares, nails and spikes, muskets and cannon, and about four hundred acres per family. They suggested two thousand acres in every township be used for the support of a clergyman and a thousand acres to support a schoolteacher.

When Jonathan Beecher disembarked, he fairly expressed the sentiments of the 'True Blues': 'As soon as we had set up a kind of tent we knelt down, my wife and I and our two boys, and kissed the dear ground and thanked God that the flag of England floated there, and resolved that we would work with the rest to become again happy and prosperous.' Eventually, 14,162 persons were shipped to the St John, 10,014 of them officially listed as Loyalists and their dependants. There were 1578 servants among them, including 220 blacks. Children under ten numbered 2340. Loyalist Edward Winslow was a direct descendant of the Edward Winslow of the *Mayflower* and he would soon be sending his son, aged nine, to boarding school in England. On one ship's passenger list, Elizabeth Strang classed herself as 'Young Lady' but that was probably only a temporary label in a country where men outnumbered women more than two-to-one.

During winter in makeshift quarters, tempers often flared between the new arrivals – many of them still smarting from their losses in both dignity and property – and the old hands asserting proprietorial rights around the harbour that boasted history going back to Champlain and the La Tours. The trading partnership of Simonds, White and Hazen – branching into lumber, lime, flour, fish, ship-building – had been established at Upper Cove for more than two decades.

In the early spring, the Loyalist farmers took boat upstream, over the Reversing Falls where, twice each day, the racing tides rise to cover the ledge over which the river spills, briefly reversing the flow. Across the wide Indiantown basin and into the lake-like Long Reach, they made their way towards the wilderness lots that they had drawn in the lottery. Settlements centred at Kingston, Sussex Vale and Gagetown, and the surveys carried the new grants from Maugerville right up to the site of present Woodstock. Eighty-four navigable miles upstream where the Nashwaak joins the St John, Fredericton, the capital-to-be, was settled by ex-members of the Loyalist regiments.

The grants had been made on the basis of one hundred acres for each head of family, plus another fifty acres for each member of his family; only those who had actually fought for the Crown were treated more liberally – 1000 acres for majors and colonels, 700 for captains, 500 for lieutenants, and the sergeants and corporals 200 acres each. Eminent Loyalists had asked for estates of up to 5000 acres but the British, remembering their recent experience, saw dangers in the establishment of another landed upper class in America. Nevertheless, some huge grants survived from pre-Loyalist times and those lucky enough to have money could buy.

Major John Coffin, of the King's American Regiment, put together the 6000 acres of Alwington Manor on the Long Reach, where the River Nerepis joins the St John. Coffin was one day rowing his daughter to town when a huge bear swam out to their boat. The squire could not outdistance the animal and waited until it put a paw over the gunwale, then killed it with an oar; he asked a neighbour to tow the carcass to the manor house, and resumed his journey.

As they became available, roof shingles and sawn boards were supplied to each head-of-family but the walls of the first cabins were made from the trees cut from their lots by the settlers themselves. When supplies of glass were exhausted, oiled paper was stretched over window openings. Middle-aged fathers had to draw upon the muscles of their youth as they swung axes and dragged the endless logs to the burning heaps. Walter Bates, formerly of Stamford, Connecticut, told in his journal of the beginnings of Kingston, New Brunswick – it was the story of most of the Loyalist settlements:

After examining about sixty miles of the inland waterways, an appointed committee from the sixty-five families who had travelled from New York in the good ship *Union* found a tract of timber land that had not been burned on Belleisle Bay, about thirty miles from the harbour of Saint John. We all agreed to proceed thither ... We set sail above the Falls and arrived before sunset. Nothing but wilderness before our eyes; the women and children did not refrain from tears. Next morning every man came on shore and cleared a way and landed all our baggage, women and children, and the sloop left us alone in the

wilderness ... We soon discovered a situation at the head of the Belleisle Creek suitable for our purpose of settlement with Church and school.

Before the lots were exposed for draft it was agreed that one acre off each adjoining corner of the four first numbers should be allotted the place for the Church and that lot No. 1 should be reserved for the parsonage ... Every man was jointly employed clearing places for building, cutting logs, carrying them together by strength of hands and laying up of log houses, by which means seventeen log houses were laid up and covered with bark, so that by the month of November every man in the district found himself and family covered under his own roof and a happier family never lived upon this globe enjoying in unity the blessings which God had provided for us in the country into whose coves and wild woods we were driven through persecution.

Pressure for provincial autonomy built up almost immediately among the educated and self-reliant Loyalists, who chafed at control from Halifax. Sir Guy Carleton supported their initiative in London and, when New Brunswick was carved out of Nova Scotia in the summer of 1784, he supplied his brother Thomas, Colonel of the 29th Regiment, as the first Governor. When Thomas chose inland Fredericton, safe from naval attack, as his capital, the injured pride of the bustling towns on the sea was soothed by their amalgamation into the city of Saint John. With a New Yorker, Gabriel G. Ludlow, as its first mayor, and the son of the last royal Governor of Massachussetts as its first sheriff, it began its career as the Loyalist metropolis of Canada.

The first roll of Saint John citizens reveals the solid talents of the immigrants – eighty-seven registered as carpenters, forty-three as shoemakers, and twenty-three as tailors. To balance the eighteen who designated themselves 'Gentlemen,' there were eighteen masons, fourteen bakers, five tanners, two silversmiths and one clockmaker. A knot of Loyalists about the future site of the city of Sydney won Cape Breton separate provincial status at the same time as New Brunswick was created but, after a stormy struggle, the island rejoined Nova Scotia in 1821.

As he watched the refugees pouring into the British-held New York enclave, Sir Guy Carleton had doubted that Nova Scotia could absorb them all. Ship after ship sailed under the protection of warships for Halifax and the Fundy harbours, but the influx continued as it became only too obvious the fledgling states were permitting a witch-hunt for anyone of suspected Loyalist sympathies, active, passive, or just merely accused by jealous or plundering neighbours. Carleton began to consider the western reaches of Quebec, along the upper St Lawrence and the lower lakes. He sent for Captain Michael Grass, now dispossessed of his farm near New York, whom he knew had been a prisoner of the French at Fort Frontenac during the Seven Years' War.

Grass assured Carleton that territory at the head of Lake Ontario and along the Bay of Quinte offered lands highly suitable for settlement, and agreed to lead an expedition of two hundred families to Cataraqui, the site of today's Kingston, Ontario. Five ships sailed from New York on September 8, 1783, reaching Quebec a month later and proceeding to an assembly point at Sorel. The Governor-in-Chief of Canada, Lieutenant-General Frederick Haldimand, had sent his Surveyor-General, Samuel Holland, up the St Lawrence that spring to survey the land from the Long Sault (at Cornwall) to the beautiful sheltered sleeve of Quinte. A contemporary report enthused: 'The Loyalists may be the happiest people in America by settling this country.' In October, Governor Haldimand concluded a treaty with the Mississaugas and bought for the Crown the sparsely inhabited land extending from the Cataraqui River to the Trent – private purchases between Indians and settlers were wisely forbidden in British Canada.

Captain Grass led his settlers upriver and through the Thousand Islands in the spring of 1784, followed by other parties from New York. Overland convoys continued to arrive via the Hudson and Mohawk valleys, often as quasi-military units under command of officers from the disbanded Loyalist regiments. A few, mostly elderly, were sent under a safe-conduct pass by the Americans as 'useless consumers.' Some sturdy individualists put their families down on empty

An 1870 New Brunswick city was literally carved out of the forest. The cabins were made of notched logs and the chinks filled with wood chips, moss and clay. Photo courtesy PUBLIC ARCHIVES

land in eastern Quebec. Others entered Canada at the Niagara Peninsula and some at Detroit, where the British retained the frontier forts for a full thirteen years after the peace treaty. When Haldimand was succeeded by Carleton – now returned as Lord Dorchester – he could report with satisfaction that he had settled 6152 Loyalists. In total, perhaps eight thousand came into the lands that within five years would be reorganized as the British province of Upper Canada.

Sir John Johnson, who had brought his Royal Yorkers to Montreal in 1780, was given charge of the settlement programme. Fourteen townships had been laid out by Samuel Holland in which free land was allotted on the same basis as in the Maritimes. Later, the heads of families who had improved their original grants were given a further two hundred acres and the officers' acreage was greatly enlarged.

Running westwards from the present Quebec-Ontario border, the first five townships went to Johnson's soldiers, segregated at their own wish into the five main religious groups represented in the ranks. Captain Grass' party was awarded the first of the Cataraqui townships. Apart from the same stock of tools and seeds supplied free in the east, the British government now allowed the Loyalists – 'who surely had some claim to our affection,' in Lord North's words – basic provisions for three years. Military doctors staffed regional hospitals and, where possible, school-teachers were provided.

The loyal Iroquois from New York, the allies of the Johnsons and Butlers, were resettled on a magnificent tract of the Grand River Valley, six miles wide on both banks from source to the Lake Erie exit, twelve hundred square miles in all. Brantford, Ontario, today recalls the estate of the great Mohawk leader, Joseph Brant. Another group of Iroquois took a land grant at Deseronto, on the Bay of Quinte.

One has to envisage an Ontario shore where huge trees grew so thickly to the water's edge that there was seldom open space enough to place a cabin. The trees had to be felled with ship axes too light for efficient tree-felling, and at the beginning there were no horses or oxen for hauling. Trees were killed by girdling and fires were built at the base. Green wood was fashioned into rough furniture, and fireplaces made of flat stones. Cabin floors were at first of rammed earth and later of adzed logs. As the walls of notched logs rose, the women and children hurriedly plastered all chinks with wood chips, moss and clay – the Canadian winter lurked just beyond the fierce heat of summer. Where the family was large enough, the walls were carried higher to provide a sleeping attic, entered by a ladder at one corner of the living room – kitchen. A platform of poles, sometimes laced with cord, served as a bed with a mattress of corn husks or feathers from duck and pigeon.

Indian corn, turnips and pumpkins were grown amid the stumps that first season, and wild rice and maple syrup harvested. Game and fish were luckily plentiful. On his lot at Athens, near Brockville, Joseph Slack killed 192 deer, 34 bear and 46 wolves. Squirrel meat was salted down in barrels made from hollowed-out logs.

Most adults had one fine outfit carefully packed in a brass-studded trunk, together with perhaps a few items of chinaware and treasured books, but most soon wore clothes cut from the trade blankets or from buckskin obtained from the helpful local Indians. Very few Loyalists had any cash money at all and, for years, little hope of earning any. They tried cheerfully to turn work into play by organizing interminable 'bees' at which everyone pitched in to get tedious chores done. There were husking bees, logging bees, stumping bees, quilting bees for the women and girls, sewing and spinning bees. As the needles or apple-paring knives flew, the women exchanged, savoured and elaborated every scrap of gossip – for news from the outside world they depended upon the Yankee pedlar with his pins and combs – while the sweating men manhandling the burnt-over logs paced their bee with draughts of scorching whisky, at sixpence a quart. The day ended with a huge meal – a potpie, venison haunch, wild ducks in season, whole salmon and lake trout, doughnuts, mince and pumpkin pies, hard cider to wash it all down.

Within a remarkably short time, travellers on the frontier were reporting the appearance of tidy farmlets, blue smoke rising among the hardwoods from straight chimneys, gaily curtained windows, the smell of baking bread, farm animals clustered about the barns. There had been periods of dire want when desperate men offered their entire 'farms' for fifty pounds of flour – with no takers. The 'hungry year' of 1788-89 was long remembered; some settlers were reduced to eating their dogs and horses and, in Prince Edward County, five deaths were attributed to starvation – one of them a women found with a live baby at her breast. But the new season brought a renewal of hope and energy.

Sawmills whined on rushing creeks and grist mills were soon operating at Brockville, Kingston, Napanee, Lake-on-the-Mountain, and Niagara. Some rudimentary bush roads were open and, at the top of the Bay of Quinte, Asa Weller was offering his team of oxen to pull boats across the isthmus at Carrying Place. Settlements were thriving at Windsor, Hamilton, Port Hope and Belleville spaced a day's wilderness travel all along 'The Front.'

After three years of wide-ranging debate at Westminster, the province of Quebec had been divided into Upper and Lower Canada, the one mostly British, the other mostly French, each with its bicameral legislature. The coming of the Loyalists had ensured the separation of Canada from the United States, and greatly increased the diversity of people in British North America. As a special 'mark of honour,' all those who had taken their stand openly for King and Empire before the treaty of 1783 were carefully checked and listed and granted the right to inscribe the initials 'U.E.L.' (United Empire Loyalist) after their names.

With Newfoundland, the British American colonies now numbered seven, but the great south-west, connected with Canada for a hundred years, the land between the Ohio and the Mississippi, though held by British forces and used by Canadian traders, was surrendered to the United States up to the Great Lakes. It was an act done as part of the new British policy of courting the friendship of the United States. It meant, however, that the dream of a Canadian empire of the interior, always so bright and yet so tenuous, was ending. Canada was to be made up of a thin southern land base and a vast northern wilderness. It was to take another generation to confirm that decision.

PART III

Chapter Ten
The great migration

From Greenock, on May 21, 1821, the emigrant packet *David of London* slipped down the Clyde bound for Canada with four hundred destitute Scots. As the sails filled and the mountains of Argyll rose across the firth, the bagpipes skirled a plaintive farewell forever. But there were few tears and fewer regrets – they were leaving a grinding poverty and abject hopelessness for what seemed to be the veritable Promised Land. The open Atlantic greeted the crowded ship with high seas and freezing temperatures and the crowded settlers groaned in seasickness under the battened hatches. In the Gulf of St Lawrence, the weather turned so hot that a passenger later wrote, 'many nearly suffocated from the smell and heat below.' The voyage to Quebec took thirty-six days, during which three newborn babies were buried at sea.

From Portsmouth, on April 25, 1833, the *England* sailed for Montreal direct with two hundred passengers drawn from the surplus peasantry on the Sussex estates of the Earl of Egremont. They were allotted a pound of meat and a pound of bread a day, and those over fourteen years got a weekly half-pint of brandy diluted with three parts of water. It seems to have been a happy ship, a passenger recording in his diary on May 15, 'the people enjoying themselves dancing on deck to the violin.' Sixty-six thousand Britons entered Upper Canada that year.

From Dundalk on May 30, 1847, a small unnamed ship sailed for Quebec with 112 ragged, hungry and sick evicted tenant farmers from County Meath. A journal left by the single cabin

passenger reveals a hellish eight-week journey as dysentery and a fever 'of a peculiar character' raged through the steerage – the lower hold. Food and water for only fifty days had been taken aboard and there was nothing extra for the raving and moaning fever victims who were unceremoniously dumped in the ocean as they died. After a month at sea, fifty were sick and 'the effluvium of the hold was shocking.' The selfless ministrations of the captain's wife – there was no doctor on board – helped reduce the death toll but more died later at the Grosse Isle quarantine station, below Quebec, where all immigrant ships were checked.

These three vessels, from Scotland, England and Ireland, can represent the hundreds of sailing ships, big and small, that carried a million British settlers into Canada during the thirty years of 'the Great Migration,' from 1820 to 1850. If anything, their stories present too rosy a picture of conditions during that historic exodus, when the starving surplus people of an old and corrupt society were shipped with less care than cattle across the Atlantic where, within a near-miraculous generation, the survivors beat back a wilderness, prospered, multiplied, and played a major part in bringing this country to the threshold of Confederation.

When all the wars and alarums of the Napoleonic years were quelled, immigrants poured into British North America from thirty-six ports in England, twenty-one in Ireland and eighteen in Scotland. The door was open, land was free to all comers and the timber ships were eagerly seeking 'living ballast' for the western journey. Some chose Nova Scotia, Prince Edward Island and New Brunswick, but the great majority came into the Eastern Townships of Quebec, the Ottawa River country and the lake-bound peninsula of Upper Canada. The Canadian population of under 500,000 in 1815 quadrupled by 1851 to 2,300,000 – and helped by the fabulous birth-rate of 53 per 1000, leaped to 3,174,000 a decade later.

The Loyalist refugees from the American Revolution had changed the character of Canada, and the repulse of the several American invasions during the War of 1812 had confirmed its positive existence, but it remained for the humble victims of the Industrial Revolution to supply the vital thrusting human numbers that alone could give verisimilitude to a new nation. The special qualities of Canadian life were now to be compounded from the inwardness of the French, abandoned by their motherland, the lingering memories of the British for the land they left behind (though it had rejected most of them), and something fresh and strengthening from the virgin soil of the New World itself.

Several momentous events and influences in a swiftly changing Europe had made an enormous supply of humanity suddenly available. All over England and the Scottish border shires the clanking machines had now superseded the hand-work of the factories, particularly in the textile mills which still provided Britain's largest exports. As many as 70 per cent of the 'hands' in factory or cottage industry became redundant and 'Luddites' were smashing machinery in a pathetic effort to save their jobs. The collapse of a war-contract economy following Waterloo brought wholesale recession, and the consolidation of properties for more efficient farming uprooted the peasant tenant and threw as many as one-third of the rural population on to the relief rolls. In Scotland, the crofters were still being evicted to allow sheep to have the full run of the glens; the most notorious of the 'clearances' was that of the Duke of Sutherland who, in 1814, put fifteen thousand off the lands to which he claimed sole title as hereditary chieftain. Even the lauded Reform Bill of 1832 offered the working classes no hope of help through political representation – it gave the franchise to only 1.2 million in a population of 24 million.

In Ireland – then still wholly an integral part of Great Britain – the situation was simply appalling. Three million peasants, traditionally impoverished in their almost total dependence upon the potato, were facing unvarnished starvation as their mainstay food was attacked by blight and, in 1846, was almost totally destroyed. A survey in Donegal showed that a community of nine thousand possessed exactly ninety-three chairs and ten beds. Evicted from their hovels for non-payment of rent, women and children were literally dying in the roadside ditches while the men, semi-crazed with anger and hunger, roamed the lanes like animals. Emigration was the single

An intriguing collection of books, chests and other cherished memorablia were brought by the more fortunate settlers to the Canadas to remind them of the families and friends left behind. Photo by PETER VARLEY

hope and they clambered aboard anything that would float in their eagerness to get to 'Amerikay' where, incredibly, there was said to be work and food for all.

In the provinces of British North America, the wilderness was indeed beginning to smile. The Loyalist surge had been followed about the turn of the century with a second wave from the United States, the so-called 'Late Loyalists' – experienced men, land-hungry, go-getters, bringing such significant names as Massey, Lundy, James, Doherty on to Upper Canada rolls. The first Doherty was offered a land grant above the village of York, bounded by Queen, Yonge, University and College streets of today's Toronto – and he turned it down as 'too wet,' taking five hundred acres at Dixie instead. Other 'American' immigrants – Robinson, Merritt, Jarvis, Ryerson – had come west from New Brunswick when Lieutenant-Governor John Graves Simcoe, the Colonel of the Queen's Rangers during the revolution, set up his capital in Toronto.

Montreal, the centre of the big-spending Nor'Wester fur traders, the 'lords of the lakes and forests' as Washington Irving called them, was reaching for metropolitan style with the first city water system – sixty-three homes connected by wooden pipes to a Mount Royal stream for $14 a year.

In his *Journey to the Western Islands of Scotland*, Dr. Johnson had found an 'epidemical fury of emigration' and, by the late 1820s, twenty-five thousand Highlanders were in Cape Breton and Nova Scotia's land was mostly taken up. The lush valley of the St John was filled.

Along the north shore of Lake Erie, the remarkable Thomas Talbot, formerly aide to Colonel Simcoe, was beginning to piece together his private barony that would eventually stretch from the Detroit River to his 'capital,' St Thomas. Born at Castle Malahide near Dublin, descendant of dukes and earls, Talbot was an eccentric but benevolent despot who liked to cook his own meals wearing 'a smock frock, practising all the menial offices of a peasant' – to quote the incumbent administrator. 'Such a mode of life,' Lieutenant-Governor Peter Hunter added, 'might suit a republic but is not fitted to a monarchical government.' Talbot liked to wear a sheepskin coat and a fox cap, complete with ears and tail.

The key to his success was the Talbot Road, to connect his lands with York (as Toronto had been named) to the east, Sandwich (Windsor) in the west, and London in the Thames Valley to the north. He granted sections along the proposed roads to settlers on the requirement that they clear, level and maintain the stretch of highway along their frontage – thus access was steadily given to new areas of wilderness. Simcoe had used the same system to extend his famous Yonge Street, from York to the large lake he named for his Royal Navy father. Talbot eventually put fifty thousand settlers on his lands and 'fathered' the present counties of Essex, Lambton, Kent, Norfolk, Oxford, Elgin and Middlesex.

On the shores of Lake Huron, across the shoulder of the south-western Ontario peninsula, John Galt, a well-known Scottish novelist and friend of Byron's, had fallen in love with the 'Huron Tract' during a visit in 1803. Back in Britain he organized the Canada Company, which secured a million acres of forest at $1.25 per acre. Eventually, Galt's company held two million acres, and, although he personally was ruined in health and fortune, he had the satisfaction of founding (with the aid of the redoubtable Dr. William 'Tiger' Dunlop) the cities of Guelph and Goderich. The city of Galt, once Shade's Mills, was named by the Hon. William Dickson, a schooldays' friend of Galt's.

Other important settlements were founded, or speedily expanded, in the years before the War of 1812 temporarily cut off the stream of immigrants from Europe. On the upper St Lawrence, from west of Montreal Island down to the Bay of Quinte, the loyal Highlanders from New York who had been settled after the American Revolution were joined by several further shiploads of dispossessed Scots direct from the homelands. Five hundred came from Glengarry, the ancestral home of the Macdonnells in Inverness-shire, and left the name of their remembered glen on the new county. Others set about clearing the hundred-foot pines, the elms, oaks, maples and chestnuts from the river frontage that would become the counties of Stormont and Dundas. One early list of settlers shows 84 Macdonnells, 35 Grants, 28 Campbells, 27 Frasers, 25 Camerons, 23 Andersons and 20 Rosses.

Many of these Scots joined the North West Company, tilting against the Hudson's Bay traders for the furs of the Athabasca Country, and pushing ever farther into the far west. Several are enshrined in the history of the fur trade; one, for instance, was the Simon Fraser whose name will last as long as his wild river roars down its British Columbian gorge. From these ranks, too, came both John Strachan, the first Anglican Bishop of Upper Canada, and Alexander Macdonnell, the first Roman Catholic Bishop of Upper Canada. Another Macdonnell, John, died with Brock at Queenston in 1812, and another, George, captured the American fort at Ogdensburg and supported the fire-eating Charles de Salaberry's Voltigeurs as they turned back the Americans on the Chateauguay River.

When Napoleon was on St Helena and Europe began the era of the Pax Britannica, the intolerable pressures of the hungry despairing hordes could no longer be safely contained. Migrants already settled in Canada were beginning to send home earned money to pay passage for indigent relatives, and the reports sped from lip to lip of ample food and firewood, of land for the clearing thereof, of clear streams and lakes where the fish belonged to the man who caught it, of steady wages in the timber trade and in the rising towns. Sometimes assisted by governments, sometimes by wealthy gentry more sensitive and charitable than their fellows, sometimes by towns and parishes eager to clear their welfare rolls, a floodtide of ragged, undernourished, mostly illiterate people washed towards the western ports. They filled the steerage, the holds of the ships that would return full of the huge squared timbers of the Canadian forests, while those who could pay (by no means all were paupers) took hastily partitioned cabins or waited for space in the comparatively few vessels fitted out for regular passenger trade. Fishing boats leaving for the Grand Banks would take some of the hardiest to Atlantic shores for ten shillings – they offered no accommodation, merely sleeping space on the open deck.

As the decade of the 1820s opened, the great migration rose to full spate. With people clamouring for every berth, earlier legislative efforts to regulate overcrowding were watered down or merely ignored. The Passenger Vessel Act of 1803 had ruled that a ship could carry no more than one passenger for every two tons of the ship's register; by 1828 three passengers for every four tons were permitted, and in 1836 the ratio was three for every five tons. At the three/four ratio, each passenger on an average ship would be allowed only twenty inches of deck space – worse than on some of the African slave ships. In the steerage – usually about 75 feet long by 25 feet wide – a double tier of family berths were knocked up within the $5\frac{1}{2}$ feet of headroom on both sides of a narrow aisle. Each berth, 10 feet wide by 5 feet long, was intended for six passengers. But what was 'a passenger'? Infants under a year were not counted at all, children under seven years were rated as 'one-third adult' and those under fourteen as 'half adult.' Since the fares were calculated on this basis – the rate for an adult began at £2 – parents swore that strapping lads of seventeen were not yet shaving. Almost every ship had stowaways, often teenage children of parents who had paid a fare and who hoped to conceal the freeloader during the trip. Boys were nailed into casks of ship's biscuit, even barrels of salt, and discovered when case-hardened bo'suns up-ended the containers.

Unscrupulous captains used every device to outwit customs inspectors who did, at times, attempt to enforce passable humane standards. Two ships of 550 tons were discovered to contain about seven hundred passengers each – they had only the regulation two tiers of bunks when they left England but a third had been erected from stored timbers as soon as the ships cleared port. Another vessel registered at 334 tons loaded 505 passengers. Adequate policing was virtually impossible: Liverpool, the main emigration port, had only three inspectors and three doctors in a year when 174,188 people were counted as sailing in 568 ships.

Much of the abuse arose from the system by which emigration brokers bought up the entire steerage of a ship and then made their private deals with ignorant passengers, easily swindled.

They sold them shoddy tools, solemnly assuring them they would pay several times the price for the same article in Montreal or New York and they directed their ticket-holders to stay at certain taverns while they waited for a ship to sail. If an emigrant seemed to have money 'his' ship might be delayed for a month until the broker's sidekicks running the tavern got most of it in inflated board and booze bills. An attempt to fine captains a shilling a day per passenger for undue delays could never be enforced.

Many sailing ships lay at anchor off shore where they could more easily catch a wind, others were towed out of the harbours by the new steam tugs. Departures could be sudden, causing chaotic scenes as parents desperately tried to keep their family groups and their baggage together. Even as the crews were casting off the cables, shouting groups from some forgotten inn or boarding house came running, the men jumping into the rigging. A journalist reporting a sailing noted: 'Here and there a woman became entangled, with her drapery sadly discomposed, and her legs still more sadly exposed to loiterers on shore. Many a package thrown from the dock missed its mark and fell into the water where it was rescued and handed up by a man in a small boat.' The emigrants carried a fantastic collection of chests, cooking utensils, bed-covers, live ducks, clocks, scythes, sacks of potatoes, a rolled carpet, and, after Victoria took the throne, 'portraits of Her Majesty, Prince Albert and the Royal Children.'

Conditions in the steerage during the voyage varied from barely tolerable to utterly wretched. During the frequent storms, with women and children sick and screaming in fear, water pouring down through the hatches and sloshing six inches deep, the pumps squealing, the ship pitching for dark days on end – the scene called for a Dante Alighieri. Hastily promoted captains could not make best use of available winds, and the ships were mostly just clumsy commercial 'bottoms' built to haul maximum cargo; some were so small that passengers could reach down to touch the tops of waves, and promenade decks were described as 'two steps and overboard.' Rations of the lowest quality ran desperately short when ships were blown weeks off course to the Azores, or Greenland. On other occasions, good food was allowed to spoil by inexperienced or callous cooks. Referring to putrid beef served on his ship, a Presbyterian parson wrote, 'I have never seen anything like [it] presented to human beings.'

In the dark crowded holds, pilfering was common and women were often molested; vigilante committees of nightwatchmen were formed by husbands and fathers. Members of the crew with access to the luxuries of fresh water and the cooking galleys could easily buy favours from peasant girls who, in the prevailing standards of their class and times, rated many things above simple virtue. A passenger in the *Hebe* in 1832 wrote that the crew were 'a set of vile abandoned wretches.' Not until 1847 did the shipping laws insist on separate berths for males and females, unless married. One Scot remarked dryly: 'There was no separation for the sexes; yet it is surprising how soon myself and all the other passengers, the females included, became reconciled to it.'

The five hundred passengers of the *Thomas Gelston* from Londonderry to Montreal were kept below decks for nine weeks, and cholera was raging. Most captains tried to enforce minimum standards of cleanliness and 'housekeeping' in the steerage – bedding had to be aired whenever the weather allowed, floors had to be scraped and swept – but passengers straight from the meanest hovels brought lice aboard and every variety of illness, and observed only the most rudimentary sanitation habits. 'The between-decks were like a loathsome dungeon,' a government enquiry was told. 'When the hatchways were opened, the steam rose and the stench was like that from a pen of pigs.' Ships were infested with rats, and infants were often bitten while sleeping.

On the fever ships, almost every day brought death. Regulations gazetted by both Canada and the United States required a medical examination before any emigrant was allowed aboard ship but these were perfunctory at best. Some of the prospective settlers died in their berths even before the ships cleared the home harbours; mothers desperately concealed symptoms in their children for fear they would be refused passage. Cholera arising from filth was the main killer of children – its incubation period is only two or three days, and it kills in three to five days – and there was no

The old clapboard Blue Church near Prescott, Ontario, is famous as the burial place of Barbara Heck, founder of Methodism in North America, who moved to this area after the American Revolution. Photo by JOHN DE VISSER

remedy in that time and place. The three children of a Yorkshire surgeon emigrating to Cobourg, Upper Canada, died on the same day. In one Irish ship, of a family of eleven, only one was left, a small forlorn boy walking around the deck proudly wearing his father's jacket.

The Canadian authorities at Quebec were appalled by the death ships coming up the St Lawrence and they had neither the funds, the equipment nor the experience to deal adequately with the situation. Wrenching scenes occurred almost daily at the Grosse Isle quarantine station in the summers of epidemic as victims of cholera, smallpox, 'ship fever' (typhus) were carried ashore. Within the span of a few days in 1832, more than fifteen hundred died at Grosse Isle; during 1847, to be known as 'the plague year,' nearly 17,500 of the 100,000 who sailed from Britain for the United States or Canada died on the ocean or shortly after arrival.

A dozen ships at a time were swinging at anchor downstream of Quebec, the captains exhorting both sick and well to 'clean ship' in the hope of getting quick clearance. To avoid complications with the authorities, some skippers would disembark delirious sick under darkness on any adjacent shore and leave them to fend for themselves. The story of the *Larch* from Sligo provides a melancholy example of the worst: of her original 440 passengers, 108 were buried at sea and 150 were reported sick at Grosse Isle.

Ruthlessly, it can be said that the weak were culled from the hordes of the great migration and only the strong passed up the St Lawrence to add to the widening diversity of the Canadian people. For some, the entry to Canada was very different. Those who could afford the luxury of a cabin, at rates of from £5 to £40 depending on the ship and the scale of provisions, were known as 'colonists' – certainly not 'emigrants.' They were warned by friends who had preceded them to Canada to bring, if at all possible, some servants with them as the natives had far too lofty an idea of their status to give satisfactory service. Even recently arrived immigrants 'immediately were seized by the most absurd notions of independence and equality.' One tourist from Derbyshire averred that 'his English blood almost boiled in his veins' when he was placed at table with two servant women at Niagara Falls. 'I never expected,' he added in shocked tones, 'to find the levelling system introduced into the British provinces to such an extent.'

Born at Leydon Hall, Bungay, Suffolk, Major Samuel Strickland came out cabin-class in the brig *William McGillivray* in the spring of 1825. He enjoyed the voyage, shooting at whales, admiring icebergs, playing draughts with the officers. He took up land on the Otonabee River, near the village of Peterborough, lively heart of the successful Irish settlement established by the New Brunswick-born Peter Robinson. For three years Strickland was an officer of John Galt's Canada Company and his propaganda led two young half-pay officers of the 21st Fusiliers, Lieutenant Thomas Traill and Lieutenant John Moodie to bring their wives – Strickland's sisters Catherine and Susanna – out to Upper Canada in 1832. Samuel wrote two volumes of his own experiences in *Twenty-seven Years in Canada West* but it was to be the books left by his sisters that would capture a wider public.

Susanna Moodie's memoirs, *Roughing It in the Bush* and the later *Life in the Clearings*, are minor Canadian classics, illustrating how an English gentlewoman accustomed to servants and the deference of the lower classes, at first found adjustment very difficult amid the stumps of Douro Township, but later came to admire and appreciate the basic worth of many of the rough-hewn settlers around her who had simply not had the chance to acquire her considerable culture and graces. Moving into the Loyalist town of Belleville when her husband was appointed the first Sheriff of Hastings County in 1840, Susanna wrote many pieces for the local *Victoria Magazine* and for Montreal's pre-eminent *Literary Garland*, which also published the work of Catherine Parr Traill and another sensitive newcomer, the Dubliner Anna Jameson.

Catherine Traill peppered her many books with lots of practical and sage advice for British women who might follow her to Canada. Writing guides for emigrants was almost a cottage industry, but, considering the problems of transport, some of the recommendations were of dubious value – one author suggested his readers bring a piano. Mrs. Jameson's husband was

A portrait of Catherine Parr Traill who wrote guides for emigrants filled with sage advice and pioneer recipes for survival in the bush. Photo PUBLIC ARCHIVES

appointed Attorney-General in Upper Canada in 1833 and she came out to join him in 1836 – but only for a few months. Long enough, though, to fire off some sharp literary shafts at the early pretensions of provincial Toronto. William Lyon Mackenzie, shop-keeper turned publisher, was also referring to 'our upstart aristocracy.'

When Charles Richard Weld, librarian of the Royal Society, toured Canada in the 1850s he was directed to Peterborough to see how transplanted British squires had fared in the forest clearings. As a class they seldom did well, for no matter how bravely they faced up to backwoods democracy, they were too long removed from the basic yeoman skills required to turn bush into farm. 'Tiger' Dunlop warned in his advice to emigrants: 'A man of fortune, in my opinion, ought not to come to Canada. It is emphatically 'the poor man's country' ... I can conceive of no possibility of its becoming for centuries to come a fitting stage for the heroes and heroines of the fashionable novels of Mr. Bulwer or young D'Israeli.'

Weld found Samuel Strickland, now a colonel of militia, running a kind of bush college near Lakefield for aspiring farmers from 'good' British families. Sections of two hundred acres were still available free to anyone who would erect a dwelling and clear one-fourth of the maple forest. Cleared and fenced land, on the other hand, was already bringing as much as £10 an acre.

Travel writer Weld left a description of the roads of the time as he went by buggy to meet Strickland:

> Holes masked by mud were of constant occurrence. Into these our vehicle plunged with a crash, threatening to reduce it to atoms; but much to my surprise, it was on each occasion dragged out by the willing horses, apparently uninjured. Worse was the dreadful corduroy composed of large logs, over which we bumped with a dislocatory motion. We frequently turned aside into the bush, preferring to rough it through the tangled underwood ... occasionally we drove in the bed of the river when it afforded an easier route. So bad, in short, was this road that although we had only a dozen miles to drive, we were five hours on the way.

All was as it should be, happily, at Colonel Strickland's outpost of empire. Weld ended his visit, noting: 'I must say, social conviviality never degenerated to coarseness; and though the red hunting shirts, looming through tobacco smoke, gave the company a brigandish appearance, gentlemanly conduct was as strongly maintained as if the scene of our merriment had been a London drawing room.'

The Durham boats brought the swelling number of immigrants from the timber ships up the St Lawrence summer after summer. Although many thousands drifted into the United States never to return, those who remained settled all the province from Glengarry to Amherstburg, and from Hawkesbury to Bytown on the Ottawa and beyond. Others pushed inland from 'The Front,' up the Mississippi to Perth, the Rideau to Smith's Falls, the Trent to Rice Lake, the Scugog to Lindsay, the Humber to Brampton and Barrie. Scots, Highland and Lowland, Irish, Orange and Green, English, yeomen and gentlemen, they came by thousands to the Canadian bush and cleared it to make the rural landscape of Ontario so British, yet so Canadian.

In the 1850s the latecomers, and the sons of the early comers, had moved into the Bruce Peninsula and were reaching out from Tobermory to the lands of Manitoulin across the Lucas channel. As the settlement of Muskoka and Parry Sound was already demonstrating, the farm lands of Ontario had been occupied by 1855. Some of the sons went into trade and some – like Frank Smith – did very well for themselves. Smith had come from Armagh at age ten in 1832. He set up as a grocer, prospered, became Mayor of London, then a banker and street-railway builder, then a Senator, a cabinet minister and, as Sir Frank Smith, a pillar of Conservative society.

The overall result of the Great Migration was, of course, to make people from the British Isles much the largest group in Canada, a fact reported in the first census of 1851. It showed that Canada West exceeded Canada East in population; the French Canadians had passed permanently into a minority in the country their forebears had pioneered.

The Mill of Kintail was established at Almonte, in the Ottawa Valley, by Loyalist Daniel Shipman in 1823, the same year the town became a settlement centre for Irish immigrants. Photo by JOHN DE VISSER

PART IV

The innocent time

INTERLUDE:
The making of the countryside

The central personalities in Canadian history for about a century after 1800 were the lumberjacks and the farmers, the timber baron and the grain buyer. No longer is there one simple, heroic character like Champlain to personify an epoch. Rather there are semi-mythical persons who stand for a host of typical types.

One such was the 'Main John' of New Brunswick timber drives, the prototype of all timber bosses or foremen. Another such was, perhaps, 'Agricola' (John Young), voice and representative of the yeoman farmer of British North America. Still another was William Price, British timber baron and founder of a company which, as part of the great Canadian firm of Abitibi, still endures. Yet another was William Gooderham, grain buyer, distiller and miller, a businessman who moved into the chief enterprise of the colonies. The techniques these men set in motion were each different from those of the fur trade, and wholly European. The once-vital tie with the Indian and the wilderness was cut by the sharp steel edge of the axe and the plough.

The great change arose out of the wars in Europe, giving the Canadas a profitable occupation for the long harsh winters and a means to transform the wilderness and the way of life of British North Americans. In the struggle with Napoleon, Britain had to maintain fleets on world-wide duty – thus she had either to keep the Baltic open or turn to North America for the masts, spars, and other timber that would build and repair her shipping. Twice Britain coerced Denmark into leaving the entrance to the Baltic open. But in 1806, Napoleon, then master of all Germany, shut off the northern supply of ship's timber and naval supplies. The Jeffersonian embargo cut off the American supply.

At once, timber factors, foremen and workmen financed by the merchants of Britain descended on the St John, or the Restigouche and the Miramichi, and on Quebec, to organize the cutting and shipping of timber. It was actually a great enterprise of war, as organized, as drastic and as sudden in its way as the bombardment of Copenhagen. Overnight it gave British North America what was for almost a century the greatest of its industries.

The timber companies had first to buy from local cutters, then also to obtain felling rights from the Crown, something readily done from colonial governments that were poor with an abundance of land. While the war lasted, they sought masts, spars, and the special woods for ship-building, oak and white pine especially. When Napoleon was finally crushed by Wellington, the timber trade remained and became its historic self, creating great fortunes as it supplied building materials for the onrushing Industrial Revolution.

Where the flashing bit of the broadaxe cleared the forest, the sturdy pioneer settler soon ventured, the embryo market towns began to develop at the junctions of the wagon trails, at the water's edge of both sheltered sea cove and navigable lake and river. Windships took the tall straight timbers to Europe, but the steamboat

Because the international stretch of the St. Lawrence River endangered Upper Canada's security, the Rideau Canal was built in 1832 and paid for by the British taxpayer. Photo by PETER VARLEY

was in service here as early as anywhere. Two years after Robert Fulton's successful demonstration on the Hudson, the Molsons of Montreal launched the 6 hp *Accommodation*. The fare: a sizable $9. By 1817 the 700-ton steamer *Frontenac* was plying from Kingston to York, Burlington and Niagara.

Compared with its millennia of wilderness tranquillity, British North America was rapidly becoming a set of widely separated, racially diverse, bustling and varied communities. They possessed neither uniformity nor coherence. What unity existed derived from a common allegiance to the Crown of Britain, and for most that tie was at best a formal one. Neither in their economics, their languages, nor their settlements were the colonists unified. Only the imperial government, its military and naval power, the use of English as the language of government and trade, gave a framework to the British possessions in North America. Yet a mere fifty years were to work a prodigious and astonishing change and create a unified nation in the Confederation of 1867.

What, then, promoted unity – if anything did? One thing was, of course, the Gulf of St Lawrence, on which all the colonies touched; the other was the mystique of the British Empire itself.

The Empire was a constant presence in the colonies. Each colony had its imperial governor and his suite, small but British. Each of the major towns had its detachment of troops, while the great ports – Halifax, Quebec and Montreal – had garrisons of hundreds of men, even in peaceful times. The red-coated units marching through the streets, the men and officers walking out or driving in *calèche* or *carriole*, in riflemen's green, artillery blue, or sapper's scarlet with gold pipings, were standard figures of afternoon or evening by the Citadel, or on the Plains, or in the Place d'Armes. The bugle calls and the noon guns were even more persuasive reminders of the imperial presence. And British North Americans knew, some with pride, some with mingled indifference and resentment, that the North American colonies were part of that power which, in the phrase of the American orator, Daniel Webster, 'has dotted the whole globe with her possessions and military posts; whose morning drum-beat, following the sun and keeping company with the hours, circles the earth with one contentious and unbroken strain of the martial airs of England.'

The soldiers joined in local sports, got up plays, their bands offered concerts, they escorted local girls – and sometimes married them.

It would be too much to say that all Canadian women loved a soldier, but there were few who didn't welcome their society. The gaiety soldiers brought to the life of the garrison town reminds us that the growing society of the Canadian provinces was now maturing, with women roughly equal in numbers to men. That, of course, was not true in the lumber camps, where neither women nor liquor were allowed. But the lumberjacks came home each spring on the river 'drives' to gladden the hearts of their womenfolk.

Throughout the provinces, women played the part in life, from the governors' ladies to the farmers' wives, which society in the nineteenth century expected of them. It was not an heroic role, such as that of Madeleine de Verchères defending the mill against the Iroquois, or of Laura Secord slipping through the forest in the War of 1812 to warn of the American attack. It was, however, an expanding role. Not only did they discharge the rites of social life and the duties of household management in proper Victorian fashion – some made names for themselves in creative work. One was Catherine Parr Traill with her exquisite and scientifically exact paintings of the flora of the Upper Canada backwoods. Another was Isabella Valancy Crawford, with her firm, perceptive poetry. And the growing number of common, or public schools, in their need for teachers, turned more and more to young women, as depicted in William Harris' painting, *The School Teacher*.

Military pay, readily spent, was always an important element in early Canadian economics and the needs of strategy dictated major public works that put cash into the pockets of contractors and labourers. The St Lawrence between Montreal and Lake Ontario flowed across a spur of the Canadian Shield that caused a fall of 226 feet over several rapids; it was an impossible fight upstream for any kind of boat, and no considerable cargo could be taken down except the timber rafts. Then, too, the international stretch of the river from Cornwall to Kingston endangered the security of Upper Canada in the event of another war with the United States. Canals were obviously needed to improve the navigation of the St Lawrence, particularly for wheat going down to Montreal, and another route was needed farther inland for defence. Yet such massive works were beyond the revenue and credit of the colony.

The Rideau Canal from Bytown (now Ottawa), by the Rideau and Cataraqui rivers to Kingston on Lake Ontario, was built by 1832 and paid for by the British taxpayer. The bill reached £800,000, after an original estimate of £169,000. This route gave a means of conveying troops and military supplies secure from the international section of the river, but its economic utility proved to be slight. The great matter of canals around the rapids of the St Lawrence remained unattempted until the union of Upper and Lower Canada in 1841. At that time, the new provincial government of United Canada, from its capital at proud Kingston, took over the private company that had cut a shallow canal from Port Weller on Lake Ontario to Port Colborne on Lake Erie, bypassing the barrier of Niagara Falls.

Economic and population growth brought with them serious problems, and the yeast of democracy was fer-

The garrison soldiers made important contributions to the prosperity and good times of the local population wherever they were stationed. Photos by PETER VARLEY and THE BANK OF CANADA

PROCLAMATION.

BY His Excellency SIR FRANCIS BOND HEAD, Baronet, Lieutenant Governor of Upper Canada, &c. &c.

To the Queen's Faithful Subjects in Upper Canada.

In a time of profound peace, while every one was quietly following his occupations, feeling secure under the protection of our Laws, a band of Rebels, instigated by a few malignant and disloyal men, has had the wickedness and audacity to assemble with Arms, and to attack and Murder the Queen's Subjects on the Highway—to Burn and Destroy their Property—to Rob the Public Mails—and to threaten to Plunder the Banks—and to Fire the City of Toronto.

Brave and Loyal People of Upper Canada, we have been long suffering from the acts and endeavours of concealed Traitors, but this is the first time that Rebellion has dared to shew itself openly in the land, in the absence of invasion by any Foreign Enemy.

Let every man do his duty now, and it will be the last time that we or our children shall see our lives or properties endangered, or the Authority of our Gracious Queen insulted by such treacherous and ungrateful men. MILITIA-MEN OF UPPER CANADA, no Country has ever shewn a finer example of Loyalty and Spirit than YOU have given upon this sudden call of Duty. Young and old of all ranks, are flocking to the Standard of their Country. What has taken place will enable our Queen to know Her Friends from Her Enemies—a public enemy is never so dangerous as a concealed Traitor—and now my friends let us complete well what is begun—let us not return to our rest till Treason and Traitors are revealed to the light of day, and rendered harmless throughout the land.

Be vigilant, patient and active—leave punishment to the Laws—our first object is, to arrest and secure all those who have been guilty of Rebellion, Murder and Robbery.—And to aid us in this, a Reward is hereby offered of

One Thousand Pounds,

to any one who will apprehend, and deliver up to Justice, WILLIAM LYON MACKENZE; and FIVE HUNDRED POUNDS to any one who will apprehend, and deliver up to Justice, DAVID GIBSON—or SAMUEL LOUNT—or JESSE LLOYD—or SILAS FLETCHER—and the same reward and a free pardon will be given to any of their accomplices who will render this public service, except he or they shall have committed, in his own person, the crime of Murder or Arson.

And all, but the Leaders above-named, who have been seduced to join in this unnatural Rebellion, are hereby called to return to their duty to their Sovereign—to obey the Laws—and to live henceforward as good and faithful Subjects—and they will find the Government of their Queen as indulgent as it is just.

GOD SAVE THE QUEEN.

Thursday, 3 o'clock, P. M.
7th Dec.

☞ The Party of Rebels, under their Chief Leaders, is wholly dispersed, and flying before the Loyal Militia. The only thing that remains to be done, is to find them, and arrest them.

R. STANTON, Printer to the QUEEN'S Most Excellent Majesty.

menting. There was social frustration in both of the Canadas and political distress also – and there was to be rebellion. Government in Upper Canada was in the hands of those who had proved their worth by success, or had it bestowed by family or by governmental connection. The result was not really the 'Family Compact' denounced by the fiery and demagogic William Lyon Mackenzie, but it was an 'Establishment' in a small and poor society. Those of radical persuasion, whether American or British in origin, resented a system of government that put both economic and political power and influence in the hands of a relatively few of the 'best' people.

The Mackenzie 'reformers' were driven – or perhaps coaxed – to arms by a final exasperation caused by the devious methods of the allegedly reforming Governor, Sir Francis Bond Head, in 1837, and by the economic distress of that year of slump. They had then to suffer the humiliation of being put down by the militia, itself a democratic force, since every man from sixteen to sixty was liable in law for service. Mackenzie himself fled to the United States where, after trying to establish a 'provisional government,' he was jailed for a year at Rochester. When readmitted to Canada, he continued his 'John Wilkes' role as elected member for Haldimand County. Sharing his exile and his return to Canada was a daughter, Isabel Grace, who was to be the mother of a Prime Minister of Canada, William Lyon Mackenzie King.

The Lower Canada rising, always a more dangerous and troubling confrontation, swirled about the controversial figure of Louis-Joseph Papineau, Speaker of the Legislative Assembly, a former militia officer in the War of 1812. Again, the main issue – owing a delayed debt to the French Revolution – was a confused struggle against an entrenched oligarchy, although Papineau himself was not an advocate of responsible government. The British commander, Sir John Colborne, a Waterloo veteran, warned of approaching civil war and then took appropriate steps. He cleared groups of rebels from barricades at St Denis and St Charles on the Richelieu River. Papineau then fled across the u.s. border and left his supporters to their fate.

Colborne caught up with the biggest *patriote* force at St Eustache, just west of Montreal, and, in a tragically bloody skirmish, about seventy *habitant* rebels, or dissidents, were killed. Papineau remained in the United States until 1839, trying to encourage the Americans to invade his Quebec, then went to France; he returned to Canada under an amnesty in 1844. The Church had steadfastly opposed the rising.

With the rebels gone, the moderate reformers could speak up, and one of these, Robert Baldwin, advanced the idea that would end the constitutional gear-grinding: the idea of responsible government. That is, the government of the colonies should be made wholly British on the nineteenth-century model, in which the cabinet, or executive government, would remain in of-fice only as long as it was supported by a majority of representatives in the Assembly.

The wealthy Irish-born lawyer, William Warren Baldwin, father of Robert, had first put the idea to the Duke of Wellington in 1828. It was given powerful impetus in the Durham Report, the recommendations of 'Radical Jack' Lambton, the first Earl of Durham, sent out as Governor-General in 1838 to investigate the discontent and suggest an improved system of colonial government. Although in North America only five months – and in Upper Canada only eleven days – Durham proposed union of the Canadas with a large measure of 'responsible' government.

But the country would never be wholly British, of course. Lower Canada was to remain, as Sir Guy Carleton had decreed, peopled mostly by the French race. That meant two further external ties. One was slight: the tie with France. It was made up only of a seldom exchange of persons, of books, of ideas – ideas mainly religious and conservative. But it was a tie, and might strengthen with changes in either Canada or France. The other tie was with Rome, and it was strong indeed.

Within the colonies bordering on the Atlantic, sea and land were nearly equal endowments. By the middle of the century Nova Scotia, together with New Brunswick, was one of the great shipping communities of the world – another New England or another Norway. While the mighty naval fortress of Halifax dominated the Atlantic community in wealth and power and social style, its glittering pre-eminence was resented by the plain 'Yankee' farmers of the Annapolis Valley, across the peninsula. The descendants of the New Englanders who had taken up the lands of the exiled Acadians were rural in their way of life, Congregationalist or 'New Light' in religion, and democratic in their tradition of rule by town meeting. Much of the political history of Nova Scotia would turn on this opposition between the capital and its distant countryside.

New Brunswick, at least the older half of it, lived by the river and by the forest. The river was, of course, the historic St John. Its broad and beautiful valley now boasted rich square fields and angled meadows surrounding wooden houses in colonial style, and high gabled barns. Around the great bend by Gagetown to Fredericton, the pioneers were making the countryside their own, pushing their farmsteads down the narrowing valley toward the borders of Maine.

Settlement on Prince Edward Island was a different story, told in softer and more comfortable accents. By some freak of geology, almost the entire island was rich, red soil, free from stone, lightly timbered. Here was a new Eden, the 'Garden of the Gulf,' with only the winter ice of Northumberland Strait to give the rose its thorn.

Served by canal and railway, the tame giant of the steam piston, the packed stone roads of John McAdam, the heartland of the St Lawrence and the Great Lakes

The 1837 Proclamation asking for the delivery to justice of William Lyon Mackenzie and the other rebel leaders after their unsuccessful revolution attempt at Montgomery's Tavern in Toronto. Photo ONTARIO ARCHIVES

was transformed by the 1870s, the countryside packaged into the forms and patterns it mostly retains today. From November 1859 there was through rail connection in all weathers from Sarnia to Atlantic ports. The seemingly limitless West was opening. But those middle decades of the widowed Queen's rule, marked by the heartbreaking tragedy of the American civil war and the heartlifting achievement of the creation of the Canadian nation, were still dominated by the family farms that had waxed wealthy shipping out wheat to a Europe embroiled in the Crimean War.

No longer, though, except on a few extreme frontiers in the Laurentians of Quebec or Ontario, were farms the lonely clearings of pioneer days. The fertile lands from Cape Breton to Lake Superior had been found, cleared and were mellow cultivated soils. Men were beginning to desert the unkindly shoulders of the Shield as they caught 'Manitoba fever.'

In the making of the countryside, the very look of the land was changing. The fields now tended to be larger, and the leveller nature of the western terrain allowed the adding of field to field from horizon to horizon, broken only by woodlots, valleys and occasional islands of hills. The old marginal agriculture of valleys and hillsides, of clearings in the forest and fences of picked stones, was opening towards the sweep of the mid-continent.

PART IV

Chapter Eleven
Wooden ships, iron men

The Age of Wood brought Canada its first real riches and its most romantic era. The magnificent trees of the eastern forests – often growing too close for an axe to be swung in comfort – supplied the timber trade and a remarkable flowering of craftsmanship, industry and artistry inspired the building and sailing of the stately windships. After scattered beginnings in the eighteenth century, the building of wooden ships rose to an exciting climax in the middle decades of the nineteenth, fought gallantly against the relentless onrush of steam and steel, then faded and was lost. The statistics of the port of Montreal tell the story: in 1854, of 180 overseas arrivals, only six were steamers; in 1907, of 742 arrivals, only eighteen were sail.

In the golden years of the windships, British North America with a mercantile marine of 7196 vessels ranked fourth among the ship-owning nations of the world. In one season, nearly five hundred ships were built in Canadian yards and many of them were sold abroad: in 1843, for instance, of 156 ships of 500 tons or more registered in the British port of Liverpool, 136 had been built in Canada. Saint John, Lunenberg and Yarmouth were famed across the seven seas for their square-riggers of tamarack, spruce and pine but the Nova Scotiamen, as they were widely known, were built in just about every town and village close enough to water. The bowsprit of a rising vessel often jutted over the waterfront streets. Until suitable lumber was exhausted, Prince Edward Island contributed nearly 2500 vessels, including at least two square-riggers.

Canadians were in demand everywhere as designers, builders and skippers – Donald McKay, who brought the American clippers with their 'cloud of sail' to perfection, was born near Shelburne in 1810; Samuel Cunard of Halifax owned forty sailing ships by 1839, running the mails to Boston, Bermuda and farther abroad; Joshua Slocum, the first man to sail alone around the world, was raised on the Bay of Fundy. These men went to sea at twelve and were hard to kill – Roderick Graham of New Glasgow was washed overboard by a huge wave while rounding the Horn; the next wave threw him back on board.

During that time of iron men and wooden ships, commerce was touched with a seldom grace. The barques, barquentines, brigs and schooners were built for work, to carry cruel loads in the highest seas, but there was some magic lent by the clean beauty of the forest and kept alive in the careful hands of the self-reliant men who took the trees and turned them into ships. Some laboured with the whipsaw to take planking from log, while others used broad axe and adze to shape the keel timbers from trunks, straight as pokers, eighty feet long. Figureheads and cabin beams were carved with natural art. The fresh tang of woodchips, pine, cedar, spruce, maple,

The bowsprit of a rising vessel often jutted over Maritime streets and, as the fresh tang of lumber laced the salt air, the tap of the caulker's hammer echoed through the shipyards. Photo courtesy PUBLIC ARCHIVES OF NOVA SCOTIA

birch, beech and oak, and the hot whiff of tar, laced the salt air about the shipyards, the tap of the caulker's mallet marked the minutes of the day, and all the provinces of the Maritimes throbbed with the pulse of progress.

There was a long and lovely twilight in which the rakish schooner danced across the oceans like some doomed heiress at the ball, before the cheaper Bessemer steel, the improvement of the marine steam engine, drove sail from the sea. One by one, the yards along the Bay of Fundy and the Atlantic shore fell silent, the gulls perched undisturbed on the lofts, the sons of Nova Scotian bluewater skippers disappeared down the hatchways of clanking steamers. A defiant Lunenburg would still create such a thing as the schooner *Bluenose* in 1921 – perhaps the most beautiful working ship ever built – but she was, in truth, designed to bring back from the States the International Fishermen's Trophy, which she did, and was then sold unsentimentally to haul freight around the Caribbean. She foundered on the rocks of Haiti; it was merely the delayed postscript of a bittersweet tale.

The timber trade for a century was a great pump siphoning both money and men into British North America. When Napoleon bent all Continental Europe to his will in 1807 and blocked British access to the forests of the Baltic, the Royal Navy reserved the pick of the Canadian forests for the masts, spars and planking. Dependent upon sea power, the British were seriously threatened. The broad arrow of the War Department was cut into the best Canadian sticks, whether the property was in private hands or not. A mast seventy feet long by eighteen inches in diameter was worth £10; at first, anything less than sixty feet long and a foot square wasn't thought worth the taking. But with workers pouring into the cities of Europe to man the new factories of the Industrial Revolution, the demand for building timber was insatiable. The very trees that the Canadian pioneer cursed as he felled and burned on his backwoods section brought good money once hauled to the mill and ripped into deals. As the square-riggers took the timber to Britain they brought back surplus population – the 'living ballast' of the great migration.

The Intendants of the French regime had given a tentative start to the lumbering business by cutting some of the Laurentian hardwood and shipping it to France. Water power was harnessed for sawmilling at natural falls and the first timber rafts were sent down the Richelieu to Quebec from the Lake Champlain country. Jean Talon launched a 120-ton vessel at Quebec in 1666, and six years later a 400-tonner was built and sailed to France. The French government sponsored a shipyard on the St Charles River and subsidized the construction of several cargo vessels for the West Indies trade. When the final years of the wars with Britain brought heavy maritime losses, keels were laid for several warships, including the 22-gun *Caribou*.

Governor Edward Cornwallis got British shipbuilding under way at Halifax in 1751 with a bonus of ten shillings per ton for new construction, and a Nova Scotian shipping register was begun in 1764. But it was not until William Hazen moved up from Massachusetts to Portland Point, at the mouth of the St John River, in the first Loyalist wave that there was significant progress. The firm of Simonds, White and Hazen, associated with that merchant prince of the Maritimes, Joshua Mauger, is granted fatherhood of the Atlantic shipbuilding industry – although only modest vessels were attempted until after the American Revolution. Exports of squared timbers, cut in the winter and hauled out by oxen, had begun from Pictou as early as 1774 and, by 1803, fifty ships were loading from that Northumberland Strait port.

The Loyalists from the New England states had brought their lumbering and shipbuilding skills with them and, exploiting the Empire preferential system, were soon trading timber to the West Indies in their own ships. Sawmills to supply local demand had been operating for years but an export market quickly developed when the supply of masts and spars from the Thirteen Colonies was cut off. Saint John exported a million shingles in 1785, and recorded the launching of a ship of 300 tons. (The non-nautical reader should remember that, with shipping, 'tonnage' relates to size, not weight. One hundred cubic feet of cargo space equals one register 'ton;' the term derives from the French *tun*, a cask being originally used to indicate how many casks of brandy a ship could

The romantic days of sailing ships were briefly re-created when Lunenburg craftsmen built the schooner Bluenose in 1921. Photo courtesy PUBLIC ARCHIVES

370.
DRIVING LOGS
UPPER OTTAWA

carry across the Channel to England.) Within an eight-year span, New Brunswick built more than 160 bluewater craft; in the years between 1806 and 1823, Nova Scotia launched 228. It was just the beginning of the golden age.

With the timber trade roaring, logs tumbled down all the many tributaries of the St John, from the hilly interior and the narrow valleys of the border territory, the Madawaska and the Aroostook. Competition for the dwindling stands brought the real threat of a shooting war when New Brunswick and Maine loggers disputed territorial rights on the Aroostook – a quarrel that was eventually settled, as such disputes almost invariably were, largely in favour of the United States.

From the height of land, the northern shoulder of the Appalachians, the other great New Brunswick river systems, Miramichi and Restigouche, flowed to the Gulf of St Lawrence on the North Shore, through forests known since Cartier's first voyage. Here there was little good land, but tremendous pineries rivalling or surpassing those of the St John. More perhaps than anywhere else in America, this was the cradle of the lumbering industry. There was abundant labour in the returned Acadians and the immigrant Irish. Here the peavey for rolling logs was invented; here the term 'Main John' for the lumber gang boss was used; here perhaps was the germ of the Paul Bunyan (*Bonhomme* ?) legend. Here, certainly, the techniques and terminology of the trade were brought to as high a pitch as anywhere.

The timber trade gave lavishly to New Brunswick, but there was a price to pay as well. It tended to create a province of a few great enterprises and a mass of poor farmers and lumberjacks. This was so even in the St John Valley, despite its many prosperous farms on the good land and the practice there of small men combining to cut a timber 'berth' of their own. Lumbering was the great trade of the Loyalist province, and lumbering both lent itself, under the government of the day, to the acquisition of great forest holdings, and called for much capital and enterprise to organize the winter cutting and the spring timber drives. Fortunately, the towns were soon large enough to support professional men and local merchants who formed a political class that could at least keep some rein on the more aggressive and autocratic of the timber barons. In Halifax, the self-taught Joseph Howe used his newspaper *The Novascotian*, to rally popular power in the battle for responsible government, the most influential Canadian journalist of his own, or any other, time.

In the more remote lands of the St Lawrence and the lakes, demand for the seemingly inexhaustible white pine was much slower in developing. Charles Meares had built a mill capable of sawing deals – three-inch planks – at Hawkesbury on the lower Ottawa River by 1804, but for fifty years it was the square-timber trade that dominated Canadian lumbering. When Napoleon attempted to starve Britain of wood, the government encouraged its merchants to invest in the Canadian forest, and the colony acquired a second, bigger business to back up the fur trade.

In many ways, timber was more complicated and difficult; the sheer bulk of the product, for one thing, posed problems new to a pioneer society, and credit facilities were cramped or simply non-existent. The Admiralty signed contracts with British principals who then established agents at Quebec; these men both bought timber that was rafted down to them, or themselves financed the cutting crews in the shanty settlements along the Saguenay and the Ottawa.

Independents with some resources of their own cut, hauled, rafted, shipped and sold their own timbers to dealers in England, under the protecting tariff that remained high against Russian and Scandinavian wood until 1842. But, repeating the pattern of the Maritimes, the basic dynamics of the trade soon produced a coterie of 'lumber kings' financing and controlling the inland supply, and rafting it down the rivers to the log ponds at Quebec – Wolfe's Cove was a well-known assembly for shipment abroad.

The Ottawa soon asserted its pride of place among Canadian rivers. Where the fur canoes had shot the rapids to Montreal for more than two centuries, great rafts of logs bound into 'cribs' now tossed and creaked their way downstream at the break-up of the winter ice. Philemon Wright, who had a sawmill and flourmill operating at Hull by 1804, had taken the first raft of squared

Driving logs on the upper Ottawa River. Note the smoke from the fires of the cookhouse on the lumber raft in the background, the lumbermen's home away from the forest. Photo courtesy METROPOLITAN TORONTO LIBRARY BOARD

timbers down to Quebec in thirty-five days in 1807 and, a decade later, was plying the river in his own steamboat, the *Union*. In the 1830s, three hundred rafts went down the Ottawa each season.

Many of the lumbermen who felled the huge white and red pines were settlers working from the shanties all winter to get some precious cash money, some were younger sons from *Canadien* farms, but later many were recruited from the the footloose, easygoing Irish who had come out with the migrations of the famine years. They were all called shantymen, paid a dollar a day and enormous meals, wearing a typical 'uniform' of flannel shirts, blanket-cloth coats, heavy grey trousers and spiked boots. Most picked up the Quebec habit of the brightly hued *tuque* – the woollen hat, that made gay splashes of colour in the white winter woods.

For men almost totally without the required forestry skills, they did exceptionally well – man can adapt remarkably quickly when he has to. Weavers from the old handlooms, for instance, soon showed double-handed skill with the heavy broad axe – they had become practically ambi-dextrous from throwing the shuttle. Even when the axe slipped, the Irish were philosophical. William Singer, a bricklayer turned lumberman, wrote home: 'I cut two of my toes off; Mr. Silcog sewed them on again; they seem to be getting on very well ... If I was to cut my right leg off I should not think of returning for I could do much better here with one leg than in Corsley with two.'

The long log shanties were lined with sleeping bunks, the centre empty except for red-hot stones, or open fires, on deep sand hearths. After dinners that seem gargantuan today – one sheep to ten men, a blueberry pie each – they bawled tear-jerker ditties, army songs and reels that almost lifted the bark roofs. Every so often, that most appealing of voices, the true Irish tenor, would rise clear and set every man keening for the 'Mountains of Mourne.' Ireland's national poet Thomas Moore had written the unforgettable lyrics for his *Canadian Boat Song* – 'Row, brothers, row, the stream runs fast/The rapids are near, and the daylight's past' – in 1804, listening to the *voyageur* song of his paddlers on the St Lawrence.

When they made up the cribs, or rafts, of squared logs on the ice of any of the Ottawa's nine main tributaries or its nine main lakes, the fancy-free among the shantymen prepared for the drive to the St Lawrence and Quebec. Sleeping 'lairs' and a cookhouse, bedded in sand, were built on the biggest rafts, and sails rigged to add favourable wind to downstream current. Eventually, wide chutes were constructed at the major rapids to allow the rafts a comparatively smooth, if swift, descent – 'riding the chutes' became a scheduled thrill for distinguished guests from overseas, including adventurous members of royalty.

On the run down to Quebec, the men began to blow their season's wages on whisky and rum in frontier towns like the infant Bytown, the Ottawa terminal of the canal from Lake Ontario that would be chosen by Queen Victoria as the new nation's capital. Their favourite pleasures, accord-ing to a contemporary report, were drinking, boasting and fighting. As the boisterous shantymen squandered their pay in Quebec, while the timber ships hauled the squared logs into their holds through special hatches in bow and stern, the God-fearing residents of that handsome capital of fifty thousand kept their daughters at home and their doors bolted.

An enterprising pair of Scotsmen, appropriately named Wood, gambled on the ultimate in timber ships, to avoid a British entry tax on sawn timber. They ordered built the largest ship in the world, the *Columbus*, 301 feet long, 3690 tons, rigged as a four-masted barque. The idea was to sail her to the firm's yard on the Clyde and then break her up – there was, of course, no tax on salvaged ship timbers. It worked like a charm and the Woods ordered another floating lum-beryard, the *Baron of Renfrew*, even bigger – 5880 tons. A terrified pilot wrecked this one in British waters, but the canny operators collected the biggest marine insurance cheque paid to that time.

The story of the Ottawa in the Age of Wood was repeated, in a minor key, on all the rivers feeding Lake Ontario with its sluiceway of the St Lawrence. A visitor to a sawmill on the Otonabee, three miles from Peterborough – only one of several in the district – was shown 136 saws working day and night converting fifty logs into planks every hour. Before 1850, Upper

An outfitter's store in Lunenburg. During the Golden Age of Sail, it was the outfitter who raised capital, hired crews and provisioned the ships. Photo by JOHN DE VISSER

Canada had nearly two thousand mills, mostly in local trade, but some, like the Hawkesbury mill on the Ottawa, employing eighty men. With the eastern American forests now thinning out drastically, demand for sawn timbers for building in the States was soaring.

Within a thirty-six-month span, two men arrived at the Chaudière Falls intent on making a million from the timber of the Ottawa. Both succeeded beyond their wildest dreams, laying down a potent formula for Horatio Alger who would soon publish his first rags-to-riches story. Ezra Butler Eddy had started work at age fifteen in Vermont, had failed as a dairy farmer, before he moved to Hull in 1854 and began making wooden matches by hand; when he died in 1906 he was called 'the greatest matchmaker in the world.' John Booth left his father's farm in the Eastern Townships with a total capital of $9 to work on the American railroads, but in 1857 he started making shingles in a small mill powered by the boiling Chaudière. It was the flashpoint of a career that made him a multi-millionaire, with four thousand square miles of timber rights, and his own railroad stretching from Depot Harbour in Parry Sound on Georgian Bay to Alburg, Vermont, almost five hundred miles. The rail line brought Booth $14 million when taken over by a fore-runner of the Canadian National.

Across the continent, the rain forests of British Columbia – with some Douglas firs topping 250 feet – had awed James Cook and his officers in 1778, but the resources were barely scratched by regional needs until the Panama Canal was cut in 1915, offering cheap ocean transportation to Europe. By the end of the First World War the accessible forest lands of the east were mostly cut over and the B.C. softwoods were totalling more than half of all Canadian production. Another generation and another world war later, the B.C. percentage had risen to 75 per cent, and exports exceeded $600 million in value.

Before the nation itself was officially born, Canadian timber had built cribs for canals, trestles for the railroads that were leaping across America, a million summer porches and church pews, lake scows, sloops and schooners, the boardwalks where fashion strolled, furniture colonial-style, docks and countless bridges in half a hundred countries. But nothing made from wood in those times could match the ships that came down the ways of the Atlantic yards. Frederick W. Wallace, a Scottish immigrant who wrote about the Canadian windship as another man might address his mistress, left this verse:

> They built 'em in Annapolis, Windsor, River John,
> Jest as able packets as you ever shipped upon.
> Yarmouth ships, Maitland ships, hookers from Maccan,
> The kind o' craft that took the eye of any sailorman.

We can now only imagine the heartlifting sight of the square-rigger or schooner, towering masts bending under full canvas, clean wind snapping the halyards, thrusting along with bright curling bow-wave, the 'bone in her teeth.' But, in 1875, the apogee of the golden age of sail, Nova Scotia alone had 2787 windships on the provincial register. Inside, the larger vessels had captain's quarters panelled in fine woods and furnished with loving care – often wife and young children went to sea with Papa. Sometimes a piano or organ was provided, and the fashionable copper bathtub. The *Muskoka* from Windsor had its own dinner service, the plates imprinted with the ship's flag and name.

Steam, at first, *helped* sail – the early steam tugs could tow a sailing ship out of harbour on schedule without the wait for a favourable wind. But Captain George McKenzie of New Glasgow scorned their help and sailed his ships right up the River Clyde to old Glasgow, winning a silver plate for his seamanship. The rakish clippers developed for the Australian and Californian trade could run at over four hundred miles a day by the 1850s, a speed not matched by steamers until nearly the end of the century.

The combination of steam-and-sail, as in first the Canadian-built *Royal William*, then in the

British *Great Eastern* (at 22,500 tons she boasted paddle-wheels, screw *and* 7000 feet of canvas on six masts), was followed by the twin-screw steel steamers which could cross the Atlantic in seven days or less, and, finally, by the *Turbinia*, the first of the steam-turbine ships that introduced the era of the ocean liner, the floating hotel. By 1859, Sam Cunard had won a baronetcy for taming the Atlantic, and the Allan Line of Montreal was offering weekly steamer sailings from Liverpool. The Allan brothers were pioneers in steam-turbine liners with *Victoria* and *Virginia*, and the later luxury ships, *Alsatian* and *Calgarian* . Like the competing Beaver Line, they were absorbed into the Canadian Pacific transportation empire in 1915.

As the graceful wooden ships fell to shoals and to decay and were not replaced, the Maritimers fell back upon their memories. The *Marco Polo*, celebrated as the fastest ship in the world, had been swept ashore by a gulf gale at Cavendish, Prince Edward Island, after a career of thirty-two years. Built in Saint John by James Smith, the beautiful clipper took nearly a thousand emigrants from England to Australia, under Captain 'Bully' Forbes, in seventy-six days. He made it back to Liverpool in the same time, a week faster than the steamer *Australia*. Even a collision with an iceberg couldn't slow up the *Marco Polo*.

Around Minas Basin, that cradle of Canada, legend still enshrines the launching at Maitland of the largest square-rigger ever built in Canada. William Dawson Lawrence came to Nova Scotia as a baby with his County Down parents, helped his father on a stony farm, then took his axe, fiddle and Bible and got a job in a Dartmouth shipyard. With capital of £30, he scouted his timber standing in the woods, cut and hauled it, and built his first ship, the *St Lawrence*, in 1853. Twenty years later, he gambled everything he had made, and more, in building the *W.D. Lawrence*, 2459 tons, to his own plans. With a mainmast towering two hundred feet high, it carried eight thousand square yards of canvas, and cost a total of $107,452.98 – a fortune for the times. The wiseacres said a wooden ship so big could not survive Atlantic seas, and four thousand people turned out to watch her launched into the crest of a new-moon tide.

The owner sailed in his namesake on its maiden voyage to England, with his son-in-law as captain. They crossed half the world with coal for Aden, then guano from Peru to Belgium. Canadian ships were taking cotton from New Orleans, coal from Cardiff to Yokohama, tea from Bombay and wool from Melbourne. Lawrence sold his leviathan to Norway after eight years, realizing a net profit of $140,848 from his project.

Spencer's Island is another Minas village, now slumbering quietly on the upper shore, near Parrsboro. The first ship built there by Joshua Dewis was the trim 100-foot 200-ton brigantine *Amazon*, launched in 1861. Except that her young captain sickened and died on her maiden voyage, she had a rather uneventful career for seven years until wrecked at Cow Bay, Cape Breton. Salvaged and repaired by Alex McBean of Glace Bay, she was sold to Americans in 1872. Within a year she was the most famous ship afloat.

Renamed the *Marie Celeste*, she had set out from Hoboken for Genoa with 1701 casks of alcohol. Captain Benjamin Briggs had taken his wife, Sara, and their two-year-old daughter, Sophia, along with the crew of seven. Every anthology of mysteries of the seas tells how the ship was found twenty-seven days later, between Portugal and the Azores, totally deserted. Three sails were still set, two had blown away, the longboat was gone. The compass was broken, the dishes washed and neatly put away in the galley, the ship's papers missing. There had been no fire, no explosion, and the cargo was intact.

The Attorney-General at Gibraltar was understandably highly suspicious, and formulated elaborate theories to explain the tragedy. But neither he nor any of the hundreds of men who have since pondered the story of the *Marie Celeste* have come up with a satisfying answer to the riddle. The little ship from Spencer's Island kept her secret and finally left her bones on a reef in the Caribbean.

PART IV

Chapter Twelve
The pioneer seasons

It was the springtime of Canadian history, so let us look at the beginnings of the pioneer year in spring. The teenage Queen Alexandrina Victoria had begun her reign and all was new and shining. While her marriage to cousin Albert prospered in nine children who were to take almost all the thrones of Europe, while she gave regal substance to the era of peace and progress that still carries her name, Canada itself multiplied and matured and began to stand – if a little humbly and bashfully – in the company of nations.

The season began in the sugar bush. *Canadiens* had learned from the Indians how to tap the sugar maple and boil down its sap for syrup and sugar. Later colonists learned the art wherever the sugar maple grew, and the sugaring in March was the first task of the warming year. The trees were tapped, the patient oxen hauled the collecting vats, the sap boiled day and night in the sugar camp, casks of syrup and boxes of sugar were prepared for family use and for sale, and the children had their taffy pulls in the late spring snows.

The year had begun with sweetness and the light was swiftly growing as the days lengthened towards summer. The sugar maple did not grow in Newfoundland or along the Atlantic coasts of Cape Breton and Nova Scotia. There quite another enterprise was beginning, the catching of bait for the summer fishing from the capelin shoaling in the bays and inlets. As the sullen winter waters smoothed and lightened under the gentler winds and more prevailing sun of summer, the boats put out from shore along the miles of rocky coast, the schooners drove out by Yarmouth and Lunenberg for the Banks. And there appeared the sails of the New England, British, French and Portuguese fishing fleets, bankers and sack (supply) ships, to harvest the teeming cod of the continental shelf.

While the ships rode the swing of the Atlantic, back on land, at the head of bays, in the Annapolis Valley, around the marshes of Tantramar, in the intervales of the St John Valley and in the river bottoms of the interior, the black ploughed fields, sown by hand, were green with spring wheat. The timothy, the red top, and all the abundances of marsh grasses were shooting to quick perfection under the urgent sun.

The time for haying was soon upon the settlements, and the men with scythe and whetstone, in steady rhythm mowed down the deep swathes of grass. The women, bonneted against the sun, with rake and fork, tugged and built the sweet-smelling, sun-dried hay into winnow and coil (or cock). Then it was carted to the barns to fill the lofts to bulging, unless the spring had been dry.

On the higher ground above the meadows, or in the dyked lands of the Acadian sea-marshes, or in square clearings in the forests along the St Lawrence and the lakes, the field crops had been ripening to harvest. Of these the chief was wheat, whether on British or French farms. For Canada from the first was a land of wheat. Most of British North America was too cool to ripen corn – except from Montreal to Detroit – and in any case the French settler brought with him the deep attachment of Mediterranean man to wheaten bread as the staff of life. So the spring wheat crop was the first sown, the largest, and the most carefully watched. Oats and barley, they were for oatmeal and the livestock, flax for linen – but none had the importance of wheat.

It was the Indians who taught the pioneers how to tap
the special maples for the sap from which they made
sugar and syrup. Photo by JOHN DE VISSER

In August the scythes, sometimes in earliest times the sickle, in later time a short-handled scythe with a 'cradle' of light wooden rods to sweep the cut grain into bundles ready for tying as sheaves, these went down the standing grain in heavy rhythm, laying the grain for the binders. It was the women and children, who swept the mown grain into armfuls, twisted light handfuls of stems into bands to bind the sheaves which stood again in stooks (or shocks), thickly or thinly as the crop was good or bad. It was a labour, a ritual, of rural life at least as old as Ruth, although here it was not the corn but the land itself that was alien.

Early authors began the task of making the country familiar by writing of it. A nephew and namesake of Oliver Goldsmith wrote the *The Rising Village*, in which he described a Nova Scotian rural landscape:

> Here the broad marsh extends its open plain,
> Until its limits touch the distant main;
> There verdant meads along the uplands spring,
> And grateful odors to the breezes fling;
> Here crops of grain in rich luxuriance rise,
> And wave their golden riches to the skies;
> There smiling orchards interrupt the scene
> Of gardens bounded by some fence of green;
> The farmer's cottage, bosomed 'mong the trees,
> Whose spreading branches shelter from the breeze;
> The winding stream that turns the busy mill,
> Whose clanking echoes o'er the distant hill;
> The neat white church beside whose wall are spread
> The grass-clad hillocks of the sacred dead ...

The verse applied to much of pioneer Canada in that Victorian summer. As the nights lengthened again and the frosts began, the fruits of the orchards were gathered – chiefly, but not only, apples – and were sliced and strung to dry in the sun. Still later, as the pale October sunlight grew even cooler, the butchering of the chosen bullocks and pigs began, to be cured or placed in 'ice-houses,' or simply hung for winter's frost to keep. Selected cowhide was soaked in the lye of the tanning trough in preparation for next season's boot repairs. The cutting of fuel in the woodlots, or on the hillsides, completed the preparations for the long winter hibernation, the annual dormancy of British North America.

Looking back, the pioneer year seems an unhurried, uneventful folding of day into week, week into month, with only the steady widening of the farmland, the improvements to the farmhouse, the growing tall of the children to mark the years. But the letters, diaries and memoirs of the settlers themselves show that it wasn't like that at all! In fact, there was so much 'going on' in the backwoods, such a level of individual participation, cheerful and open, that it is the urban life of today that seems tame and tasteless by comparison. But, certainly, pioneer life in Canada was no sylvan idyll: there was hardship and hunger, sickness and suffering; there was drunkenness, with untaxed rye whisky the refuge of the despairing; and, in a society heavily weighted with the unlettered poor, a coarseness of speech and behaviour that revolted the sophisticated.

Each spring, by Ste Anne's, at the westerly tip of Montreal Island, where Thomas Moore listened to the *voyageurs* sing 'their parting hymn,' simple folk gathered to watch the ceremonial departure of the nabobs of the fur trade for the summer rendezvous in the Northwest. No mayoral procession of limousines and motorcycles could be half as colourful. The scene is described by Samuel Thompson, a London printer who had arrived with his brothers, Thomas and Isaac, in 1833 in the square-rigger *Asia* :

The despot of the Northwest, Sir George Simpson, was just starting for the seat of his government via the Ottawa River. With him were some half-dozen officers, civil and military, and the party was escorted by six or eight Nor'west canoes – each thirty or forty feet long, manned by some twenty-four Indians, in the full glory of war-paint, feathers and most dazzling costumes. To see these stately boats, with their no less stately crews, gliding with measured stroke, in gallant procession, on their way to the vasty wilderness of the Hudson's Bay territory, with the British flag displayed at each prow, was a sight never to be forgotten.

The touch of spring also brought out that other aristocrat of the forest, *Euarctos americanus*, the black bear. Since the seigneurs of the French regime settled the fringes of the Quebec forest, the bear and the wolf had been the twin curses of the pioneers. The bears were 'thick as blackberries' in the woods of Upper Canada and, when their preferred diet of insects, honey, berries or fish was hard to come by, they raided the clearings. They took particular delight in the piglets, often penned close to the settler's cabin. Gideon Richardson, a pioneer along the Penetang road in old Huronia, finally moved his pigpen within yards of his door and kept a log fire burning all night between the porkers and the forest. A heavy shower one night doused the fire and the bears moved in. The Richardsons turned out to defend their stock and, at the height of the mêlée that followed, a rearing bear threw a pig clear through the cabin door.

Humour seldom lightened the stories of the grey wolf. Growing up to 175 pounds, six feet long from nose to tail-tip, baring inch-long fangs, they could pull down a moose, and domestic stock stood no chance with them. Common through all lightly settled areas, they took calves, sheep, even horses were attacked. Hunting in packs of up to thirty animals at times, howling eerily to the moon, they terrified women and children left in remote cabins. From the earliest days, there was a bounty on their hides – and there still is.

'In the summer of 1837,' a pioneer of Orono recalled, 'the tracks left by wolves were as common as sheep tracks are now.' On the Thames River, David Dobie reported hearing three packs howling at the same time. At Markham, eighteen sheep were killed in one night on one farm, while a single wolf slaughtered six in as many minutes in daylight at the Islay settlement on Lake Simcoe. Young steers were pulled down and milk cows had to be destroyed in Chingacousy Township when they came home with their udders bitten by running wolves. If a herd of cattle was attacked, the oxen formed an outer ring with lowered heads, while the cows and calves were protected in the middle.

Men carried a gun, and if possible a burning brand, when they had to walk a forest trail at night. If wolves closed in, the usual precaution was to climb into the crotch of a tree and wait until daylight dispersed the animals. A human death attributable to wolves was reported by David Dobie in the days when London, Ontario, boasted just two brick buildings. One night after a barn-raising bee, where the usual free whisky keg was supplied, one man passed out on the way home and was left by his companions to sleep it off by the roadside. When he had not reached home next morning, a search party went out. All that was found at the place where he had been left were a few shreds of flesh and clothing.

Game and wildlife were everywhere in the pioneer summer. White-tail deer were so numerous in the Bowmanville area that H.L. Powers, one of the founders of Kirby, shot 119 in his years there; marksman Cyril Davidson shot seven in one day. Samuel Strickland once had seventeen deer hanging in his barn. Rabbits and hares, squirrels and raccoons raided the crops in field and kitchen garden. Porcupine, beaver and otter were all present, and were all eaten in scarcity. A stroll with a gun in the woods in the late afternoon would usually bring meat to the table.

Wild turkeys, partridge, ducks, pheasants and pigeons filled the iron cookpot, the turkeys running up to thirty pounds when replete with the nuts of the fall. The passenger pigeons came in flocks that literally darkened the sky at noon and they would strip a peafield in minutes. The

settlers shot them, caught them in nets slung between the trees, knocked them down with sticks. J. L. Warnica, a pioneer at Innisfil, near Barrie, recalled getting twenty-nine pigeons with two shots – one barrel fired as the birds fed on the ground, the other as they rose. In the nesting groves, the birds could be merely shaken from the boughs; others fell to the ground when branches broke under the weight of the roosting thousands. The women skinned the birds, discarding everything except the plump breasts which were put down in salt for winter treats.

Eagle and snake were then common, with rattlers among the sunny rocks of the Niagara Gorge, around Burlington Bay and along the limestone outcrops of the Bruce Peninsula. Some pioneer wives from southerly American states had learned to snatch the reptile up by the tail and crack him like a whip.

Foxes regarded the pioneers' poultry as a sheer gift and themselves supplied a sporting target. Well-to-do colonists, and officers from the garrisons, organized fox hunts English-style as early as 1826 in Montreal, and at Toronto and London in 1843, the beginning of the traditional Canadian admiration for the jumping thoroughbred.

Sports and amusements for everyman turned on the simple facilities of village and homestead. Pleasures were boisterous and uncomplicated, often muscular and sometimes savage. Chopping contests, putting the stone, hurling the hammer, gave local strongmen their chance to shine. Where the kill-joy religious sects didn't rule, card-playing, music and dancing were enjoyed. Cock-fighting and dog-fighting, even bear-baiting, could be found, and all-in wrestling and bare-knuckle fighting were common. The honour of a township could turn on a half-nelson – the citizens of Marysburgh on the Bay of Quinte challenged Adolphustown across the channel to a three-man team wrestle to settle the question of which town was 'top dog' on the bay. Adolphustown won, in straight falls.

Regattas were held on Quinte's sheltered reaches, on the St Lawrence, the lakes of the Ottawa and the Kawarthas; at these events the voyageurs and Indians demonstrated their canoe speed and endurance. Match races between the best local horses were arranged with spirited betting and, when the fields of blackened stumps gave way to pastures, ploughing contests were held, sponsored by the swiftly expanding farm-machinery companies.

These were the days when people as couples, or singly, danced with vigour and abandon; to a swift and singing violin, son, father and even grand-daddy heeded the caller to 'take your partners and away we go,' stepping and strutting, swinging and whirling in breathtaking reels and 'sets.' Everyone knew such numbers as *Old Dan Tucker* and *The Wind Shakes the Barley*. A dance was often the payoff for a summer's day of steady labour at the work bees, and the youngsters wouldn't stop till dawn. The courtships begun in glances while husking corn or stringing apples could flower under beaming parental approval. A favoured young man would soon be noticed sitting around the fireside, smoking pipes with the girl's father and older brothers, undergoing quiet but thorough investigation while chewing over the regional news.

Sunday was 'sparking' day, the traditional time of courtship. And being permitted to 'see' the girl home from church was the unmistakable sign of acceptance. As the young lovers strolled hand in hand down the summery meadow trails, the inevitable mischievous young brothers contrived to play tricks upon them. A wedding sent the families, the hamlet, the whole district into a happy stir and bustle. When the hungry years were past, mothers and daughters baked for days – breads, pies, tarts, doughnuts, gingersnaps – and plotted to minimize the inevitable consumption of whisky. Tables were set under the trees of the orchard, or in the barn.

After the ceremony, the new husband handed his bride into the buggy and led off a processional triumph around the local roads, all the wedding party following, accepting the good wishes of the whole district – the forerunner of the modern honeymoon. They might be held up by a group of gallantly disappointed bachelors, who had stretched a rope from tree to tree across the path, demanding a ransom – the price, a kiss from the blushing bride.

Efforts to conceal the destination for the wedding night seldom prevented the arrival about

A barn-raising bee, where all the neighbours helped.
While the men laboured outside, the women prepared
for a feast and dancing as a reward for the day's
work. Photo courtesy ONTARIO ARCHIVES

midnight of the 'shivaree' boys, beating skillet lids, tin kettles, ringing horse-bells, whooping and hollering, until paid off with liquor or a five-dollar bill to blow at the nearest tavern. If the bridegroom wasn't popular, a spoilsport might climb the roof and throw a wet sack over the chimney to fill the house with smoke.

Elections were held when the crops were in and usually provided the most raucous, riotous week of any pioneer year. There was a single polling station in each district which opened at 1 p.m. every day, the mornings being given over to last-minute speeches by candidates on the 'hustings,' a raised platform of rough boards protected from sun and showers by a sloping roof. Important leaders arrived with an impressive hiss of steam by the swiftly expanding railroads, exhorted the awed populace, took a glass or two with local pooh-bahs, then rolled on to the next poll. The competing parties erected tents nearby and laid in wait for the electors to ride in from the clearings.

Monday to Saturday, there was free lunch and free whisky and some 'undecided' voters tied on a week-long 'toot' as they deliberated between the candidates. At an election in Peel in 1848, an eyewitness remembered that 'whisky flowed as freely as the waters of the Credit.' As the closing of the voting book grew near, when the poll was thought to be close, bribery was always likely. Samuel Jones of Durham County recalled an election in Newtonville: 'On one occasion, rival factions, each led by banners and fife-and-drum bands, met in the middle of the road. What might have been anticipated happened; banners were torn to ribbons, drums smashed, and some heads were cracked as well. Something worse occurred on one occasion, when one man voted, as another thought, the wrong way. The offender was struck on the neck with a club and dropped dead.'

It was an open vote, often cast in the leading local tavern. If a man upon whom free booze had been showered voted for the other side's candidate, he might find himself thrown into the nearest creek. A win at the polls set off a fresh round of celebrations. A fierce election fight between James Morton, a rich distiller of Lennox County, and Sir Henry Smith, the Solicitor-General of Upper Canada, resulted in a win for Morton – who was supported by an up-and-coming young lawyer called John A. Macdonald. Morton's victory party at Adolphustown drew 'ten acres of teams; oxen were roasted whole and feasting was kept up for two days and two nights.'

All through the year, the swilling of hard liquor was the vice of pioneer Canada, usually explained by its role as an antidote to the hardships of life in the timber trade or on the wilderness farm. Rye whisky or rum lubricated every social wheel, and there was created the curiously acceptable image of the 'hard-drinking man,' staggering, pugnacious and foul-mouthed in his cups, that has not been entirely lost from the land.

'When I was a young man,' recalled Neil McDougall of Kincardine, 'the man who did not take his liquor was looked upon as a milksop.' The explanation as given is only part of the truth. Not only the failures, ignorant labourers and backwoodsmen were drunkards. There was something in the boozing cult of a large body of men from humble backgrounds of beer and cider leaping at a bound to the level of the squire's decanter of brandy, without the opportunity of acquiring moderation or taste on the way. Where German settlements took root and stuck to beer, there was no liquor problem.

With crude distilleries at just about every site that offered surplus grain and running water, liquor of a high potency was suddenly available at from 15 to 50 cents a gallon. A bushel of grain could produce three gallons. Often it was provided free at stores and auctions – an open barrel with a tin cup on a chain – as an encouragement to trade. The effect of cheap whisky on some sections of the pioneer population was little different to that later widely regretted among the innocent Indians of the prairies.

There were once nine distilleries between Toronto and the now-connected suburbs of Richmond Hill, and Yonge Street boasted sixty-eight taverns from Kempenfeldt Bay at Barrie to Lake Ontario, one for each mile with three to spare. In Upper Canada in 1842 there were 147 registered distilleries and 96 breweries. Toronto itself in 1850 had 152 taverns and 206 beer beverage rooms for a population of thirty thousand. A pioneer writing back to a British magazine said that it was 'a moderate man who does not exceed four glasses in the day.' Cases were known of a glassful of whisky stirred into the children's porridge pot 'to warm their stomachs.'

Two distilleries at Delaware and another at Mount Brydges kept the central Middlesex area well supplied, and a busy crossroads anywhere in the colony might have a drink shop at each corner. The inns were required by licence to offer accommodation for a man and his horse, on the British pattern, but the average establishment was merely a front for the sale of liquor. Writing home before 1835, an immigrant reported 'every inn, tavern and beer shop filled at all hours with drunken, brawling fellows, and the quantity of ardent spirits consumed by them will truly astonish you.' Whisky was five cents a grunt, a 'grunt' being as much as you could swallow in one breath. At Stayner, a well-known store kept a barrel open to all customers until the 1860s.

When Indians coming down from Lake Simcoe and Georgian Bay traded their treaty goods for liquor, the authorities began to distribute all money and goods right on the reservations. One young half-breed, eighteen years of age, had died after drinking a pailful of whisky in three swallows on a bet. Of the cases of sudden demise investigated by a coroner, excessive drinking was by far the most frequent cause of death.

A drunken quarrel led to the first hanging in Toronto. Two friends, Dexter and Vandaburg, shared a bottle during reaping and an argument arose. It ended with Vandaburg dead and Dexter found guilty of murder. At the public gallows, Dexter refused to climb the steps, even though asked politely, 'Do go up, Mr Dexter,' by Bishop John Strachan. Eventually, the poor wretch was placed on a cart and driven under the scaffold so that the noose could be adjusted about his neck. Then with a crack of the whip the cart was driven away and the body left swinging.

Appalled at the degradation caused by cheap colonial whisky, temperance societies were active in Nova Scotia as early as 1828 and within eight years a convention of thirty societies was held in Montreal. The Sons of Temperance, the Order of the Good Templars and the Ladies' Total Abstinence Society were influential in getting local option legislation passed by 1864, and extended to all provinces in 1878. Drinking was severely curbed – many townships, cities and even hamlets voted to go 'dry' – but strenuous efforts to introduce total prohibition in Canada were always to fail.

After Sir Robert Peel formed his 'Bobbies' in London in 1829 the idea of a paid police force slowly took hold in the colonies, but it was many years before there was any semblance of adequate protection in Canada. A vigilante group called the Cavan Blazers enforced a brand of rude, but often effective, justice in Upper Canada's Durham County. One disagreeable citizen awoke one morning, ready to depart with his waggon full of grain in sacks for Port Hope, only to find the waggon, still loaded, sitting astride the ridge pole of his barn. In matters 'injurious to the community' the Blazers acted quietly to 'settle all such matters without delay, without cost, and with much less ill-feeling than follows upon legal proceedings.' Some young hired hands contemplating flight when they learned their country girlfriend was 'expecting,' decided upon matrimony after all when the Blazers took an interest. A preacher who railed against them in his pulpit was stopped in the gloom at a crossroads one night and required to alight from his buggy to kneel and pray in the dust – for the success of the Blazers' efforts to maintain law and order.

When the first snows introduced the last phase of the pioneer year, the womenfolk were in a final flurry of activity in 'putting down' all possible fruits, berries and meats for the long winter ahead. Kitchens were festooned with strings of drying apple chunks, and 'Mom's apple pie' was just as much a standard on the Canadian frontier as on the American. They were the unsung heroines, bearing their babies in bush cabins often without medical aid, working alongside their men in the fields, spinning flax and wool, weaving and stitching through the evenings after 'himself' had drowsed off before the pineknot fire. Two young sisters from Galway earned local renown as axewomen in the Sunnidale district; they could match most men in the bush and were

seen walking seventeen miles to the store, returning each with a full sack of flour or ninety pounds of potatoes on the shoulder. One of the girls was killed when struck by a falling yellow birch.

The ingenuity of the pioneer women was boundless. They made drinks from mountain sweet, corn syrup, cherry bark, birch and maple sap, beets, hops and wild raspberries. Susanna Moodie left us her recipe for making 'coffee' from roasted dandelion root – a drink she rated 'far superior to the common coffee we procured at the stores.' Medicines were compounded from gentian root (for rheumatics), May apple (sore throats), Seneca snakeroot (fevers and pains in the bones), burdock roots (indigestion), crow's foot (dysentery), balm of Gilead (boils), yarrow (malaria), spikenard and hemlock tips (for colds) – when all else seemed ineffective, wormwood tea was offered. Plantain leaf was the most popular poultice.

Surgery was rough-and-ready, with the patient usually befuddled with whisky. When Thomas Mason of Haliburton was crushed by a falling tree, his left leg was broken and his throat ripped open, exposing the windpipe. Mrs James Hewitt, a neighbour, took her darning needle and thread and sewed up the throat and Mason survived past his 102nd birthday. When an axeman's head was laid open in the bush at Newmarket, it was stitched up on the spot. Not much could be done in a similar accident in Halton, near Oakville – the victim's head was sheared cleanly from his body. The germ theory of diseases and vaccination therapy was generally unknown until Louis Pasteur's publications in the later years of the century. All cold, fresh air was kept from the sick – everyone knew that poisonous vapours arose from swamps – and blood-letting was still widely practised to reduce the malignant 'humours' of the system.

The merry scenes of winter travel and fun so well-known in the Quebec paintings of Cornelius Krieghoff were duplicated in Ontario during those same years before Confederation, with perhaps just a touch of British reserve. The settler's sleigh was often made on the farm, set close to the snow, while the townsman's *carriole* stood high on handsome wrought-iron runners. As the year-end approached, the party spirit quickened along the concession roads with the jingling of sleigh bells in the crisp air announcing the arrival of gaily-scarved family friends. Pioneer John Thompson summed it up in his diary in a Dickensian phrase: 'Christmas, all people idle and feasting.'

PART IV

Chapter Thirteen
Of mind and spirit

It is impossible to overrate the importance of religion in the Canadian chronicle. Most of what is best and worst in Canadian history can be traced to organized religion. Difficulties encountered by foreigners, even adjacent Americans and related Britons, in swiftly understanding the 'Canadian thing' are often rooted in our religious heritage. For in the formative years, our churches created and controlled our schools, and the schools made the men who created the modern state. A country of missions to begin with, Canada in its farthest reaches is a country of missions still.

All the first peoples from Europe were Christian – although the term has to be stretched to breaking to include the average frontiersman. The Christian faith – at first only Roman Catholic, then also English Catholic, or Anglican – had, however, soon taken several forms. But, in the beginning of the Canadian spiritual and academic life, the main influences were those of the parish schools and Jesuit colleges of pre-revolutionary France, and the Anglican grammar schools of eighteenth- and nineteenth-century Britain. The world of the time offered none better. Two thousand years of struggle and splendour, and the striving and inspiration of the greatest minds and spirits of all recorded history, were thus invoked.

Canada joins the minority of northern hemisphere countries which have escaped the scarifying revolutionary experience. And, therefore, it has given acknowledgement of the only force comparable with revolution: religion in itself. Whether it was the Roman Catholic Church among the

The pioneer kitchen was seldom seen in repose, for each season brought its round of activities from the preserving of precious summer fruits to the concocting of medicines and teas. Photo by DON NEWLANDS

conquered French, or the fugitive Highlanders, or the starved-out Irish peasants, or the Church of England – perhaps the chief opponent of the French Revolution, as it was the chief victim of the American – or the evangelical 'Bible thumpers,' all had the common spirit of resistance to the revolutionary spirit. Only the Presbyterians and the Congregationalists had the root of revolution in them, but the former became part of the Canadian establishment from the first and the latter were a small and uninfluential minority. Methodists, as they interpreted their special doctrine of grace, might be conservative or reformist, rarely revolutionary.

The churches all asserted, with varying emphasis, the essential Christian doctrine, that man has an immortal soul and that his future life depends upon his conduct in this transitory one. This was the inescapable reference point for all behaviour and all thought. It might lead to applications that now can seem only quaint: that the French had a special mission in America; that the British victory in the Napoleonic wars was of divine ordination; or that God, whose eye was on the sparrow, was equally concerned in so small a matter as the stealing of apples or the kissing of a girl in a corner. The point is that it gave an orientation to Canadian life – and the great change that has occurred in modern times is that that orientation has ceased to be generally effective.

The religious experience is usually said to have begun in the raising by Jacques Cartier of his famous cross at the Gaspé in 1534, and in Humphrey Gilbert's proclamation of the Church of England in Newfoundland in 1583. But Cartier actually raised five or six crosses on Canadian soil and, probably Protestant in his own family, his motive was doubtless to honour his King and patron and, more simply, to establish French hegemony. Putting aside romantic myths, neither Cartier nor, later, Champlain came with a missionary motive: the former sought a seaway to the riches of Cathay; the latter was at first but one of several seeking to exploit the wealth of the Canadian forest. As a well-known Canadian churchman put it, 'Visions of gold preceded visions of God ... it was commerce over conversions for a century.'

Only after his fourth voyage did Champlain openly interest himself in religious affairs – and then it was to seek the support of the rich and well-connected Jesuits in saving the tottering colony. He suggested that for the sum of 3600 *livres* missionaries could come to Quebec to convert the natives and, probably, take a percentage of the fur profits. On that occasion, the Jesuits refused the St Lawrence, sending Fathers Enemond Massé and Pierre Biard to Acadia instead, where they were soon captured and returned to Europe by the English raiding up from Virginia.

Champlain turned to the Franciscan Récollets, the humble Grey Friars, and Fathers Joseph le Caron and Jean Dolbeau arrived in 1615, being joined later by the literary Brother Gabriel Sagard. They were the pioneer priests of Canada, for a decade travelling hard by canoe into Huronia and the Montagnais country on the north shore of the lower St Lawrence, striving to construct a written language from the jawbreaking, totally unknown dialects, choking down the stinking *sagamite* of the Indian canoemen, stumbling on the portages of the Ottawa as they tried foolishly but gamely to prove that Renaissance European man was a match in the wilderness for the Stone Age *sauvage*. While the first of the *coureurs de bois* showed the Indian that the European had feet of clay, the mere handful of priests struggled to claim that he was rather the lieutenant of the supreme *Manitou*.

The Indians were to be always curious and always unconvinced of the white man's God, and the brilliant Franciscan, Father Chrestien LeClercq, would state it clearly if cynically in one sentence: 'They would be baptized ten times a day for a glass of brandy.' To the Indian, there was a spirit in the river, in the fish that swam there, and in the stone that could rip the bottom from the canoe; in his view, the Christian story was interesting but thin, and in its central compassion so obviously unrelated to the law of the wilderness.

The Society of Jesus came in 1625, finally, when it persuaded the Duc de Ventadour to buy the vice-royalty of Canada from his uncle, the Duc de Montmorency, and to finance the establishment of six Jesuits in the land. They were led by Jean de Brébeuf, Charles Lalemant and the same Massé who had earlier attempted to plant the Roman rite in the Maritimes. The newcomers got an early taste of Canadian barbarism when the Récollet Nicolas Viel, returning that summer after two solitary years in Huronia, was drowned by his Indian paddlers in the Des Prairies River, behind Montreal Island, for the value of his few pitiful possessions. The spot has been known as the Sault du Récollet ever since. The Jesuits were treated coldly by the traders but made welcome by the Grey Friars until, when the Kirkes captured Quebec for England, all priests were shipped back to Europe.

When the colony was returned to France in 1632, after an intensive diplomatic campaign by Champlain and the supplication of Ursuline and Carmelite nuns who knelt in perpetual prayer, the Jesuits returned alone to the St Lawrence to begin their years of trial and triumph. Encouraged by the increasingly devout Champlain, they planned to set up a theocracy in Canada, an ecclesiastical monopoly to balance, if not indeed outweigh, the commercial monopoly of the traders. Generous gifts of land were made to the church which eventually held more than a quarter of all seigneurial grants. The forerunner of all French Canada's *collèges classiques* took its first few students in 1636. In Acadia, where the Capuchins had charge of missions until 1654, the first school was begun in 1632.

Father Paul le Jeune, who would be the Jesuit Superior in Canada until 1639, began sending back to France the annual reports, meaty, discursive and often inspiring tales, that would become famous in France and then in all the Christian world as the *Jesuit Relations*. Published for forty-one years, they focused the attention of the educated classes, then in the midst of a spiritual revival, on the struggling colony across the Atlantic, providing a steady reservoir of funds and dedicated personnel. These were the golden years from Henri Quatre to Louis Quatorze, from Montaigne to Molière. The *Relations* were far from impartial, but without them sympathy and support for the unrewarding and dangerous wilderness colony may well have withered and died, and without them our knowledge of the first half-century of New France would be meagre indeed.

In his first report, Le Jeune told of celebrating his first mass in 'the oldest house in the country, the home of Mme Hébert.' The sturdy Héberts were among the thirty-four French who had stayed on in Quebec during the three years of the British occupation. 'Tears fell from the eyes of nearly all,' Le Jeune wrote, 'so great was their happiness.' He immediately also revealed himself as the educator: 'I have become teacher in Canada: the other day I had a little Savage on one side of me, and a little Negro or Moor on the other, to whom I taught their letters. After so many years of teaching, behold me at last returned to the A B C, with so great content and satisfaction that I would not exchange my two pupils for the finest audience in France.'

Jean de Brébeuf returned in 1633, and the next season resumed his mission to the Hurons, with Antoine Daniel and Ambroise Davost. Champlain and his associates had perforce chosen the semi-agricultural Hurons as their middlemen in bringing the beaver out of the western hinterland. Where the Récollets had tried to draw the Indians into the settlements and catechize them there, the Jesuit policy was to attempt to keep the natives aloof from the worldly French settlements, to establish self-contained missions within the tribal areas. It was an idyllic dream, to create the perfect society with the relevation of the Old World and the innocence of the New. Brébeuf had written a Christmas carol for the Hurons:

Within a lodge of broken bark
The tender Babe was found;
A ragged robe of rabbit skins
Enwrapped his beauty round;
But as the hunter braves drew nigh,
The angel-song rang loud and high:
Jesus your King is born;
Jesus is born.

Sainte-Marie Among the Hurons was the largest of the Jesuit missions in Huronia. This careful reconstruction captures the aura of labour and dedication brought by the Jesuits to the wilderness. Photo courtesy
ONTARIO GOVERNMENT TRAVEL BUREAU *(next page)*

Jean De Brébeuf

...uste par les Iroquo...

Le 16 de mars l'an

1649

In 1639 the Jesuits built the palisaded village of Ste Marie on the southern shore of Georgian Bay, two miles east of the present town of Midland, Ontario, to be the central hub of a group of controlled mission villages. It was fort, church, hospital, school, and dwelling – fortified because of the growing threat of the Iroquois thrusting ever more aggressively towards the north-west in their need for furs to trade to the Dutch and English. Building materials, tools, pigs, chickens and cows were transported to Ste Marie over the eight-hundred-mile canoe route, with its fifty portages. A canal complete with the first lifting locks in the Americas was constructed to allow loaded canoes to enter the fort through a portcullis in the high wall of sharpened logs. At a time when the entire population of New France totalled 250, there were fifty-eight Europeans at Ste Marie, including twenty-two soldiers. At the peak there were eleven mission villages in Huronia and the adjacent Petun and Algonquin territory.

But it was, in the end, just a dream with a cruel awakening. To the horror and grief of the priests, they brought scourges like smallpox, influenza and dysentery to the Indians who had no immunity to European diseases, while other tribes not in close and continual touch with white men remained healthy. The Iroquois, further emboldened by the reports of many Huron deaths, finally attacked en masse in 1648, murdering Father Daniel at the door of his chapel – thus the little-known Daniel, the schoolteacher from Dieppe, became the first of the Canadian martyrs. Seven hundred Hurons were taken for the intricate ritual of the torture stake.

The following spring, having wintered in the bush, the Iroquois rolled up the Jesuit missions, taking Brébeuf and Gabriel Lalemant at St Louis, on the Hog River. Their agony at the stake at St Ignace is a sombre Canadian classic, celebrated in the traditional manner in the epic poem by E. J. Pratt. Father Paul Ragueneau eventually led the remnants of the Huron race – no more than three hundred – and sixty surviving Frenchmen back to the dubious safety of Quebec. In all, eight Jesuits were put to death by the Iroquois and all were canonized in 1930, giving the Canadian Roman Church that most sustaining of draughts, the blood of martyrs.

The power of the press, the challenge thrown down to the zealous by the *Jesuit Relations*, brought Canada the honoured teacher, Marguerite Bourgeoys, and Jeanne Mance, Canada's first nurse, in a group of one hundred immigrants to Montreal. *Mère* Bourgeoys founded a day school at Notre-Dame-de-Bonsecours in 1658, and eventually a great teaching order with her nuns stationed at Pointe-aux-Trembles, Lachine, Batiscan, in the protected Indian villages and as far afield as Louisbourg. She became chaperone to the 'King's girls,' sent out as brides for the settlers. The hard-working Jeanne Mance founded the Hôtel Dieu in Montreal in 1645.

Their renown is shadowed by that of the little widow Marie Martin, *née* Guyart, who had come to Quebec as one of three Ursuline sisters with Mme Marie-Madelaine de la Peltrie, a rich and devout widow from Alençon. They set up Canada's first convent, a boarding school for the daughters of settlers and Indians, and a second school at Trois-Rivières. Under her name-in-Christ of Marie de l'Incarnation, the widow Martin had become by her death in 1672 'the spiritual mother of New France' and the confidante of governors, intendants, generals and bishops. Even the austere Laval, reaching Canada in 1659 as the first Vicar-General of the Pope in New France, was responsive to her gentle power and persuasion.

In François-Xavier de Laval de Montigny, named the first Bishop of Quebec in 1674, the church found its flinty champion who would spend his life, gallantly if doggedly, in the Jesuit theocratic dream. The aristocratic and autocratic Laval was a member of the Sovereign Council – he would have thought the puissant member – from 1663 and, until his retirement in 1688, he harried a string of Governors and administrators, forcing the recall of two of them. His running quarrel with the equally aristocratic, equally arrogant Governor Frontenac stretching over a quarter of a century is legendary.

Laval attempted to enforce the total prohibition of the sale of brandy to the Indians and applied a stern Jansenist curb to all secular entertainment. He ordered two boys publicly flogged when they saluted the Governor in advance of himself. More a prince of the church than a father to his

A memorial to Jean de Brébeuf, a Jesuit from France
who founded the Huron Missions on Georgian Bay,
was killed by the Iroquois in 1649 and later canonized.
Photo by M. MILNE

145

flock, Laval nevertheless founded the Quebec Seminary to provide a flow of Canadian-trained priests for the parishes created by 1683, began the system of craft schools to teach vocational skills to the sons of settlers, and personally ensured the independence and the very real power of the church hierarchy. Laval refused to follow the traditional system of France in placing his priests permanently in a parish, insisting that they move as missionaries, returning to the seminary at his call. The scheme was suited to the thin and scattered population of New France, and also particularly to the maintenance of the Bishop's authority.

From Laval's seminary was to arise the Université Laval of today, with its dual charter from royal and pontifical authority, and its mushrooming off-shoot, the Université de Montréal. From that small beginning grew the seventeen seminaries of modern Canada, with their ten thousand graduates in the priesthood.

The importance of church in education was equally marked among the first Protestants in Canada. King's College, established by the Anglican Church in Windsor, Nova Scotia, in 1788, was the first university established in the British Empire after the loss of the American colonies (it still grants its own divinity degree, in association with Dalhousie University). The Rev. Henry Jones had opened a school at his church at Bonavista, Newfoundland, in 1722, the earliest Protestant school known within the territory that is now Canada. The Rev. John Jackson, a ship chaplain, had begun services at St John's at the turn of the century.

The first Anglican services are traditionally said to be those conducted by Robert Wolfall, 'minister and preacher' with Sir Martin Frobisher's voyage of 1578 in search of the North-West Passage. Wolfall no doubt used the English prayer book authorized by Elizabeth I, the first version of the Book of Common Prayer, still in substance used in all Anglican churches today. Good Queen Bess had ordered Wolfall 'to serve God twice a day.' Another favourite reference is to Sir Francis Drake's prayers during his voyage of the same year, when he claimed San Francisco Bay for the Queen under the name of New Albion. The narrative runs: 'The General and his Company fell to Prayers, and by lifting up their Hands and Eyes to Heaven, signified that their God, whom they ought to worship, was above in the Heavens, whom they humbly besought, if it were his pleasure, to open their blind Eye, that they might come to the Knowledge of Jesus Christ.'

These quotations precede Humphrey Gilbert's pronouncement at St John's in 1583, already mentioned, establishing the Anglican Church in Newfoundland. But Gilbert was lost at sea on his return voyage to England and his solemn declaration was lost in the gales that swept the Avalon. There is a footnote to history which records the arrival in Conception Bay in 1612 of the Rev. Erasmus Stourton, to minister to a colony expected of Milords Bacon and Baltimore, granted a charter by James I. Stourton went back to England in 1628 and Baltimore went, well, to Baltimore, Maryland.

The temporary barony of Nova Scotia, held by Sir William Alexander from 1621 to 1632, was always closely in touch with the Puritan Protestants of Massachusetts where a theocracy of another stamp was evolving. Captain John Smith, the hero of Jamestown, Virginia (est. 1607), always thought of his 'New England' as stretching from Cape Breton to Florida. The association continued, briefly, during the resumption of French authority in Acadia, with Father Gabriel Druilettes paying a fraternal call on Pastor John Eliot, at Roxbury, Massachusetts. The austere old Protestant had taught himself several Indian dialects and had invented an Indian alphabet in which he had published the Lord's Prayer, the Ten Commandments, and, eventually, both the Old and New Testaments. Eliot had been a leading figure in the negotiating of an Indian peace that was to last for forty years. The Jesuits at that time had just been swept out of Huronia and were planning, with a steely courage, their mission to the Iroquois.

After 1713, following the Treaty of Utrecht which delivered most of the modern Maritimes to Britain while guaranteeing freedom of religion to Roman Catholics, the growth of the Church of England was slow but steady. The garrison chaplains at Annapolis Royal and at the Gut of Canso preached and kept school for the British military families, and in 1720 a 'large church of Firr and

The Quebec Seminary shown here was founded in
1663 by Laval, later named the first Bishop of Quebec.
Laval's early efforts resulted in the foundation of 2
major universities and 17 seminaries. Photo courtesy
INFORMATION CANADA

spruce wood' was raised in St John's. The Rev. Killipatrick made a shaky start on Trinity Bay. But from the founding of Halifax in 1749, the Anglican presence was protected and permanent.

The Society for the Propagation of the Gospel in Foreign Parts, the S.P.G., had promised Governor Edward Cornwallis six clergy and six school teachers, two of whom arrived immediately, the Revs. William Anwyl and William Tutty. St Paul's Halifax, the oldest Anglican church still standing, was opened the following summer, with Tutty preaching the first sermon. General Wolfe worshipped there before the battles for Louisbourg and Quebec. He took with him as chaplain to the 48th Regiment the Rev. Michel Houdin, a Quebec-born former Roman Catholic priest who had converted to the Anglican ministry in Trenton, New Jersey. Houdin knew the Canadian capital intimately and, since he reported later that Wolfe had promised to reward him for his 'contribution to the victory,' romantics ask: was it a French Anglican who showed Wolfe the cleft at Anse-au-Foulon where the first of the Redcoats gained the Plains of Abraham?

Rev. John Ogilvie, a New Yorker, chaplain to Sir William Johnston, was called to surrendered Montreal by General Amherst, to preach the first Anglican service there, on September 14, 1760. Anglican ministers' wives, often ladies of the English upper classes, favoured literature as a cultivated pastime and one of the first in Quebec, Frances, wife of the Rev. John Brooke, wrote and published 'the first Canadian novel,' *The History of Emily Montague*. It gives a lively and witty picture of the life and amusements of the garrison families.

In Nova Scotia, the Church of England had been proclaimed the 'established' religion (that is, the official faith of the state) and a misguided attempt was made to achieve the same result in Quebec by the appointment of some French Protestants as parish priests, by prohibiting novices from entering the Roman Catholic religious orders, and by setting up an exclusively Protestant school system. Many influential thinkers of that time believed that the root cause of the American Revolution had been the failure of Britain to establish the Church of England in the Thirteen Colonies as a unifying force. The first British Governors of Canada, Murray and Carleton, were, however, sympathetic to the permanent *Canadien* population, especially so to the influential seigneurs and to the church hierarchy.

A Roman Catholic Bishop, Jean Oliver Briand, was appointed by Murray in 1766 – under the title of Superintendent – while the selection of an Anglican Bishop was deferred. Briand helped keep tempers cool by having prayers said in his parishes for the long life of King George. The Quebec Act, 1774, guaranteeing the security of the Roman Catholic Church and other traditional characteristics of *Canadien* life, came just in good time to deny the Americans a possible corps of active supporters in their invasion of the following year. And when revolution ripped France asunder, the ultramontane priests of Canada drew their flocks about them in the riverside villages and looked ever more steadily to Rome.

One Sunday during the American Revolution, Yankee rebels marched with loaded muskets into Trinity Church, on New York's Wall Street, and demanded that the Rector, Irishman Charles Inglis, omit the prayer to the King or be shot. He continued the time-honoured service without a pause, and the patriots lost their nerve. The same Inglis, after the Loyalist exodus to Canada, was consecrated Bishop of Nova Scotia in 1787, the first Bishop appointed anywhere in the British Empire overseas. His jurisdiction covered the whole of British North America, the first Anglican Bishop of Quebec, Jacob Mountain, not being appointed until 1793.

The Loyalist families welcomed Inglis joyfully as a bulwark against such forces as the 'New Light' Methodism of the young American immigrant Henry Alline, still stirring the illiterate backwoods with ecstatic conversions. Since 1767, Presbyterian James Murdock had been preaching on a circuit out of Horton. Schisms that had racked the Protestant churches in Britain were sometimes bridged under the different conditions in Canada, establishing a precedent that would lead, eventually, to the formation of the United Church, now claiming more than 20 per cent of all Canadians as adherents.

Bishop Inglis had begun his college at Windsor, Nova Scotia, as a 'King's university,' a pattern

Flags decorate the walls of St. Paul's in Halifax, founded in 1750, and the oldest Anglican church in Canada. Photo by JOHN DE VISSER

later followed at Fredericton in 1828 and in Toronto in 1843. The prototype had been founded in New York in 1754, the institution known today as Columbia University. Inglis held his first confirmation, for 125 candidates, in St Paul's Halifax on June 20, 1788, then set out on his 'Visitation' to his huge charge. At Saint John he laid the foundation stone of Trinity Church where the Loyalists hung the royal coat of arms they had taken from the Boston Courthouse – it can be seen in the modern Trinity today. Anything but a democrat, the Bishop opposed free seats in church 'because they made it possible for men of the worst character to sit down beside the most religious and respectable characters of the parish.'

Sailing grandly in *H.M.S. Dido*, Inglis visited Prince Edward Island, the Gaspé, and the four 'new' parishes of Quebec, Three Rivers, Sorel and Montreal. At Quebec, he confirmed two sons of the Governor, Lord Dorchester, and further discussed the thorny matter of a system of public education. At Montreal, he took over a Jesuit chapel, renaming it Christ Church – the predecessor of the present Christ Church Cathedral. The Jesuit estates had been sequestered by the Crown after the Pope had suppressed the order in 1777.

At the end of his western journey, Bishop Inglis met the strapping Rev. John Stuart, a six-foot, four-inch Pennsylvanian, just completing his second year at the new Loyalist settlement of Kingston. Stuart had been a missionary to the Mohawk, and was a particular friend of Chief Tyendinaga, the Iroquois ally of the British better known as Joseph Brant; he now had charge of the Western Settlements mission, stretching the lengths of Lakes Ontario and Erie.

The previous summer, Stuart had travelled to the lands on the Grand River given to the Mohawk, baptizing seventy-eight infants and five adults in the church just built at Brantford at the order of George III. In celebrating Holy Communion, Stuart used the Bible and the silver vessels that Queen Anne had sent to the Christian Mohawk in New York. The church, now known as Her Majesty's Chapel of the Mohawks, is the oldest in Ontario and, with its adjacent Indian school, is a site of pilgrimage.

The story of religion in Canada is particularly rich in missionary endeavour to both Indian and Eskimo. On the prairies, in the old North West, in Labrador and the Arctic, great figures appeared: the Anglicans' Bishop Bompas and John West, the Oblate 'Apostle to the Blackfeet' Father Albert Lacombe, the selfless Methodist teacher James Evans who invented the Cree syllabary, the Presbyterian James Robertson who once commented that for the Canadian mission field he would prefer that 'a man know less Latin and more horse.' It was on Lacombe's pleading that the federal government established the first Indian residential schools.

When Bishop Mountain – *Jacob* Mountain, to distinguish him from his son *George*, also later Anglican Bishop of Quebec – made his first pioneer travels he cemented cordial relations at York with the first Lieutenant-Governor of Upper Canada, John Graves Simcoe, a pillar of the church, and at Newark (Niagara-on-the-Lake) he encouraged the S.P.G. missionary Robert Addison, who was trying to build St. Mark's Church on the frontier. Addison succeeded, only to see his church burned by the Americans in 1813. The Mountains, father and son, held the bishopric for fifty-eight years.

For much of that time they were sturdily supported in Ontario by the Aberdeen schoolteacher-turned-cleric, John Strachan, swiftly becoming the leading personality of his province. Strachan was a feudal but heroic figure, struggling to plant in a semi-wilderness colony a social and religious system already under attack in the mother country. Like Simcoe before him – and many thousands since – he failed to grasp the full significance of Ontario's American heritage. The fathers of the boys he taught at Kingston and Cornwall, most of the elders in his pews in 1812 at St James' in York, were certainly Loyalist in heart but they were, first, American colonial in mind. The opposition and interplay between these two forces, combining, as we can now clearly see, in the acceptance of a constitutional monarchy, were to be the cause of endless conflict, bickering and bigotry in the fields of faith and education, and, finally, to bring an attempted civil war.

Simcoe's hopes for the establishment of the Church of England in Upper Canada and sole

Father Albert Lacombe, an Oblate priest, worked among the Indians of the west, in particular with the warring Cree and Blackfoot, for whom he wrote various books in their languages. Photo courtesy GLENBOW-ALBERTA INSTITUTE

Anglican possession of the valuable clergy reserves of land were cherished equally by Strachan, who was appointed the first Bishop of Toronto in 1839. Yet these designs must fail, if only because already the majority of English-speaking Canadians were Presbyterian, Methodist, Congregationalist, Baptist, Quaker or Mennonite, and the great migration of mid-century brought thousands of Roman Catholic Irish into the province. Thus Strachan and his minority of Anglicans, however well educated or well intentioned, became fatally identified with the rich and propertied, the 'Family Compact' of relished legend. It was an era of seemingly unbridgeable social gulfs; several of the 'good' families built, staffed and maintained their own private churches – the Sibbalds of Lake Simcoe, Sir James Gowan, the Pinheys of the Ottawa Valley.

Where Strachan was signally successful was with his first love, learning. The view of education within a religious setting was universal at the time, and the fact that the Anglican concept was exclusive – although certainly no more so than the Roman Catholic in Quebec – should not detract from the very real quality and ardour of Strachan's endeavours to enrich the culture of his adopted country. A graduate of Aberdeen and of St Andrews, he was first president of King's College, resigning when it was reorganized undenominationally as the University of Toronto. The following year he founded the University of Trinity College, until recently independent within the University of Toronto, and became its first chancellor. At a time when governments did nothing to support elementary education, when the few schools were often taught by men who had failed at all else, Strachan demanded and got £6000 a year for the 'common schools' and was mainly responsible for setting up the first General Board of Education. Having received his share of bouquets and brickbats, he was honoured in the Confederation year with the biggest funeral Toronto has ever seen.

The champion of the Nonconformist churches in the duel in English-speaking Canada with the Anglicans for control of education and religious freedoms was Adolphus Egerton Ryerson. Raised an Anglican, he entered the Methodist ministry and in 1829 became the editor of the Wesleyan journal, the *Christian Guardian*. Until 1831, only Anglican and Presbyterian clergy were permitted to perform the marriage ceremony and Methodists were particularly suspect because they were under the jurisdiction of the General Conference of the United States – one of the periodic waves of anti-Americanism was sweeping Canada.

Although Ryerson belaboured the 'Compact' on behalf of the 'Dissenters' – as all of the non-episcopal sects were then known – and supported legislative reform, he personally opposed the rebel leader William Lyon Mackenzie, and eventually left as his *magnum opus* a two-volume history of *The Loyalists of America and Their Times*.

At a time when the hard-riding evangelists among the Dissenters (the Rex Humbards and Billy Grahams of their day) were labelled 'the saddlebag brigade of itinerant preachers' from their sermons on the stumps of the backblocks, and 'a set of ignorant enthusiasts' from their scant theology, the persuasive intellectual Ryerson was able to weld their mostly inarticulate congregations into a political force which, although never formally organized, was easily strong enough to tame and then topple the Anglican elite. Curiously for a man devoted to the principle of schools open to all, irrespective of class or creed, Ryerson supported the early development of Roman Catholic separate schools outside Quebec – an issue that would within a few years imperil the unity of the nation.

Ryerson became the first president of the Methodist university founded at Cobourg in 1841 – now, as Victoria University, federated with the University of Toronto – and then, for a span of thirty years, Chief Superintendent of Education for Upper Canada. In that chair, he created the public school system of Ontario basically as it is now known. At Kingston, in 1877, the Presbyterian George Munro Grant was Principal of Queen's University, and an oracular consultant to his friend, John A. Macdonald.

In these ways, the affiliation of religion and politics – more marked in Canada than elsewhere in modern times – was developed. It would lead eventually to the founding of a major political party

The unique and beautiful Sharon Temple built in 1825 at Holland Landing, Ontario, by a dissident Quaker group, reminds us of the freedom of religious expression accorded to all sects in Upper Canada. Photo by DON RITCHIE

(the CCF, now the NDP) by a Methodist, the Rev. J.S. Woodsworth; to the undermining of Duplessis fascism in Quebec by Archbishop Charbonneau, and to a trio of Baptist parsons assuming the premiership of provinces in the West.

PART IV

Chapter Fourteen
The beckoning West

For two and a half centuries while eastern and central Canada were taken and turned to the uses of man, the rolling vastness west of Lake Superior and north to the Arctic shore lay virtually empty. Only the Indian bands moving with the buffalo and caribou, and the wintering partners of the fur trade, left scant track across the domain of plain, slough, river and lake, of hidden valley and northern forest, a territory larger than all Europe.

Although Henry Kelsey had brought back his news of the open and fertile prairies in 1692 to the Hudson's Bay Company factors clinging to the rocky rim of Hudson Bay, the company had done little to meet its duty under its grant of Rupert's Land of establishing a colony.

There was, in truth, a small permanent settlement inland at Cumberland House, established by Samuel Hearne in 1774 near the entry to the Saskatchewan River system, but it was merely a few huts and a summer garden around the frontier trading post. Some groups – the *Bois Brûlés*, soon to be called *Métis* – descended mostly from the sons of French *coureurs de bois* and Ojibway women, were living in the valleys of the Red and Qu'Appelle; but although a few of them farmed in a desultory way the great majority lived the semi-nomadic life of the buffalo hunter and freighter. Not until the turn of the nineteenth century, when the H.B.C. came fully alive to the threat of the thrusting Nor'Westers from Montreal, did the ancient Company of Adventurers allow the first true settlement in the lands now encompassed by the wide and wealthy provinces of Manitoba, Saskatchewan and Alberta.

The pioneers came into the West painfully slowly at first, shuttlecocks between the fur-trade rivals, victimized, abused, even massacred. Then the trickle became a stream as the lands in the East were filled, as the American territories in the warmer south were taken up, as the younger sons of the settlers of Upper and Lower Canada sought land grants of their own. As the boundless confidence of the railway age flowered in Canada – as perhaps nowhere else – the flood-gates opened and a rising tide of humanity rode by rail on to the prairies.

When the already established provinces of British North America suggested in 1857 that the Hudson's Bay Company's private kingdom be now made available for settlement, the white population of the central territory was below six thousand. By 1871 it was 18,995 and at the next census, 1881, it had risen to 65,954. The Canadian Pacific Railway reached Calgary by 1883, met the British Columbian construction in Eagle Pass in 1885, and the road to the West was wide open. By 1901, population had risen to 419,552 – and that was just the beginning.

The next decade and a half saw the prairies, so recently the 'great lone land,' filled as if by magic with a great toiling influx of people from twenty different homelands, speaking half a dozen tongues, all grasping eagerly at the chance of a new start in the new nation. Within ten years, nearly two million immigrants entered Canada, the population of Manitoba doubled and that of both Saskatchewan and Alberta multiplied five times over.

In the saga of Canadian settlement, no chapter holds more fascination than the opening of the West. Where the sea of grass rippled to hazy horizons, everything was on a grand scale. Never lawless in the storybook manner – the Mounties were out there before the rush – it was still 'wild' enough for any man, with two armed uprisings within fifteen years, vicious whisky traders, horse and cattle thieves, the last baleful flickering of Indian savagery, tales of endurance and starvation beyond number in the earliest days. Asked how they got by as frost or grasshoppers hit the first

Groups of Métis who were mostly descended from the coureurs de bois and Ojibway women, lived a semi-nomadic life as buffalo hunters for the fur traders.
Photo courtesy PUBLIC ARCHIVES OF CANADA

155

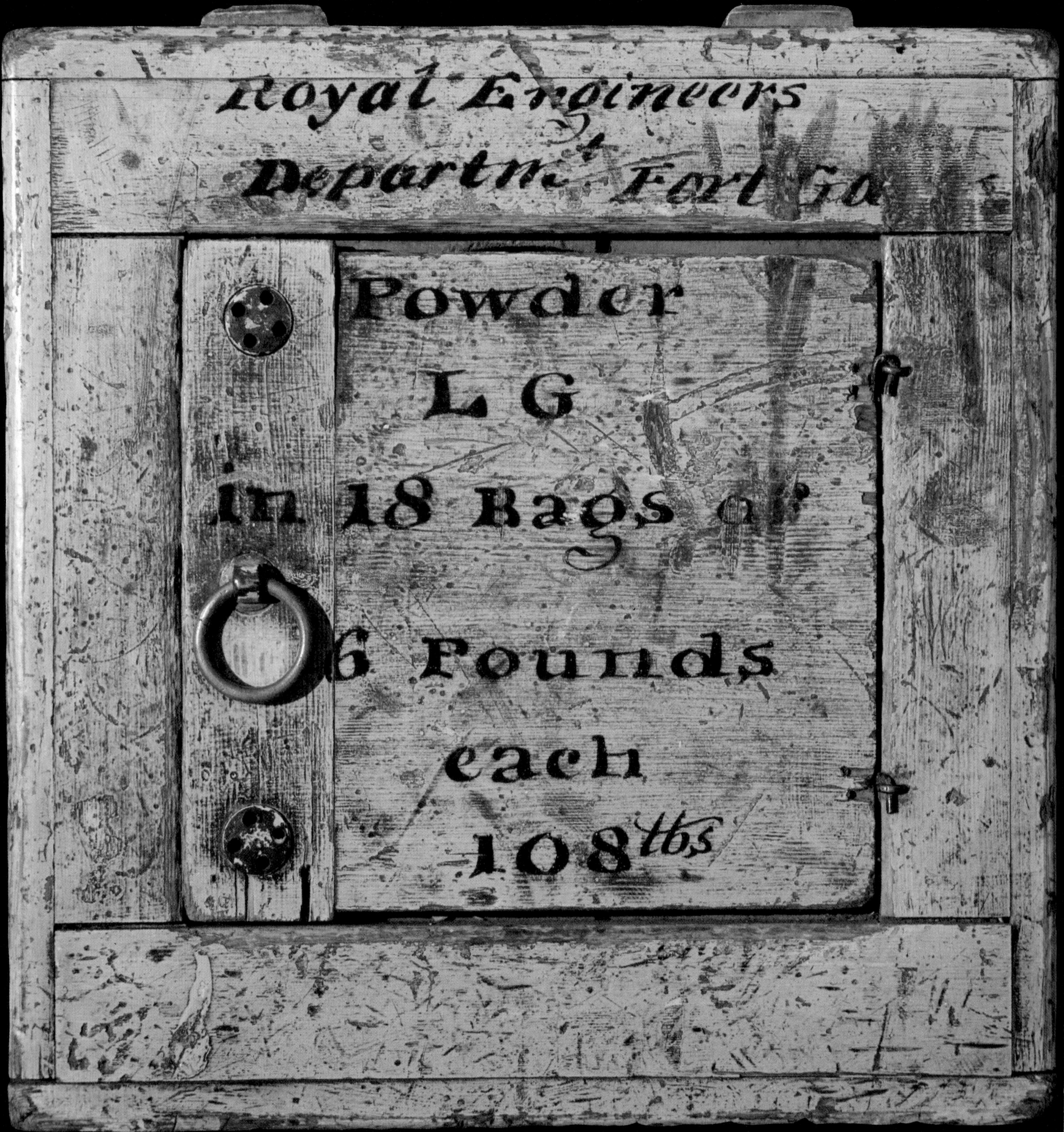

Royal Engineers
Departm.t Fort Ga[...]

Powder
L G

in 18 Bags of

6 Pounds

each

108 lbs

sparse crops, a pioneer said: 'Nobody had nothing, and we all shared it.'

In these years, the character and the very look of the Canadian were changed forever. Until the 1880s, the typical westerner was Anglo-Saxon, the overspill from Upper Canada and the mid-west of the United States. By the turn of the century, the arrival of Scandinavians, Germans, Ukrainians, Poles, Dutch, Hungarians, Jews and other Europeans by the many thousands was bringing the West and the whole nation an astonishing and welcome diversity.

The old patterns of French royal regime and British imperial colony were to be drawn into a new mosaic of peoples. Upon the more formal courtesies and traditions of the foundation races was laid a simple cheerful helpfulness, an earthy response, the neighbourliness of humble men and women drawn together by a common challenge and adversity, despite all barriers of language, ethnic custom and religion. Some peasants walked in with their precious boots tied by strings about their necks and, at another extreme, some gentlemen brought blooded horses to ride to hounds. In their sons and daughters, the class strata of Europe, the ancient national border and blood feuds, were diluted and then dissolved. Despite the census-taker's dreary insistence on reaching back to European racial lines, the people called themselves 'Canadians.'

It is particularly satisfying that idealism played its part in the launching of settlement. If any one man is to be credited with the formal beginning of the taming of the Canadian West, he must be Thomas Douglas, the young Scottish nobleman, friend of Sir Walter Scott's at Edinburgh University. Succeeding to the Earldom of Selkirk and a considerable fortune at twenty-eight, he was deeply troubled by the plight of Scottish and Irish tenant labourers then being forced off the land to make way for large cattle and sheep runs. He may have been prompted in his unusual democratic concern by the peasant poet, Robert Burns, known to be a visitor at the Douglas family seat on St Mary's Isle. Young Selkirk had visited France to study the revolt of the oppressed there and had been sickened at the excesses. The best hope for the dispossessed Highland crofters lay in emigration, he decided, and he proceeded to devote the remainder of his life (he died at forty-eight) and all his wealth to that cause.

The French Revolution had been inspired by the American, and Selkirk could not see a good and godly life for his people under the Stars and Stripes of the rapidly expanding republic. When he read the *Voyages* of Sir Alexander Mackenzie, a bestseller of 1801 recounting the epic crossing of British America, Selkirk knew he had found the new homeland.

In egalitarian times, debunkers muddy his motives by trying to cast him as a wilful, even greedy, aristocrat forwarding the campaign of the lordly Hudson's Bay Company against the deserving Canadian enterprise of the North West Company. Certainly, Selkirk became embroiled in the 'fur war' after 1812 in the defence of his colony on the Red River but, ten years earlier he had written to the British government proposing settlement on the prairies: 'At the western extremity of Canada, upon the waters which fall into Lake Winnipeg ... is a country which the Indian traders represent as fertile, and of a climate far more temperate than the shores of the Atlantic under the same parallel, and not more severe than that of Germany and Poland. Here, therefore, the colonists may, with moderate exertion of industry, be certain of a comfortable subsistence, and they may also raise some valuable objects of exportation.'

Selkirk's climatic information may have been faulty but his prediction, in 1802, came considerably closer to the eventual truth than the later and more pessimistic analyses of a stream of scientific experts. Much of the territory he advocated covered the bed of the glacial Lake Agassiz, some of the richest soil on the continent.

When the authorities in London turned him down, Selkirk proceeded at his own cost the following year and brought eight hundred Scots not to the distant Canadian West but to fourteen hundred acres he had acquired on Prince Edward Island. In the spring of the following year he waited at Kingston, Upper Canada, for the arrival of a second contingent for whom he had purchased a tract on the shore of Lake St Clair. It was not until the competition of the Nor'Westers began to draw blood that Selkirk and the Hudson's Bay Company became allied.

This wooden gunpowder chest accompanied the 6th Regiment of Foot, sent as a show of force to Fort Garry in 1846, at the request of the HBC, alarmed at the prospects of trouble. HBC COLLECTION, LOWER FORT GARRY NATIONAL HISTORIC PARK

Ironically, it was the merchant princes of the fur trade in their sumptuous Beaver Hall in Montreal who convinced Selkirk that he should persevere with his earlier plan to create a settlement in the Winnipeg basin. The Nor'Westers had a weakness for hobnobbing with titled visitors and they waxed enthusiastic about the fertility of the Red River Valley, about the security of food supplies based on their 'pemmican factory' operated by the Indian and Métis hunters. In this same period, the Bay company was aghast at its dwindling profits; it had to pass its dividend in 1810 and the value of its shares had fallen from £250 to £60. Three years earlier, Lord Selkirk had married Jean Wedderburn-Colvile and now, with his wealthy brother-in-law Andrew, he acquired enough stock to exercise control of the Hudson's Bay Company.

By 1811 the company was convinced that a farming settlement at the strategic junction of the Red and Assiniboine rivers – where La Vérendrye had once built Fort Rouge – would cut costs by providing a domestic food supply for the Bay trading posts. It would also serve as a retirement location for pensioned workers. From their fabulous land holdings, the Governors carved out a 116,000-square-mile principality and gave it to Selkirk for ten shillings and his promise to settle a thousand families there within ten years.

It was called Assiniboia and it contained 74 million acres – five times the size of Selkirk's native Scotland. It stood at the near centre of the Canadian land mass, stretching from latitude 52°N – halfway up Lake Winnipeg – down the length of the Red River, deep into the modern states of Minnesota and North Dakota. From Lake of the Woods in present-day Ontario, it ran westward clear across Manitoba into portions of Saskatchewan. Miles Macdonell, a former captain in the Royal Canadian Volunteers who had settled at Cornwall after his Loyalist family had fled from New York, was chosen by Selkirk, and appointed Governor of the new territory. They offered settlers a free grant of land, free transportation, freedom to worship as they pleased. The first three ships, carrying a total of 105 pioneers and Bay personnel, sailed late from Stornoway, in the Hebrides, on July 26, 1811.

The delay was caused mostly by the harassment of the colonists by the agents of the North West Company, itself predominantly a Scottish organization. They saw the proposed settlement as a direct threat to their 'pemmican factory,' admittedly being operated on lands included in the Bay's original 1670 grant. It's obvious Selkirk never dreamed the Nor'Westers would dare oppose his scheme so openly and it would soon become equally obvious that the Montreal Scots underestimated the man whom their chief, William McGillivray, referred to contemptuously as 'this piddling lord.' Sir Alexander Mackenzie, now himself among the landed Highland gentry, attacked Selkirk's motives scandalously and one of his relatives tricked some of the settlers into joining the army; Simon McGillivray wrote articles for the Scottish papers spreading tales of scalping terror and death by starvation and ice in Canada.

It was, then, remarkable that the ships ever sailed, a marvel that the colony took hold and a near-miracle that it survived. Macdonell had planned to get to Assiniboia early enough in the season to plant a crop and erect some housing, ready for the main influx of colonists in 1812, but his late start and a slow voyage to Hudson Bay forced him to spend the first winter miserably near York Factory. By the time he was ready the following summer to push on via the Hayes and Nelson rivers for Lake Winnipeg, his party had dwindled to nineteen. They had one bull, one cow, a few sacks of seed. They reached the forks of the Red and the Assiniboine on August 30, 1812, and that was the day the settlement of the West began.

Intimidation, cold, flood, hunger, arson and even eventually armed assault – nothing could extinguish that settlement once begun. The pioneers, Scots and Irish, were met by whooping Métis daubed in war paint in the pay of the North West Company, but when the second contingent of seventy Selkirkers arrived at the Forks in October to a skirling of bagpipes they were met by kindly Indians who lifted the eleven small children up onto their ponies and guided them to Fort Daer, by modern Pembina, where Macdonell had prepared wintering quarters on the buffalo range.

A train of fur sleds leaving Lower Fort Garry in 1905 enroute to Winnipeg and the railway for shipment around the world. Photo courtesy HUDSON'S BAY COMPANY

Lord Selkirk despatched several more shiploads of settlers and, while his own people huddled about the strongpoint of Fort Douglas facing winter hunger, Miles Macdonell had watched grimly as the heavy skin bags of pemmican were transported daily into the Nor'Westers' Fort Gibraltar. Lacking funds to outbid the local Nor'West factor – actually his own cousin Alexander Macdonell – for the pemmican prepared by the Métis and Indians, and lacking horses and know-how to hunt buffalo to make his own, Governor Macdonell finally prohibited the export of food from Assiniboia for a year.

When news of this action reached Fort William and Montreal, the Nor'Westers reacted violently. Under a pseudonym, McGillivray had written earlier that the settlers 'will be subject to constant alarm and terror. Their habitations, their crops, their cattle will be destroyed and they will find it impossible to exist in the country.' Both Métis and Indians were now encouraged to menace the colony and, to prevent a possible massacre, Governor Macdonell surrendered himself at Fort Gibraltar and was sent to the east on trumped-up charges. Scared and worried, 133 of the settlers accepted the North West Company's offer of transportation to Upper Canada, and the Métis led by Cuthbert Grant moved in to burn Fort Douglas and the humble cabins.

Sixty survivors fled to Jack River House, at the northern end of Lake Winnipeg, then came stubbornly back to the Forks in early August of 1815. Like the thousands of farmers who would follow them onto the plains, they were determined to fight for their crops; while some worked to rebuild the houses, the others harvested 500 bushels of oats, 400 bushels of wheat and 200 of barley – the first sizable crop taken from the prairies. Eighty new settlers arrived that fall, with the new Governor of Rupert's Land, Robert Semple.

There was still more drama to be staged, the most tragic act of all. The following summer, on June 19, 1816, Semple and a band of twenty settlers, on foot, some of them unarmed, were killed by a band of mounted Métis and their bodies mutilated. This was the notorious Seven Oaks Massacre. Cuthbert Grant then seized Fort Douglas, and all its stores, signing an inventory in the name of the North West Company. Once again, the surviving Selkirkers fled to Jack River House.

Lord Selkirk was at Sault Ste Marie, leading another contingent into the West, when the stunning news of Seven Oaks reached him. Warned of probable attacks from the Nor'Westers, he had vainly asked both the British and Canadian governments to protect the colony. Now he was bringing with him ninety tough Swiss, German and Canadian veterans of the War of 1812. In no mood to palaver, he seized the North West headquarters at Fort William, arrested eight of the partners, shipped them back east under guard, and despatched a company with two cannon over the old La Vérendrye trail to retake Fort Douglas.

This time, the Red River colony would stand, to provide within a short half-century the stoutly beating heart of the province of Manitoba, the fifth to enter the Confederation of Canada. Selkirk himself had spent the summer of 1817 on the Red, completing a survey of the river lots – each settler got ninety acres plus ten acres of woodland – selecting sites for a school and for churches both Protestant and Roman Catholic, drawing up a plan for roads and bridges. On the spot, he assessed the needs in seed grains, cattle and hog breeding stock and committed himself personally to supply them.

Realizing that the local tribes had no understanding of the Hudson's Bay charter on which Assiniboia depended for its legality, Selkirk made his own treaty with the Saulteaux and Cree – creating the pattern that the Canadian government would eventually follow throughout the West. When he left Canada, harried by law suits, broken in health, soon to die of tuberculosis, it was estimated that Selkirk had spent £100,000. He had dreamed of a state that would some day support thirty million British subjects. Sir Walter Scott wrote of him, 'I never knew in my life a man of more generous distinction.'

The year after Selkirk's death, the conflict that had ruined him was over. The North West Company was merged into the Hudson's Bay Company and the stocky ex-clerk George Simpson built Fort Garry at the Forks and began his forty-year reign as virtual dictator of half of Canada, including the Pacific lands of the Columbia. The Governor-in-Chief of Rupert's Land by rank, he was more widely known as 'the Little Emperor.' When his headquarters was swamped in the flood of 1826, he built Lower Fort Garry twenty miles down river, inside stone walls eight feet high and a yard thick – and 'the Stone Fort' stands there today, carefully preserved, the oldest surviving building in western Canada.

Simpson was all trader, and it went against his grain to find the inherited colony a charge on his now-buoyant company. Lord Selkirk's heir had conveyed the territory back to the company. Grasshoppers more than once ruined the Red River crops and the settlers had to rely on buffalo meat for survival. Hail and drought appear in the earliest prairie records. The marking of the U.S. border across the plains severed the southern half of Assiniboia and some of the people of Fort Daer and Pembina came north to swell the population; others, most of the Swiss soldier settlers and most of the Irish, discouraged by the fierce winters, the hoppers, the floods, went south into the States or back east to Upper Canada.

Contemporary historian Alexander Ross described the Hudson's Bay guardianship as 'the cool care of a stepmother.' Schemes to run sheep on the prairie grass, to raise flax and sugar beets, to gather and weave buffalo hair all failed. But when Canada was first seeking to take over the North-West Territories, Sir George Simpson was still holding out: 'I do not think that any part of the Company's territory is well adapted to settlement.' He was opposed by, among others, the Toronto newspaper editor George Brown, an ardent champion of western settlement. Steamships from Ontario's Lake Huron ports were already reaching Fort William.

Trying to get an objective report on the fertility of the plains, the British government sent out a well-connected Irish sportsman and travel writer, Captain John Palliser, backed up by a botanist and geologist, to examine the West. For two years they roamed on horseback between the Red and the Rockies, bequeathing Canada with the classic division of the land into its three distinct levels, its fertile park belt, the 'true prairie' and 'Palliser's Triangle' – the semi-arid area enclosed today by southern Alberta and southern Saskatchewan.

It was basically a positive report. Palliser advised that a railroad scheme for the prairies was feasible and, as it happened, his party discovered Kicking Horse Pass, the high cut through the Rockies eventually chosen by the CPR. No mystery about that name: the geologist James Hector was kicked by his own horse in the pass and 'left senseless for some time.' Palliser was overly pessimistic about his own triangle, but dirt farmers who later pooh-poohed his warnings were in days to come to watch heartbroken as their farms blew away in drought and dust-storm.

Early reports of another kind on the North-West, fast becoming a Mecca for the adventurous traveller, were supplied in realistic oils by artist Paul Kane, and in the colourful travel diary of the young Earl of Southesk.

Canada sent out its own technical experts, including surveyor S.J. Dawson and chemist and geologist H.Y. Hind. At the time, the only practical access to Fort Garry was via Hudson Bay (and, in 1857, a company of the Canadian Rifles was sent in by that route to cool American expansionist sentiments) or by railroad through the states to Abercrombie or St Cloud in Minnesota and from there by boat or wagon train to Fort Garry. The first steamship, the *Anson Northrupp*, came down the Red in 1859.

Dawson plunged into the rock and river wilderness beyond the Canadian Lakehead and reported that a road *could* be built through that nightmare country to Winnipeg: and later it was, at a cost of $1.3 million. Hind returned to Ottawa from his studies, reporting 11,100,000 available acres of first-class farm lands.

When, under the deft guidance of John A. Macdonald and George-Etienne Cartier, the Quebec Conference of 1864 hammered out the basic concepts of Confederation, one of the seventy-two resolutions stated: 'The North-West Territory, British Columbia and Vancouver [the island was then still a separate colony] shall be admitted into the Union on such terms and conditions as the Parliament of the Federated Provinces shall deem equitable ... ' At the first meeting of that Par-

liament, December 4, 1867, a resolution was drafted asking Queen Victoria to command the passing of the North-West into Canadian hands. Almost exactly two years later, the Hudson's Bay Company surrendered. The price: £300,000 cash, 71,000 acres freehold around the Bay's 120 trading posts, plus another seven million acres parcelled across the West.

'We have quietly,' wrote Sir John A., 'and almost without observation, annexed all the country between here and the Rocky Mountains.' Macdonald was not, in fact, wildly eager to add extra problems so early to his delicately laced Confederation but, with regular steamer services from Minneapolis-St Paul taking out western trade and bringing in annexationist pressures, his hand was forced. A bill had actually been introduced into the u.s. Congress seeking 'the admission to the Union of the States of Nova Scotia, New Brunswick, Canada East and Canada West, and for the organization of the Territories of Selkirk, Saskatchewan and Columbia.' Although sponsored by the head of the Senate Foreign Relations Committee, the bill was dropped after Canadian protest but there was little doubt which way the prairie wind was blowing.

Haste and careless staff work on the part of the Ottawa bureaucrats, rather than any treason to Queen and country, now brought the confused uprising of the Métis, overdramatized in Canadian history as the 'Riel Rebellion.' The Métis, of partly both French and British ancestry, numbering about nine thousand throughout the West in 1870, naturally objected to being 'traded' from one entity to another and their fears about the new Dominion's respect of their land rights were fanned both by Americans and Canadian jingoists. Skilfuly manipulated, wracked by their fears, they began to see themselves as 'the first owners of the soil.' The mercurial twenty-five-year-old Louis Riel, only one-eighth Indian, the Fenian W.B. O'Donoghue at his side, led them into seizure of Fort Garry, the proclamation of 'the Provisional Government of Manitoba,' and to the 'kangaroo court' that executed a Protestant troublemaker. The u.s. consul at Winnipeg, Oscar Malmros, immediately wrote to Washington for permission to recognize the Riel 'government' and Zachariah Chandler rose in the Senate to demand that Rupert's Land be recognized as an independent state, and then annexed.

The threat and the rising were both quashed by the despatch from the east of a military force, part imperials, part militia, which toiled for ninety-six days over the Dawson route to a bloodless victory. It was only the first act in the regrettable Métis tragedy: fifteen years later, Riel returned from a u.s. exile to lead another confrontation when settlement pushed ruthlessly into the Saskatchewan River valley, again threatening the Métis way of life. This time, the Crees took up the hatchet and blood flowed at Fish Creek, Frog Lake and Batoche. When Riel was captured, and hanged at Regina – though his sanity was in doubt – he became a martyr to those French Canadians who were feeling increasingly swamped in the country their ancestors had once ruled. It was, in a way, a curious replay of the events at Red River fifty years earlier, with the power shifted to the other hand.

The West was now both open and safe. The North-West Mounted Police were enforcing the law clear to the foothills of the Rockies and all the Indian tribes had accepted the treaties which guaranteed that six million acres of Canada – one square mile to each family of five – would be held for them forever. William Van Horne, the whip-cracking chief of the Canadian Pacific, had proved the efficiency and value of his line by racing a total of 7982 soldiers and their supporters onto the plains. Where the troops had travelled, the pioneers soon followed. Branch lines were thrust to every outpost, often before there was any business to justify them. The Grand Trunk Pacific and Canadian Northern Railway both reached across the continent, giving Canada a total of over thirty thousand miles of track – about one mile for every 250 inhabitants, by far the most lavish in the world.

To lure settlers, the government now followed the American practice of offering a family head a free grant of 160 acres, a quarter-section in the new townships each consisting of thirty-six sections of one square mile, with the title being confirmed after three years' residence on the land and the cultivation of at least part of it. There was no immediate rush, and half of the grants lapsed as

A column marches through a coulee in the Touchwood Hills to confront the Métis and the Cree who were fighting against the loss of their land to settlers. Photo courtesy PUBLIC ARCHIVES OF CANADA

163

the farmers, mostly from the more clement east, struggled against the harsh and different prairie conditions. They tried planting fall wheat, but it was killed in the sub-zero winters; their spring-sown wheat took an average of four and a half months to ripen, and was usually caught by the early frosts.

Their saviour was David Fife, an amateur agricultural scientist farming near Peterborough, who imported some winter wheat from a friend in Glasgow which, by chance, included a few seed heads coming from Danzig on the Baltic but originating in Galicia, a central European province of the old Austrian Empire. He planted the seed in the spring and from the few surviving heads – a wandering cow ate most of it – he developed a russet-hued, rust-resistant wheat that matured in from 115 to 125 days. Dubbed Red Fife, it was tried out successfully in Ohio and Minnesota and, by 1890, it was the chief wheat of the prairies – the famous 'Manitoba No. 1 Hard.' The strain was improved still further by Charles Saunders, who won a knighthood for his development of Marquis wheat, with a still-shorter growing season and better yield. The research continued with the introduction of such varieties as Ruby, Reward, Rescue, Garnet, Thatcher, Selkirk and Manitou. The world recognized Canadian prairie wheat, at over 13 per cent protein, as the world's best for bread-making.

The stream of pioneers had flowed fitfully westward, tempted by the rising price of wheat. The sound of new tongues was heard. Fifteen hundred Icelanders took farms on Lake Winnipeg and called their settlement Gimli ('Paradise,' in Icelandic). Swedes came to the Qu'Appelle Valley. Promised religious freedom and exemption from military service, Mennonites settled on the Red below Winnipeg, and close to the U.S. border at Emerson, while later groups located in the Rosthern area of Saskatchewan. Charles O. Card brought the first of the steady, hard-working Mormons in from Utah. *Canadiens* repatriated from the towns of New England came to join the flock of that great Manitoba priest, Bishop Taché of St Boniface.

But, compared with the size of the land that lay empty, the stream was really just a trickle. Only nine hundred homesteads were registered in 1896. What was needed was, in fact, a human flood. Prime Minister Wilfrid Laurier found in the western lawyer Clifford Sifton just the man to bring it about. High-minded and high-handed, in full vigour at thirty-five, Sifton looked immediately beyond the traditional sources of English-speaking immigrants and made a pitch to the landless, harried, peasant farmers of central Europe. With apologies to no one, he stated his creed: 'I think that a stalwart peasant in a sheepskin coat, born on the soil, whose forefathers have been farmers for ten generations, with a stout wife and half a dozen children, is good quality.'

Like some modern Pied Piper, he drew them by their many thousands in the last few years of the old century and the opening years of the new. He spotted recruiting agents throughout likely areas of Europe, gave bonuses to shipping lines who carried immigrants, arranged free tours of the West for prominent Ukrainians, Hungarians and Germans and for influential foreign politicians and journalists. Six hundred editors came in a single party as guest of the CPR and the government. Dozens of propaganda pamphlets were prepared in ten languages, under titles like *The Last Best West*, and *The Wondrous West, Land of Opportunity*. Sifton forced the railroad companies to complete selection of their free land grants, to facilitate the release of great blocks, and prohibited the granting of any more land as construction subsidy. With 25 million acres to sell, the CPR soon joined the bandwagon.

Sifton's 'Sheepskins,' as they were often called, took up their quarter-sections on the bald prairie, and literally moved into it. The first shelter was almost invariably a 'soddy,' sixteen by twelve, made with 'bricks' of virgin turf, a yard long and a foot wide. Scarce poles supported a roof of twisted grass, or more sod, and doorways and windows were often merely blanks, perhaps curtained with sacking. In the more northerly park belt, log cabins rose chinked with clay. Inside, perhaps one treasured piece of furniture, a family heirloom, stood pathetically on the earthen floor. The first 'crop' was often buffalo bones, gathered and stacked and carted to the railhead for $7 a ton; the cash would buy oatmeal, flour and salt and the coarsest brown sugar at 20¢ per

The quiet grave of Louis Riel in Winnipeg reveals little of the mercurial personality of this Métis leader whose execution ended the major threat to the peaceful opening of the west. Photo by T. GRANT

pound. Such a supply point was Pile O'Bones, later to reach the dignity of a provincial capital under its new name of Regina.

At first, the pioneers merely survived. Water had to be found or carried. The sod had to be turned for the seeding. Hay must be gathered for winter fodder for horses or oxen; vegetables and berries 'put down.' Fuel had to be hauled for the stove, often for fifty miles. Mosquitoes, gophers, coyotes plagued them, and prairie fire and hail wiped them out. The jack rabbit was at times the only meat for the pot; a sodbuster's tribute ran:

Rabbit hot and rabbit cold,
Rabbit young and rabbit old,
Rabbit tender and rabbit tough;
Thank you, but I've had enough.

Many quit in a rage of frustration, or in dull despair, but the hardiest took hold, fought back against an implacable nature, erratic markets and that all-pervading prairie loneliness. When the neighbours were out of sight across the hazy plain, when snow lay deep for half the year, when doctors were simply unavailable, a rare human warmth arose in 'visiting' and communal caring that we still admire as 'western hospitality.'

Successive waves from the United States and from Britain carried the human tide across Saskatchewan and Alberta, bringing those territories into the federation as separate provinces in 1905. In a fifteen-year period, nearly a million streamed across the U.S. border into the three prairie provinces – again thickening the American fibre in the Canadian nation.

John and David McDougall, sons of the pioneer Methodist missionary George McDougall, brought fifty head of cattle into southern Alberta in 1873, launching the ranching business. One hundred thousand acres of range could be leased for twenty-one years at one cent per acre. The huge empty box of land cornered by Regina, Prince Albert, Edmonton and Calgary was filling in fast, and the more venturesome were pushing into the Peace River Country.

Beyond the Rockies, the story in detail was very different. Canadian life alters at the Rockies. In broad outline, however, the story was not dissimilar. It was one of expansion, settlement and development within and because of the new Canada.

On Vancouver Island and the mainland to the Rockies the fur trade had flourished and governed. With the loss of the territory of the lower Columbia Valley to the United States by the Oregon Treaty of 1846, made by warlike President Polk and peacable Lord Aberdeen, the boundary of Canada was pushed to the Pacific. Vancouver Island, with Fort Victoria as capital, was made a colony open to settlement in 1849. Under stern Governor James Douglas, upright, top-hatted, both fur trader and imperial officer, it lived drowsily until 1857.

Then the discovery of gold in the bars of the lower Fraser led to the gold rush of 1858 and to the opening of the fabulous field of the Cariboo in the early 1860s. American goldseekers poured in, bringing the possibility of annexation to the United States. But the creation of the colony of British Columbia in that year – governed as was Vancouver Island by James Douglas – the quick firm justice of Judge Begbie, the presence of the Royal Engineers who built the Cariboo Trail, kept the camps quiet and maintained British authority.

With the quick exhaustion of the gold bars by the mid-1860s, the two colonies collapsed commercially and, for economy's sake, were united as British Columbia. Rich though it was in timber and minerals and fish, it seemed unable to survive on its own. The Empire could be of little help, except for defence. What, then, was needed: union with the United States or union with Canada?

The gold fields had attracted Canadians and Canadian capital, including the Nova Scotian William Alexander Smith, who had assumed in California the lustrous name of Amor de Cosmos. A Canadian party seeking union with Canada was formed. With the backing of British elements in the legislative council of British Columbia, and of the British government, a delegation consisting

Wood was scarce on the prairie and the settler's first house was often built of sod squares which provided warmth in the winter and coolness in the summer.
Photo courtesy PUBLIC ARCHIVES

of J. S. Helmcken, Joseph Trutch and Dr. R. W. W. Carrall, was sent in 1870 to Canada to seek terms of union. They found the Canadian government, represented by Sir George-Etienne Cartier during the illness of Sir John A. Macdonald, generous beyond their wildest hope. Shaken by the Red River resistance, Cartier was determined that no penny-pinching, no lack of daring, should stop the Canadian advance to the Pacific. Laden with the largesse of Canada, including a pledge to build a railway to the Pacific, the delegates went home to recommend union. In 1871, Canada extended from sea to sea.

The sequel to this auspicious opening was much less happy. In the depression of the 1870s, the economy of British Columbia did not recover; settlers and capital came in slowly, when at all. The new province feverishly sought better terms from Ottawa, and even threatened withdrawal from Canada. The completion of the railway in 1885 brought renewed optimism, more population and trade, and led to a modest prosperity.

British Columbia was at last a Canadian province, but with strong differences. Its Pacific frontier gave it an orientation of its own. Much of its development depended on its commercial and financial ties to the south and overseas. In its tumbled world of mountain, forest and inland valleys, the distinctly Canadian drive, already checked on the prairies, was slowed and dissipated. The direct associations with the British and Americans gave rise to a class structure different to the moderate levels of older Canadian class distinctions. British Columbia was Canadian, more Canadian than one might expect, but given its history, its resources and its location, it was, in the nineteenth century, something more than Canadian.

As the century turned in the twilight years of hearty Edward VII, as the Great War darkened Europe, the flow of immigrants ceased. But, by then, the West was open and the pioneer era was closed.

The first "crop" of the Western pioneer was often buffalo bones, such as this pile pictured at Saskatoon in 1890, worth $7 a ton when gathered and carted to the railroad siding. Photo courtesy GLENBOW-ALBERTA INSTITUTE

ABITATION DE QVEBECQ

4

A Le magazin.
B Colombier.
C Corps de logis où sont nos armes, & pour loger les ouuriers.
D Autre corps de logis pour les ouuriers.
E Cadran.
F Autre corps de logis où est la forge, & artisans logés.
G Galleries tout au tour des logemens.
H Logis du sieur de Champlain.
I La porte de l'habitation, où il y a Pont-leuis.
L Promenoir autour de l'habitation contenant 10. pieds de large iusques sur le bort du fossé.
M Fossés tout autour de l'habitation.
N Plattes formes, en façon de tenailles pour mettre le canon.
O Iardin du sieur de Champlain.
P La cuisine.
Q Place deuant l'habitation sur le bort de la riuiere.
R La grande riuiere de sainct Lorens.

PART V

The treasure trove

INTERLUDE:
The rise of the cities

The cities of Canada in the main were, in a very real sense, the first form of settlement. They preceded; agriculture followed, often well behind. It is true, of course, that none began as a city full-blown. But they were centres of trade, or garrisons, not agricultural settlements. Farming usually followed to supply their needs, rather than the cities arising to supply the settlements. The latter sequence did happen to some degree in Upper and Lower Canada in the nineteenth century, and later on the Prairies, but that was the exception, not the rule. Canada, in short, began as a series of forts and trading posts and, after the long reign of agriculture from 1815 to 1930, is now again dominated by its cities, the industrial heirs of the trading posts.

What is most striking is the definiteness of their foundations, and the ready identification of their founders. Champlain and Quebec, Maisonneuve and Montreal, Cornwallis and Halifax, Simcoe and Toronto, Douglas and Victoria – the connections are as direct as those of

Romulus and Rome, if better attested. Some, of course, seem just to have grown because of some overwhelming asset – St John's and its harbour, Winnipeg and its rivers, Vancouver and Burrard Inlet. The first settlers on the site of the latter were three brickmakers, their thought confined to the clay they burned. But most Canadian cities had an explicit original purpose.

Champlain, for example, in choosing the site below Cape Diamond in 1608 for his *Habitation*, ' ... looked for a place suitable for our settlement, but I could not find any more suitable or better situated than the point of Quebec, so called by the natives' – here he placed his defended fur trading post at the point where the St Lawrence narrowed. Maisonneuve, a soldier with a commission to discharge, was carrying out the will of the Messieurs of Sulpice to establish a missionary settlement, even 'if all the trees on Montreal Island were to turn into Iroquois warriors.' The British Board of Trade ordered Colonel Cornwallis to occupy Chebucto Bay in order to confirm the British title to Nova Scotia by settlement and fortification. James Douglas was marking the limit of the British retreat from the Oregon. And Simcoe, most imperialist and far-dreaming of all, who ensured Toronto's growth by deeming it the capital of Upper Canada, thought it suitable because there an 'arsenal could be better defended than at Niagara or at Kingston.'

The balance between agriculture and industry, between countryside and city – so far as anything so complex can be measured – was even in 1921. By the census of that year the population rated as rural was 4,435,827 and that rated as urban was 4,352,122. In 1931 the balance had tipped: 4,802,138 rural and 5,572,058 urban. In 1971, 76.1 per cent of Canadians lived in villages, towns or cities.

Two historic events marked the change. One was the closing of the homestead frontier with the surrender of public lands, those not granted, to the three western provinces in 1930; the other was the stock market crash

A drawing by Champlain of his first habitation at Quebec, built in 1608, which marked the founding of that city as a centre of exploration and settlement. Photo courtesy THOMAS FISHER RARE BOOK LIBRARY, UNIVERSITY OF TORONTO

of 1929 and the end of the economic and financial world as it had been organized in Victorian times. Canada henceforth was to thrive in the measure that it could not only maintain its long-established economy but adopt the new, more sophisticated and technological industry of the twentieth century.

The pattern had been already clear when the timber trade was at its peak – when Reciprocity, that forerunner of the Common Markets, had added the American to the British market. Not only were there the old industries based on timber – shipbuilding, saw-milling, cooperage, furniture-making – or those based on farming – flour-milling, brewing and distilling, tanning, shoe and harness-making, and the blacksmith shops; besides these, particularly following the swift development of the railway, a host of new industries sprang into being: iron-founding, glass-blowing, machine-making, potteries, manufacture of sewing machines, musical instruments, textile factories, and many others.

Printing was perhaps the most advanced of all, as the steam presses of the *Globe* of Toronto in 1853 indicated. The Montreal firm of Notman's made Canadian photography internationally known. Insurance companies, banks, trust companies, mortgage firms multiplied.

A galaxy of soon-to-be famous names now appeared – Massey, Harris, Kaufman, Eaton, McMaster – to add to the roster of the lumber giants, Price, Booth, Eddy, and of the legendary names of Molson and Redpath. The economy of forest and farm had laid the foundations of a new industrial and urban society.

Some cities were cast in the role of capital. In the nineteenth century that role was perhaps more social than either political or economic, but the political quality increased steadily after Confederation, as did the economic after 1921. It is difficult to be more explicit, for the capital city in Canada, as in the United States, long had difficulty in finding how to play an essentially European role in countries without royal courts and which were themselves essentially ungovernable until the frontiers closed.

With the notable exception of Quebec City – a capital born – both the imposed national capital city, Ottawa, and most of the designated provincial capitals struggled to live up to the mantles and dignities of their high estates. The limited fate of Canadian capitals must be viewed with a certain reserved tolerance; they have rarely been taken as seriously as they took themselves, and were to some always faintly comic. However well chosen the ceremonial music, the airs of Gilbert and Sullivan and *Yankee Doodle* were always to be heard in ghostly overtone.

A good number of the market towns – a few of them as old as some of the major cities – grew swiftly themselves to a small-city status. As pioneer farming ripened towards its maturity and the science of agriculture put old land in good heart, those towns that served and depended on agriculture became secure and balanced. The countryside, organized around the horse – whether the 'driver' to take the buggy or cutter smartly to town for shopping, or the draught team to pull the grain waggons – had need of the market towns. They ranged all the way from mere 'corners,' crossroads villages, to towns beginning to verge on the self-sufficiency and self-absorption of cities. Most, however, remained sensitive to the fact that they were rural towns that existed to serve the farm folk of the country. Such towns even lived to a great extent on the produce of the local farms, butter, milk, cheese, eggs, fruit, vegetables, even flour from local grain ground in the local mill. They were often quaintly named after obscure mediaeval saints in Quebec, for much-loved places left behind in England, or Spanish towns remembered from the Peninsular War – Elora, Almonte and Cordova.

The towns in turn served the countryside and paid for food and for fuel by giving professional or craftsman services. They furnished the ordinary necessities of life in late Victorian times: salt, sugar, molasses, dried fruit, coal oil, lamps, crockery, hardware, and to ever-greater extent, textiles and clothing as machine-woven replaced hand-loomed. The smithies in particular were necessary to sharpen ploughshares, shoe the horse, weld broken machine parts, even to build the first crude wood and iron stump-pullers, or the horse-powered threshing machine. In every town the clang and tap of the blacksmith's hammer, ringing from morning to evening, was likely to be the first sound to catch the approaching visitor's ear. It heralded also the lighter industries that were to seek economical sites and surplus labour in the swelling towns.

In them also were found the local middle class, the members of the professions and the furnishers of capital. Next to the teachings of the Christian religion, the second most powerful intellectual force in developing Canada was the commitment to free enterprise, the freedom of the individual to pursue economic ends, trying all means within the law. Leading in formal social status were the clergy, priest, parson or pastor, 'the Reverend' in English usage, *'monsieur le curé'* in French. Next came the local judge, or magistrate, and the lawyers, higher in practical status than the clergy, for they were men of affairs having to do with property in all its forms. And the doctor was quickly rising to a similar, or even higher, esteem, for his craft was at last becoming scientific and helpful, as the name of James Bovell suggested and that of William Osler confirmed.

Somewhat below the professional men in esteem, but not in utility, were the men of finance and commerce. The private banker, or the manager of a branch bank, wielded great power in town and country, particularly in times of depression when loans had to be called. His coldness or warmth, his power to assess character, could make enormous differences in terms of human worry or security. Mortgages, handled usually by the

In every town the clang and tap of the blacksmith's hammer rang out as he reshod horses, sharpened ploughshares, and in a later age welded more sophisticated machine parts. Photo by PETER VARLEY

lawyers, might call for equal qualities of business firmness and human consideration if a transaction was not to become a tragedy. The storekeeper also, in times when seasonal credit was still extensively given against the harvest, was intimately involved in the lives and fortunes of town and country.

Less established as yet, but necessary parts of the town and country community, were the real-estate agents and the auctioneers. Farms were beginning to be sold outside the family, fields were sold to meet a mortgage, farm equipment and livestock, with household chattels, had to be auctioned when retirement without an heir, or foreclosure of a mortgage made a sale necessary. Like marriages and funerals, fairs and picnics, these sales were social affairs, of intimate concern and the cause of much gossip among all members of the neighbourhood.

It is the trader, then, who has been the central figure of Canadian urban history, perhaps simply of all Canadian history. It was he who, long before cities were possible, found the crossroads of river and trail that were the sites of future cities. The first traders were the factors, or supercargoes, such as Pontgravé, sent out in charge of the trade goods of a ship despatched to the rendezvous on the coasts of the St Lawrence or of Acadia. He it was who supervised the trade for furs with the Indians, and on his management, as well as on the navigation of the ship's captain, the prosperity of the voyage depended. Behind him and the whole voyage stood the outfitters, the men who raised the capital, rented and provisioned the ship, bought the trade goods, hired the crew, and to whom the profits of a successful voyage would go.

These were indeed the essential figures in the whole story of primitive trade. From the days of the outfitting of Cabot's and of Cartier's first voyages to the most recent 'grub-stake' on the Precambrian mining frontier, it was these men who made discovery, trade and development possible. It was they who furnished capital and took the risk of profit or loss.

They dealt, of course, with those who could supply the provisions and trade goods needed for the voyage. In time, some suppliers worked more or less wholly for some particular aspect of the North American trade. The farmers of southern Ireland furnished the fishing ships of Devon and Cornwall with provisions for the Atlantic voyage at the last port of call. The weavers of England's Witney and Stroud furnished the famous blankets for the fur trade. The wineries of the Charente and Bordeaux furnished the brandy of the French Canadian fur trade, while later in Canada the silversmiths of Montreal and Quebec turned out the trinkets that pleased Indian dignity.

Behind them always were the bankers, the accumulators of credit to back the outfitters. And behind the bankers were the lawyers, who built up the commercial law which tried to regularize the quick and subtle transactions of the traders and the money men.

From these astute men and their activities, from their successors over the swift generations, through world wars, times of boom and bust, was to come the whole great commercial apparatus of modern Canada and the power and personnel of the nation's financial centres.

PART V

Chapter Fifteen
A tale of three towns

The cities and towns of Canada, set in an ice-scoured land halfway to the Pole, none of them venerable in European or Asian scale and most of them born but yesterday, or the day before, are for all of that remarkable in their diversity. Where the traveller could fairly expect something of the continental Russian or Australian sameness of style and pulse, we can show cities as demure and dignified as dowagers taking tea at four, or as brazen and bold as disco girls, the sirens of the moment. There are towns that nestle on opposite banks of a pebbled stream in a soft summertime valley, linked like a courting couple by a slender silver bridge. Some are hard, grime ingrained in their boards as under the nails of the miners who labour there. Others, built for war, still glower from high ground, cocking their cannon from revelin and battlement. There are ports which have known the *knorr* and the caravel, the windjammer, the ironclad, and the ocean liner now, in its turn, slipping into the mists. Across the inland sea of grass, at river bend and fork, under mountain shadow, on the sparkling lake, stand cities savouring perhaps a history of turbulent fur-trading times, of Indian troubles and gold fevers, a pioneer memory in their porches, their white churches beside a field of leaning tombstones.

Some, certainly, resemble nothing more than a clutter of boxes spilled from a derailed freight, or a human carelessness in concrete swirling at times in smog, but many of the places where

At Fort Pitt in 1884, Cree Indians in their finery deal with fur traders. This business was always at the centre of Canadian history. Photo courtesy
GLENBOW-ALBERTA INSTITUTE

PANORAMIC VIEW OF

Canadians choose to live and work are attractive, a number charming, and a few even beautiful – like Quebec on her rock, Fredericton under the elms, and Kelowna among its blossoms. Others again ring to the clamour of business, the many-towered Camelots of the technical age.

Among all of these, we will visit briefly three: a city of the east, of the centre, and of the far west. They are small, medium and large; they are not 'typical,' they have nothing in common except their diversity, yet all have played major roles in the Canadian drama.

Charlotte of Mecklenburg-Strelitz gave George III of Great Britain and Ireland fifteen children, and probably the only contentment that unhappy and unstable ruler was to know. She also graciously gave her name to the somewhat marshy townsite of 7300 acres set aside in 1765 by Captain Samuel Holland to be the capital city of the newly British island in the Gulf of St Lawrence. Booty in the Seven Years' War, the island remained St John, after the French *Ile St Jean*, for forty years until the authorities tired of the confusion with Canada's other saintly places and renamed the colony Prince Edward Island – the Prince so honoured being the Duke of Kent, a son of Queen Charlotte's, later to become the father of Queen Victoria.

Charlottetown succeeded Port la Joie, often written Joye, established at the entrance of the harbour in 1720 by one of the rare contingents of emigrant settlers from France. The name – 'Happy Port,' in free translation – may have been simply bestowed in thankfulness after a long and rough Atlantic crossing but, although the settlement, and the island as a whole, were not to escape some of the rigours and setbacks common to the Canadian pioneer experience, this was truly a favoured place. Despite being sacked by Sir William Pepperell's New Englanders in 1745, roughly taken by Lord Rollo and his five hundred troopers in 1758, raided by American privateers during the War of Independence, the island was in fact spared open battle and bloodshed and soon its fertile crescent became known as 'the Garden of the Gulf.'

Recalling the mythology of western discovery, it was an 'isle of the blest.' By some freak of geology, it was made up wholly of tillable soil, free of stone, except for some areas of sand on the fringe of the sea. The soil was for the most part rich and red, something of a Devon across the waters. Nor was it heavily timbered, so that without too much toil nearly the whole island could be made into a farm, a patchwork of farms. The sea, it is true, was always near, for the island was long and narrow and its inlets ran far into the land. Fish abounded, with lobsters and oysters in its waters, but the island's population never followed the sea to any degree. Rather, they supplied those who did.

Although destined to play a starring part in the founding of the nation, Charlottetown could never hope for the prestige or power of sheer size. After its first century, it counted 9000 citizens; today, with 30,000, it still ranks as one of the smallest capitals anywhere. It could hardly be anything else. The island province it rules makes up just 0.1 per cent of the land area of Canada; it is, by comparison, only one-tenth the size of Nova Scotia. Its seven thousand farms are neatly packaged into a curved bow of land, 120 miles long and from three to thirty miles across. No spot on the island is more than ten miles from salt water, and on the south and east the mainland shores of New Brunswick and Nova Scotia stand up clearly across the separating and isolating, seaway of Northumberland Strait.

There was always a miniature charm, measured against so huge a country. When Prince Edward Island was given in 1769 the full dignity of a separate colony under the Crown, complete with lieutenant-governor, executive council and supreme court, the population was exactly 271, of whom 203 were French-speaking. The official salaries were not forthcoming and the first Chief Justice, John Duport, is said to have died of starvation. By 1773, when population had soared to a thousand, Governor Walter Patterson called the first meeting of the general assembly; the eighteen members met in a Charlottetown tavern and were described as 'a damned queer parliament.' Even half a century later, a visiting British writer was amused at the spectacle of the Premier serving beer in his tavern, and an Executive Councillor riding atop a load of dried codfish.

A panoramic view of miniature Charlottetown in 1878 showing the carefully planned and historically named streets of the capital of P.E.I. Photo courtesy PUBLIC ARCHIVES OF CANADA

The sleepy little capital was disturbed only by religious bigotry and by the long and frustrating fight to reverse the apportionment of the island into 'lots,' or baronies, of 20,000 acres each granted to the generals and admirals who had directed the conquest of Canada, and to current favourites about the Georgian Court, many of them Scots. The Earl of Egmont, the First Lord of the Admiralty, was prominent in this scheme, and the Duke of Richmond promoted a similar plan for Cape Breton Island. Permission was sought to move several thousand slaves north from the Caribbean to work the plantations for the absentee proprietors, who bound themselves to introduce tenant settlers and to pay a yearly rental to the Crown. Transfers of slaves were still being registered in Charlottetown in the early years of the nineteenth century.

The schemes had their root in the belief that the American Revolution had occurred partly because a landed gentry had not been established at the beginning in the New England colony. Only a handful of the PEI 'seigneurs' lived up to their obligations, but they hung on grimly to their grants and the last of them were not bought out until after Confederation.

There always was, and still is, a true-blue loyalty in Charlottetown. Lord Hillsborough, British Secretary of State, ordered Charles Morris, Chief Surveyor of Nova Scotia, to draw the detailed plan for the capital. His Lordship's own name went on the wide bay and the main river that gave a deep-water port to the capital. Its main street was called Great George Street, flanked by Queen and Prince streets. The public squares are called King's and Queen's, the three counties on the island are Prince, Queen's and King's, while sundry aristocrats are remembered in Rollo Bay, Murray Harbour, Lennox Island, Cape Egmont, Tryon, Montague, Wellington, Cardigan Bay and Alberton (for Prince Albert Edward, later King Edward VII, who visited the island in 1860). The mother country can never be forgotten in New Glasgow, New London, Dundee, Kensington, York, Dover, Tyne Valley, Suffolk and Surrey. The French, now 15 per cent of the population, have contributed St Louis, Crapaud, Souris, St Chrysostome, Gaspereaux, Grand River, Miscouche, Malpeque and Bedeque bays.

Surveyor Morris was ordered to lay out his main streets at a hundred feet wide, and all others at eighty feet – a restriction not totally followed by later city fathers. Morris allowed a hundred acres for an administrative building and another five hundred for a common. Fort Amherst was constructed over the crumbling stones of Fort la Joie where the river estuaries emptied through the narrow gut into Hillsborough Bay. The capital had to wait until 1847 to occupy Colonial House, the handsome three-storied, four-pillared stone pile renamed Province House when the island became the seventh province to join the British North American federation. It was in an elegant room on the second floor of Colonial House during the first four days of September 1864 that a federal union first became a political probability.

The Maritime provinces had scheduled the first of many meetings to discuss a regional union when Lord Monck, Governor-General, asked if a delegation could come from Ontario and Quebec to 'ascertain whether the proposed union might not be made to embrace the whole of the British North American Provinces.' This remarkable idea had been first mooted in 1858 by that remarkable man Sir Edmund Head, Oxford don and twenty-first British Governor-General of Canada.

A delegation packed with several of the great names of Confederation – John A. Macdonald, George Brown, Thomas D'Arcy McGee, Alexander Tilloch Galt, George-Etienne Cartier – arrived at Charlottetown with impressive pomp in the steamer *Victoria* to be met by PEI cabinet minister William Henry Pope in his rowboat, which also contained 'a barrel of flour in the bow, and two jars of molasses in the stern.' All the rest of Charlottetown was otherwise engaged – the first circus for twenty-one years was playing the town. The capital's twelve hotels were jammed too, the Nova Scotian and New Brunswick delegations – Charles Tupper, Leonard Tilley, and their associates – having arrived the previous day.

But the hospitality picked up. The islanders provided 'a grand *déjeuner à la fourchette*, oysters, lobsters and champagne and other Island luxuries' and a ball in the legislative chamber where, at

In this elegant room of Charlottetown's Colonial House, a federal union of the British North American Provinces was proposed in 1864, to be called Canada. Photo by JOHN DE VISSER

midnight, the guests were led to a table 'literally groaning under the choicest viands.' On board the *Victoria*, the visitors threw a lunch that began at 3 p.m. and lasted into the evening. Ontario's often unbending George Brown later wrote: 'Cartier and I made eloquent speeches – of course – and whether as a result of our eloquence or the goodness of our champagne, the ice became completely broken, the tongues of the delegates wagged merrily .'

Macdonald and Cartier were, supposedly, only observers but, in one of the happiest of the national legends, they swept the confederence into broad general agreement of the principles of an ocean-to-ocean union, setting the stage for the successful conclave at Quebec the following October. Twenty-three of Canada's leading statesmen had dedicated themselves to the construction of a new nation. Prince Edward Island, as it turned out, was a tardy entrant, but that should not obscure the ringing prediction made by one of the Confederation's 'forgotten men' – the Speaker of the PEI House, Thomas Heath Haviland: 'It may yet be said that here was that Union formed which has produced one of the greatest nations on the face of God's earth.'

In a footnote, it was proposed at Charlottetown that the new nation be called either Canada or Acadia.

At the opposite end of the land, on the shore of a tree-girt, sea-drowned valley, the corpulent American railwayman William Cornelius Van Horne rode down all opposition and brought reality to the statesmen's dream of a British nation *a mari usque ad mare*. Deciding on the lumbering village of Granville on Burrard Inlet as the western terminus for the Canadian Pacific Railway, he sent his surveyor L.A. Hamilton to lay out a new city. 'This eventually is destined to be a great city in Canada,' he told Hamilton. 'We must see that it has a name that will designate its place on the map ... Vancouver it shall be, if I have the ultimate decision.' On April 6, 1886, Vancouver it became, under the royal assent bestowed at New Westminster by Lieutenant-Governor Clement Cornwall of the twenty-eight-year-old colony of British Columbia.

The bearded 'whipcracker' of the CPR, then a vice-president of the line, soon to become a British knight and a Canadian multi-millionaire, was determined to honour explorer George Vancouver, RN, but the city that was to rise so quickly that it would seem magical could more fittingly have borne the name Van Horne. The English naval captain was certainly the first known European to enter Burrard Inlet (in 1792) but his name was already fixed on the mountainous 200-mile-long island he had visited with Captain James Cook in 1778 and where British settlement had begun at Fort Victoria, the Indian *Kusing-a-las*, in 1843.

The new city was Van Horne's creation and, right from its brash beginnings, it took on something of his personality. Everything about him was larger than life. When he was near death at seventy-two, he summed up his philosophy: 'I eat all I can, I drink all I can, I smoke all I can and I don't give a damn for anything.' He loved to gamble at high-stakes poker, while munching crackers loaded with caviar. He washed them down with straight whisky. A former Morse code telegraph operator, he never lost his touch as a 'brass pounder' and during his eleven-year reign as CPR president he would telegraph ahead from his private car for two roast-chicken dinners – and arrive to eat them both. When doctors cut him down to three cigars a day, he had special cheroots rolled for him, twenty-four inches long, lasting four hours each. When the steel ribbons of his line were tied at Craigellachie, the promise that had brought British Columbia into the Confederation in 1871 was redeemed. Against all odds of mountain passes, snow slides and torrents, political scandal, Indian troubles and personal vilification, he took a virtually bankrupt railroad and forged it into the largest and perhaps best-known transportation system in the world.

Van Horne's grandiloquence, his superb confidence, his touch of gambler's recklessness were all mirrored and magnified in his city. Given one of the world's most beautiful sites, cupped by mountains and washed by sparkling seas, Vancouver has mushroomed from wilderness to a metropolis of a million or more in a single lifetime.

Nothing could crush its spirit or curb its drive. Three months after its incorporation, it was

A huge log felled in 1885 at the site of today's Georgia and Seymour Streets in Vancouver. Sam Brighouse, centre, was one of the first pioneers to file claim on 500 acres comprising most of the present West End. Photo courtesy PROVINCIAL ARCHIVES, VICTORIA

burned to the ground in twenty minutes when a freakish squall swept in from the Strait of Georgia fanning a brush-clearing fire into a holocaust. Of the eight hundred wooden buildings centering on the Hastings sawmill and Spratt's fish-oil factory, only four were left standing. Twenty persons were known to have died, but the figure was probably higher as the town was swarming with two thousand settlers, speculators, lumbermen, railroad gangs, barkeeps, outfitters, sailors, petty crooks and harlots, many of them unrecorded in any hotel guestbook or company payroll.

Among those who sought safety in the sea was Samuel Brighouse, one of the three Englishmen whose land claim at Coal Harbour – shared with John Morton and William Hailstone – became recognized as the foundation 'Lot 185' of Vancouver. The three young immigrants – Brighouse and Morton were cousins – had come to try their luck, somewhat belatedly, in the gold fields. The strikes on the lower Fraser in 1858 and along the blue-clay creeks of the Cariboo country in 1861 had enriched Victoria and New Westminster and had forced the hasty proclamation of the new mainland colony, but little of the excitement touched Burrard Inlet. Only rough roads, little better than bush tracks, led from the provincial capital at New Westminster to the mills at Moodyville and Hastings, then beginning to rip into one of the world's most magnificent stands of timber.

In October of 1862, Brighouse and his companions returned disappointed from the Cariboo and decided to set up a brick kiln based on the clay at Coal Harbour. Morton was a potter from Yorkshire. They filed claim on five hundred acres for a fee of $555 – a parcel of land worth as many millions today. It covered most of modern Vancouver's West End, from Burrard Street to Stanley Park, from the inlet through to English Bay. The coal, visible in surface seams, had been first officially reported by Governor James Douglas (later Sir James) in 1851. Other pioneer claims were entered by Walter Moberly, Robert Burnaby, Henry Crease, John Graham and Thomas Ronaldson, and Colonel R.C. Moody of the Royal Engineers reserved 2500 acres for naval and military purposes, including the 788 acres of Point Grey and much of Stanley Park.

It is entirely appropriate within the legends of Vancouver that Jonathan Swift, in publishing his *Gulliver's Travels*, included a map that claimed this corner of the north-west Pacific as Brobdingnag, the 'Land of the Giants.' The citizens have never blushed at the provincial motto, *Splendor sine occasu* (which can be read, 'Grandeur without end'). When the eye moves from the noble Coast Mountains, it is taken by the giant trees rising in the forest still clothing a third of British Columbia's 366,000 square miles. In the 1860s, Douglas fir nine feet through at the base and 250 feet high crowded the shoreline of Burrard Inlet from First to Second Narrows, up Indian Arm and around the tidal flats of Port Moody and False Creek. Hemlock, pine, cypress, red cedar and spruce were plentiful. One eighty-acre lot on English Bay produced over nine million feet of timber.

The circle of boisterous, brawling shack towns that dotted the inlet in pre-railway days sent out to the world the biggest 'sticks' even seen in commerce. Captain Edward Stamp, the peppery proprietor of the Hastings mill, the first father-figure of the modern city, planted western pride in the centre of the Empire when he shipped a giant spar to Kew Gardens as a gift, in 1861. It stood for half a century until it became rotten and unsafe. Vancouver then sent a replacement even bigger: from a 220-footer, six feet at the butt, eighteen inches at the top, lumberjacks shaped a perfect tapering pole without a knot or other blemish. When it reached London as deck cargo, it was lowered into the Thames and floated up to Kew where it was moored until an especially high tide helped raise it to the towpath. When erected, it was the greatest flagstaff ever standing in one piece, and millions of visitors came to gaze at it. No one failed to thrill that it came all the way from Vancouver, *British* Columbia. In 1959, continuing a happy tradition, it was again replaced. Today, the forest-products industry rejoices in years of industrial peace, in an annual revenue of more than one billion dollars.

When Sir William Van Horne died in his fifty-two room mansion in Montreal in 1915, Vancouver had zoomed and zagged from boom to bust and back to boom and its population stood at 172,000. From the turn of the century there was a new elegance to counter the pioneer rawness. Chinese houseboys clipped holly hedges around the ornamented homes of the rich, and ladies in

The MacMillan Bloedel building designed by Arthur Erickson on downtown Georgia Street in Vancouver, near the site where prospector Samuel Brighouse posed with friends 100 years earlier. Photo by E. STOLLER

tailored habits drove clean-legged trotters through the glades of Stanley Park. Yacht and tennis and cricket clubs flourished, madrigals were sung, and the elite were listed in the social directory. Land was money. Frontage on Hastings Street sold for $8 a foot in 1886 and $4000 a foot in 1911.

But the course was seldom smooth. Chinese and Japanese immigrants had been the targets of vicious attacks by mobs of white labourers who feared their competition in the job market; in 1907, a year of recession, more than eleven thousand Orientals entered Canada and Prime Minister Sir Wilfrid Laurier sent his Deputy Minister of Labour, a righteous tubby bachelor who liked to be called W.L. Mackenzie King (to recall his rebel grandfather), out to the coast to survey the scene. King was sold on 'the yellow peril' and recommended a limit of four hundred migrants a year. The New York *Post* jibed in an editorial: 'Vancouver, B.C. – Yes, 10,000 B.C.' The fear was to flare again in the Second World War, when, after the attack on Pearl Harbour, all Japanese in Vancouver – even the Canadian-born – were uprooted and shipped east of the Cascades; while this move was probably unavoidable in the temper of wartime, the virtual looting of the refugees' property by forced sale was inexcusable.

All old fears and feuds have since vanished as Japan has become British Columbia's second-best customer and Vancouver, once the terminal city, now reaches for a new splendour as the gateway to the Pacific.

The beaver is preferred as the symbol of Canada in many lands that can't allow us an exclusive claim on the maple leaf. They expect to see the industrious rodent on the national or at least the provincial crests of the country identified with 'the romance of the fur trade' and everywhere conceded to be signally hard-working and thrifty. But, as it happens, the beaver is given pride of place only on the official emblem of Toronto, the great central metropolis forever bursting its bounds along the north-western shoreline of Lake Ontario.

Steadily closing on Montreal for the title of Canada's largest city – at last official estimate, Montreal at 2,761,000 was ahead by only 89,000 – Toronto with its superior rate of growth is clearly destined to take the dubious laurel for sheer size in the short future and then, from all present portents, to forge ahead into contention as one of the world's greatest cities. Its projected population by 2000 A.D. is 5,700,000. It was never a major entrepôt of the fur trade but that beaver in the crest is apt; the city had gone about the job of getting big and rich and powerful with a direct and and single-minded energy that is, at times, the envy and despair of other municipalities. Some of them, paying financial tribute to the metropolitan banks and warehouses, might add that Toronto, like the beaver, has sharp teeth indeed.

From the twelve four-acre blocks of Governor Simcoe's eighteenth-century York to the 141,187 acres of the modern city, Toronto had a development peculiar to itself. For a century it could believe that it was a provincial British city because it was, by population, a provincial British city. Its upper classes could develop the best in British Victorian and Edwardian society, a careful cultivation of manners, a discreet public charity, a polite deference to taste and learning, because it *was* in essence, a typical Victorian and Edwardian city. Nothing in the New World was ever more British than Toronto, at its best and at its worst. Yet, in this there was nothing effete, nothing languid, nothing of reliance on inherited position or wealth.

Toronto might well have been content to be the capital of Ontario after 1867; it was, however, a city as dynamic as Birmingham, as thrusting as Glasgow. The stock exchange had opened in 1855 and at the elaborate annual dinners of its members, toasts were raised to banking, milling, shipping, machinery and brokerage interests. The city had set out, as early as the 1840s, to be the spearhead of western expansion, under the leadership of George Brown, publisher of the *Globe*. It seized on the fact, which Montreal, as the gateway city of the North-West trade should have done, that the future lay in the west, and in doing so raised itself from the condition of a provincial capital to its pretension as national metropolis.

It was Toronto that led the drive, partly as leader of the agrarian need for new land, partly as trader and financier seeking wider scope, for the acquisition of the North-West. It became, in fact, a veritable capital, dynamic, productive, cultivated, vigorous in seeking wealth, sensitive to the arts and learning, as its great university revealed. Drawing ever more factories and an ever-more-varied population that in time changed a British provincial city into a Canadian and North American metropolis, Toronto reaped the heavy fruits, not only of virtue and respectability but also of foresight and vigour.

If John Graves Simcoe had had his way, the capital of his Loyalist Upper Canada would have been the New London to be planted at mid-course on the river La Tranche, which he renamed the Thames. The infant Toronto on its fine and sheltered bay he christened York, marking it, as in England, as the second city of the land. If Governor-General Lord Dorchester had had *his* way then Sir John Johnson, once of the Mohawk Valley, would have been Governor in Simcoe's place. Thwarted in that, Dorchester insisted that Simcoe establish his capital at York, the temporary site at Newark being altogether too close to Yankee cannon. In the records, York was capital from 1793, but the legislature never met there until 1797, a year after Simcoe's departure.

Dorchester had been prodded by the fur traders of Montreal, seeking in their competition with the Hudson's Bay Company to develop all avenues into the trapping grounds. 'Tarantou' had first appeared on a map in 1656, designating the area between Lake Simcoe and Lake Ontario, but it was later applied more particularly to the 'carrying place' between the Humber and Lake Simcoe, the heart of the Huron Indian country. An Iroquois village once stood at the mouth of the Humber, visited – if the thin evidence be accepted – by Etienne Brûlé in 1615, but the territory was held by the Ojibway Mississaugas when the French built Fort Rouillé in 1750. It was a stockaded trading post at the foot of today's Dufferin Street, held by a garrison of sixteen men for a decade until burned to a row of charred posts to deny it to the oncoming British.

On September 23, 1787, at the neck of land that separates the Bay of Quinte from the sweep of Lake Ontario, Deputy Surveyor-General John Collins, acting for the Crown, met three chieftains of the Mississaugas and negotiated 'the Toronto Purchase.' It was a deal to be reckoned with the legendary purchase of Manhattan Island a century and a half earlier for $24: for the sum of £1700 'in cash and goods' King George III became the owner of 250,000 acres of the present counties of York and Peel. The 'goods' included four dozen black silk handkerchiefs.

A Montreal trader, Jean-Baptiste Rousseau, known to the British as 'Mr St John,' had set up a log cabin on the Humber but when Lord Dorchester sent Captain Gother Mann of the Royal Engineers to survey the harbour formed by the arc of sandspit islands there were no buildings on the Toronto site – or 'Torento,' as it is called on Mann's town grid. He laid out a sizable settlement bounded by the Don River, High Park and the present-day Bloor Street to the north.

Simcoe's town was a less expansive place; outside the walls of his Fort York on Garrison Creek (now covered over), the capital boasted only about twenty houses. At his departure, 127 ratepayers were being assessed a total of £25.16s.3d. His military pioneer corps, the Queen's Rangers, had, however, pushed Yonge Street north through the forest towards Lake Simcoe and, with a touch of Roman grandeur, he flung roads west to Burlington and east to Kingston. With a development of harbour facilities, Simcoe thus put Toronto from its inception at the centre of a communications web covering all of southern Ontario – in his day, all of Canada west of Quebec.

Always loyally responsive to the call of duty in war, the 'Queen City' had its own baptism of fire during the War of 1812 when American forces twice raided the town. In a sensational turn of chance, the stone powder magazine of Fort York blew up as the invaders were tasting their triumph and no fewer than 260 Americans, including the celebrated commander, General Zebulon Pike, were killed or wounded.

The Americans looted and fired the public buildings, destroying the legislature on Front Street East – a site later chosen, somewhat unfeelingly, for the gas works. When General Robert Ross attacked Washington in one of the last campaigns of that struggle, the Capital Building and the White House were burned in reprisal.

The pioneer town of York – it was not incorporated as the city of Toronto until 1834 – lay within the square bounded by Gerrard and Parliament streets, Spadina Avenue, and the lake. Well-known street names of today were once carried by men important in the affairs of Upper Canada. Peter Russell, who followed Simcoe as administrator, is remembered in Russell Hill Road. Joseph Bloor was a successful brewer. Jarvis Street recalls the families begun by the cousins William and Stephen Jarvis, Loyalist office-holders and slave-owners, famed for their hospitality at Rosedale, the family seat. In an 'affair of honour' Samuel Jarvis killed in a duel John Ridout, scion of another important family.

It was Sheriff William Jarvis with a patrol of twenty-seven men who scattered the first column of the Mackenzie rebels in 1837, at the intersection of Yonge and Maitland streets. Beverley Street commemorates Chief Justice John Beverley Robinson, pupil of and lieutenant to the redoubtable Bishop Strachan who, of course, has his own avenue. Robinson strapped on a belt of thirty ball cartridges, ready to fight for 'Queen and Country.' With Lieutenant-Governor Sir Francis Bond Head, a hero of Waterloo, on his charger in the lead and two cannons bringing up the rear, the Queen's men advanced to Montgomery's Tavern – just above today's Eglinton Avenue – and blew out the flames of revolt with a few shots. The rising town of Hamilton had sent sixty-five militia, and a contemporary reporter noted: 'It was an inspiring thing to see these fine fellows land on the wharf, bright and fresh from their short voyage and full of zeal and loyalty.'

Mackenzie fled before the outraged citizenry but when he returned twelve years later some of the reforms he had sought had been granted and the power of the 'Family Compact' much reduced. He was not, as is often written, an advocate of responsible government, but the fumbling uprising he led, with the much bloodier confrontation in Quebec, brought Lord Durham out to settle 'the Canadian question' and helped put the country on the road to nationhood. Durham was deeply influenced by the constitutional ideas of Toronto lawyer-politician Robert Baldwin, another of those names still remembered in a downtown street.

In buildings, too, for anyone who cares to look, Toronto remembers its creators. William Osgoode, the first Chief Justice, left his name on Osgoode Hall, the headquarters of the Law Society of Upper Canada, built 1829-32 and still the city's most handsome structure. In a later day, the Sigmund Samuel Canadiana Gallery would grace Queen's Park, the Parliament Square, in honour of another immigrant.

The growing city impressed Charles Dickens, in Victorian times. 'It is full of life and motion, bustle, business and improvement,' he wrote. 'The streets are well paved and lighted with gas; the houses are large and good, the shops excellent ... There is a good stone prison here, besides a handsome church, a court house, public offices, and a government observatory for noting and recording magnetic variations.' Dickens read from his works on the stage of the Theatre Royal on King Street, unconcerned that Egerton Ryerson's *Christian Guardian* was running an editorial campaign on the iniquity of novel reading.

Toronto's standards were at times startling: the first masters at Upper Canada College, chartered in 1827, were mostly graduates of Cambridge and local Oxonians rated them 'not altogether gentlemen.' Those fearful of the general morality would forbid public transport on Sundays and even abolish band concerts in the parks on the Sabbath. In the Methodist churches, men and women were seated on opposite sides of the aisle:

Dickens had astutely caught the Toronto theme: 'bustle, business and improvement.' As the former 'Muddy York' on Toronto Bay swallowed its adjacent municipalities with ever-increasing appetite, replacing its blue-stocking label as 'Toronto the Good' with a gamy reputation for nude entertainment and pornographic cinema, erecting ever bigger and uglier banks and hotels while earnestly seeking cultural graces in tax-subsidized theatre, opera and ballet, the novelist's swift slogan would still ring true.

This bustling scene at Toronto's Yonge Street wharf in 1902 indicates the vigorous trading and financial centre the city would later become. Photo courtesy ONTARIO ARCHIVES

PART V

Chapter Sixteen
Cracking open the North

The world's conventional appreciation of Canada seldom properly weighs what is perhaps its most important single fact – the vast area Canadians call 'the North.' If we accept the arbitrary demarcation of the 60th parallel, which is the cut-off line of the provinces of Manitoba, Saskatchewan, Alberta and British Columbia, all the territory – mainland and islands – stretching from there to the Pole, and from Atlantic to Pacific, can be seen as 'the North.' But it is much more than that – all of Labrador, for instance, is below that line. It is, physically, to the great majority of Canadians, any place that is distantly above the southern fringe of the country (the 'banana belt,' if you relish northern jargon) where nine-tenths of the people live. Thus the North includes valleys where world champion grain has been harvested, where SRO signs go up in summer at drive-in movies, modern towns with scheduled air and rail links where white-collar mining engineers and oilmen rattle their gin-and-tonics while planning exploitation of the world's greatest single conglomeration of natural resources.

But in reaching for a fuller understanding, the stranger must also weigh the huge, relentless and peculiar pressure of the North on the mind and the spirit of the Canadian. In a way that perhaps only Russians can entirely comprehend, it sits there like a colossal frozen mass on the shoulders of the people, greater and stronger than they are or ever can be, influencing eventually all they hope to do. Some see it as the source of a national caution or timidity – more unkindly, an inferiority complex; others trace to its looming presence the brashness of 'frontier' attitudes, an uneasy stance to the challenge of one of the world's few remaining wildernesses.

Every Canadian child is raised to comprehension of limitless muskeg, taiga and tundra – of great islands lost under ice, thousands upon thousands of lakes, the spruce woods rolling like any sea, the barrens crossed only by caribou and bear. Mackenzie, Keewatin and Franklin, the three administrative districts of the Northwest Territories, they learn, cover 1,304,903 square miles, measuring more than two thousand linear miles north to south, and east to west; it is an area three times the size of Ontario, and six times larger than Texas.

The geographical centre of Canada is not marked by any flagpole or cairn because it is in the emptiness of Keewatin, about 250 miles north-west of Churchill, Manitoba. There are perhaps 35,000 people in the territories, half of them white; in 1971 the density of population, in the inane statistical code, was .03 persons per square mile. (For all of Canada, it was 6.06). Through this vacant and mysterious world, the ice enemy came again and again in the past to crush the habitable southlands – and only a minor change in our climate is needed to stir the brooding glaciers to new and terrible life.

Millions abroad – and many at home – still accept, indeed enjoy, the concept of the 'white hell' of Jack London's novels, Robert Service's poems and Farley Mowat's stories, the 'frozen wastes' of the legends of the Hudson's Bay Company and of the indomitable Mounties 'getting their man' by dogsled over waist-deep drifts. Modern generations of urban man, shivering at the epic chronicles of Munck, Hudson and Franklin, are turning only slowly, almost reluctantly, to the realization that the North is not 'the land that God forgot' but a treasure-house of raw materials just beginning to finance the next major phase in the growth and development of Canada.

There have always been individuals, the risk-takers, seeking and finding their bonanzas, and towns and then cities grew to grubstake them, to capitalize their discoveries, to handle or process their materials. These cities at the fringe of the North are very different from their more southerly cousins. Like the men who founded them, they are inured to cold and privation, to boom or bust, and they live always partly in tomorrow. A new strike in oil or gas, nickel or lead, iron or uranium will set the town ringing, land values soar, speculators and work crew fly in, fortunes are made,

The discovery in 1896 of free gold on the Klondike River in the Yukon launched the most dramatic gold rush of all because the nuggets could be washed from the soil in a basin such as this. Photo by JOHN DE VISSER

the hotels are overflowing and the bars running dry. When the market slumps, the lode is worked out, the town goes back to pork and beans – or, in some cases, empties and falls to ruin.

The gleam of copper and the hope of gold first lured men into the North. It was hunger for the precious metals of Cathay that had prompted the earliest European voyages. Minerals have been sought in Canada since Frobisher, probing for the North-West Passage, found 'fool's gold' in Baffin Island in 1575. Cartier had tried hard to locate the source of the soft copper he had found in the hands of the St Lawrence Indians, and he had taken back to France barrels of 'gold and diamonds.' Iron had been dug at St Maurice since 1740, coal mined in Cape Breton time out of mind. In 1842 the Geological Survey of Canada had been set up and the search for minerals given the necessary geological background, leading, among other things, to the finding of copper at Bruce Mines in 1847 and of petroleum by James Miller Williams in the western end of the Ontario peninsula in 1857, two years before Edwin Drake's strike in Pennsylvania.

There had been a gold rush of sorts in Nova Scotia in 1862, and another on the Chaudière in Canada East in 1863, the same years of the major strike in the Cariboo country of British Columbia. In 1866, gold was found at Madoc, in Hastings County in Ontario. By 1871, the small but fabulously rich mine at Silver Island, near Fort William, had yielded heavily for a few tense years as the shaft on the tiny islet sank below the lapping waters of Superior.

These, of course, were mere scratchings of the old territories of the Dominion and the southern edge of the Canadian Shield. Beyond lay the vast and little-known bulk of the Shield itself. Curving in a giant's arc around Hudson Bay, from Labrador to the Mackenzie Basin, making up about one-half of the entire country, the ancient rocks of the Shield hold the majority of the sixty minerals found in Canada. Fused in a mighty volcanic convulsion two thousand million years ago, the Shield would surrender to modern technology nickel, platinum, uranium, gold, copper and iron. The scale is staggering. The famed 'Iron Trough' of Labrador, a belt of folded Proterozoic rocks up to fifty miles wide, runs for six hundred miles.

The Shield, however, was not all. Beyond lay the great islands of the Arctic Archipelago, stretching towards the Pole. By the mid-nineteenth century, these had not yet been occupied or used, but the British government claimed those known by British discovery from the days of Elizabeth to those of Victoria. Explorers and whalers of several nationalities seasonally entered these starkly beautiful regions. In 1873 the discovery of coal suggested for the first time since Frobisher that the Arctic might indeed be rich in minerals. Stirred by an attempt by Americans to use the coal, the Canadian government asserted an interest in the Arctic islands and, in 1880, the British government transferred its claims – in effect, the whole huge archipelago – to Canada. Suddenly, Canada became as deep as it was wide.

Always more interested in its own West and in the cross-border trade to the south, Canada paid little attention to its new imperial wasteland. When mineral treasure came to attention again, it was the discovery of the Sudbury complex on the new line of the Canadian Pacific in 1885 and, in the early 1890s, the discovery by American prospectors of the gold and base metal complexes at Rossland and Trail in British Columbia. These were great and lasting additions to the Canadian economy but, in drama, colour and immediate economic impact, both are little known compared with the Yukon gold rush of 1897.

After the Cariboo diggings petered out, prospectors had begun to comb the valleys to the north, with scant result. The Cassiar strike of 1882 was encouragement but no more. They passed from British Columbia into the North-West Territories penetrated by the fur traders since the 1840s but otherwise unknown. Not until 1896 was free gold found on the Klondike, a tributary to the Yukon River, just below where Dawson City was to rise. At once perhaps the most exciting, as it was the last, of the great gold rushes began. The story is arrestingly told in Pierre Berton's award-winning book *Klondike.* The gold was 'free,' that is, could be washed from the soil by a man with a basin or a cradle; little capital was needed, only a grubstake, pick, shovel and basin.

Thousands of prospectors, adventurers, city men and *cheechakos* (novices) set out for the

Among the thousands of adventurers who flocked to seek their fortune in the Yukon, was the Klondike belle. Photo courtesy PUBLIC ARCHIVES

191

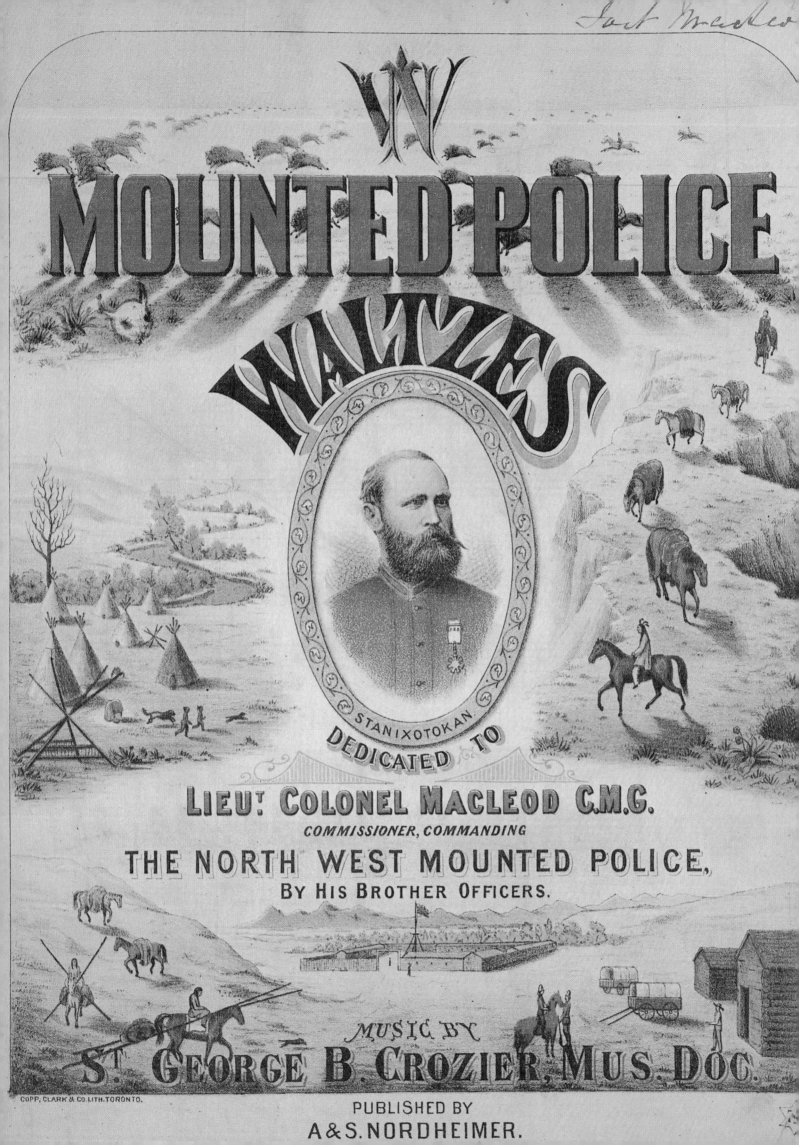

frogging to a chain of fourteen landing strips, carrying track crews, equipment, machinery, food. Seven thousand men were employed, pushing the line across canyons and through mountains as it climbed the 2055-foot face of the Laurentian Plateau; seventeen bridges were built to the halfway mark. When construction was finished in 1954, the first shipments of ore were ready to be loaded.

At the end of steel, the town of Schefferville arose, named for the pioneering Bishop of Labrador, Mgr Lionel Scheffer. Following the fine example of Arvida on the Saguenay in an earlier day, this was no huddle of workers' blockhouses and commissary around a mineshaft: in a ferocious climate – with up to thirteen feet of snow from September to June – there are streets of brightly painted single and double-family homes that could be standing in any suburb of southern British Columbia or Ontario. Here are cinema and bank, gas station, schools and shops.

Within a radius of only two miles from the spire of the handsome church lay an estimated 200 million tons of iron ore – and two million tons of it were railed south in that first season to beat the freeze-up in the gulf. Within ten years, the yearly production had risen to twelve million tons, with a top potential of twenty millions. At that rate, the known reserves of the Iron Trough alone are sufficient to supply all foreseeable needs of the Western world for several generations.

As the Canadian centenary approached, while most Canadians were content to catch only rare glimpses of their Northland in television documentaries, the frontier was being thrust back towards the very rim of the Arctic. A new railroad was pushed 438 miles from Grimshaw, Alberta, to Pine Point, on Great Slave Lake, where a concentrator was processing six thousand tons a day of high-grade lead-zinc ores. The Mackenzie Highway was completed, providing all-weather access to the bustling transportation and fishing port of Hay River, with spur roads linking to Fort Smith, Fort Providence, Fort Simpson and Yellowknife. Five million pounds of fish was shipped south from Hay River in a single year.

Carrying one of the North's most romantic names, Yellowknife, at 62° 27' N, is in every way a modern small city, nourished by the gold and other metals from the Giant Yellowknife and Consolidated Mines and by a swelling bureaucratic wages cheque. From here, truck convoys strike north on winter snow-roads for Great Bear on the Arctic Circle. On the Arctic shore itself, where the Mackenzie empties into the Beaufort Sea, the towns of Inuvik and Tuktoyaktuk (mercifully, 'Tuk' for short) boast many of the conveniences of the south, including (at Inuvik) the Utilidor, a central-heating, water and sewage complex that points the way to technical victory over the killing climate.

In Manitoba, a long extension of the Hudson Bay Railway reached out to serve the Sherritt Gordon nickel copper mines at Lynn Lake, six hundred miles north-west of Winnipeg. A series of dams on the Nelson River system boosted the provincial hydro-electric power six times over. More new harbours are operating at Port Cartier and Pointe Noire on the Gulf of St Lawrence to handle the increasing flow of minerals being won from the eastern arm of the Shield.

Reaching into central Labrador to harness the tremendous power of the Grand Falls on the Hamilton River (renamed Churchill Falls and River to honour the British wartime leader), Newfoundland initiative drove yet another wedge into the rapidly shrinking 'white hell' of the North.

PART V

Chapter Seventeen
Big wheels of industry

Confederation had been a splendid feat of reorganization of the political scheme of British North America. It created nothing new, but it so reassembled the existing political machinery as to increase its power and efficiency, especially for expansion and development. Whether it would be proof against the historic cultural and language stresses of the regions so amalgamated, it can be clearly seen as a great political merger.

Smelting in progress at Thompson, Manitoba, the instant town built as the world's only integrated nickel complex which processes the mineral completely from mine to refinery. Photo courtesy MANITOBA GOVERNMENT TRAVEL BUREAU

A similar process now began within business and industry – no less vital ingredients than politics in the shaping and conditioning of the modern state. With the rise of the cities, reorganization, growth and, in some industries, mergers were set in motion by the most able and ambitious. The age of the great outfitters and forwarders, the pioneer traders like Sir George Simpson of the Hudson's Bay Company, was beginning to yield to the industrialist, the manager and the salesman. It was the answer to the increase of demand by the expansion of the market, especially to the new West, partly by the search for efficiency, the desire to do a thing as well as possible with the least effort. Much of the history of Canada after 1867 was, therefore, to be the story of business growth, the solid realization of the flawed but serviceable ideal of an unshackled private enterprise. By the 1870s there was little that an ordinary man might want from the cradle to the grave that could not, in some degree of quality, be made in Canada.

The exploitation of the re-opened North – once the exclusive preserve of the fur trade – was only the more spectacular part of the growth of the industry on the base of the old family-farm agriculture. More important, perhaps, in terms of the way most people lived, was the rise of old crafts into new industries, and the creation of new techniques and new uses of power. Every town and village had from its early beginnings a smithy, and the blacksmith found work to do until the auto and the tractor replaced the horse. Every town and village had its wood workers, some simple carpenters, some skilled joiners and cabinet makers, who made sturdy furniture in white pine, or highly worked pieces in maple and walnut. Some of these in the nineteenth century carried their craft on to the point that it became an industry. One example is that of Jacob Hoffman, of Kitchener (then Berlin), who founded a furniture factory in which prize-winning pieces were made. .

It was a time of mechanical awakening as the stream of wonders released by the Industrial Revolution began to flow from Europe. Ideas took fire in men who insisted there must be a better, easier – and more profitable – way of getting things done. Perhaps best known of these in Canada was Daniel Massey, an American-born farmer, who in 1849 established a small foundry and machine-making plant at Bond Head, near Newmarket, Canada West. The business did well and was moved to the wider sphere of Toronto, absorbing the similar implements firm, based in Brantford, of the Alanson Harris family. Son succeeded son in one of the foremost Canadian family firms, until it merged in the Massey-Ferguson Company, an international farm implement industry and a major world corporation. From the original company, and those like it – Frost and Wood, Cockshutt and McCormack – flowed the reapers, binders, the mowers, hayrake, and threshing machines that thinned the farm hands in the fields and prepared the way for the industrialization of agriculture by the tractor and the combine. The sulky (one furrow) and gang (two or more furrows) ploughs ended the familiar rural scene of the ploughman plodding behind a team of horses. A talent that went back to the dawn of history was lost as a practical art within a generation.

The industrial explosion went much further. One by one the tall stone mills by the streams of the Atlantic provinces, Quebec and Ontario, fell silent; their great stones ceased their rumble and the water wheels were still. Their place was taken by fewer, much larger mills, powered by electrical energy and making flour by crushing the grain between serrated rollers of ever greater fineness. No more did anyone take a 'grist' to a local mill for flour of his own wheat to bake into the crusty tall loaves of the country kitchen. No more did bags of flour bear the quaint labels of some small firm owning one particular mill; a few names only appeared – Ogilvie's, Five Roses, Robin Hood, Lake of the Woods – and even they diminished over the years. With the rails now across the plains to siphon the grain, and the hydro-line leaping rock and river to bring limitless steady power, flour-milling had become a large industry, working day and night, shift on shift, more for export than for national use.

The local brew-houses and distilleries increased in size, and a few famous brands took the place of local, often unnamed, beers and whiskies. Rye whisky took its position as a noted Canadian

It was a time of mechanical awakening – from the original firms of Massey and Harris flowed the farm machinery which changed the Canadian and international rural scene forever. Photo courtesy GLENBOW-ALBERTA INSTITUTE

product – even if it was made from wheat. Company records show that the firm of Gooderham and Worts was founded by William Gooderham, miller and distiller, in 1843, one of the oldest of Canadian distillery companies, now merged into the Hiram Walker giant of Windsor, Ontario. The brewing companies of note also emerged from a similar close relation with milling and the grain trade: Molson's of Montreal, O'Keefe's of Toronto, and Labatt's of London, to mention examples of surviving names. For distilling and brewing, like milling, became ever larger industries working in ever larger plants and organized in ever fewer companies.

Industries similarly based, if with different products – cheese and butter-making, tanning, meat packing – also arose out of domestic and local skills, to become larger, national and exporting industries. Belleville, Brockville and Ingersoll were centres for dairy produce, exporting cheeses to Britain and the United States. The largest cheese ever made, 'the Canadian Mite,' 28 feet in circumference, weighing 22,000 pounds, was sent from Perth to the Chicago World's Fair in 1893 and later shipped to London for sale. These food industries were a result of the search for other products than wheat to serve the new and swelling urban markets.

Stock-raising was a necessary part of the turn to mixed farming after the passing of the wheat frontier. Cows were kept for milking and, along with pigs and sheep, for meat. In meat packing, the economies of large-scale production drew more and more local firms into larger concerns, until only a few great corporations in a few major centres became the buyers and packers. Locally cured ham and bacon, the sausages of the local butcher, gave way to the brand products of Canada Packers of Toronto, Burns of Calgary, and Swift's of Canada. The humble local butcher in his blue and white striped apron was replaced by men like Sir Joseph Flavelle. The interest in better and more productive farming brought the development of agricultural colleges at Ste Anne de la Pocatière in 1859 and at Guelph in 1874.

One great industry that was to arise at the peak of the agricultural era, and indirectly at least, out of the character and needs of that era, was the iron and, later, the steel industry. The fur trade, shipbuilding, the fisheries, the timber trade, all of these had called for iron, and they encouraged the search for ore and the forging of the metal that gave its name to the whole historical period. But agriculture, once it became the primary calling of the colonies and the Dominion they formed, was the great consumer of iron in plough and axe and scythe. So also was the rural kitchen, with its great cauldrons and the iron stoves and heaters. Bog iron locally, and that of St Maurice, for long supplied the needs of the colonies, with pig iron brought in as ballast rather than cargo.

It was, however, with the coming of the railway that the need for iron became massive. The great demand was for iron rails, but there were many supplementary demands – locomotives themselves, car wheels, spikes, fish plates, nuts and bolts. The Nova Scotia Steel Company produced Canada's first steel ingots in 1882, but in the early days of railway construction and down to the building of the Canadian Pacific Railway, rails came from Britain. In locomotives, however, and eventually even in rails and other supplies, North American conditions – frost, heat, distance, interchangeability – led to use of American imports, or to domestic production on American models.

The building of the Grand Trunk Railway – open from Sarnia to Portland, Maine, in 1859 – was to give, along with the new farm machinery, a great impetus to the local forging of iron, to the repair of iron machinery, and the building of railway equipment. As early as 1850 the Tutton and Duncan Engine Works was established at Kingston, and delivered its first locomotive to the Grand Trunk in 1856, becoming eventually the present Canadian Locomotive Company. The first Canadian-built locomotive had actually taken to the rails in Toronto three years earlier. This was the beginning of a major industry, which grew rapidly with the building of the Canadian Pacific, and reached its apex in the railway boom in the early years of this century. Not until then was the Canadian iron and steel industry to begin the massive production which made the rolling of steel rails profitable, but the beginning of the railway age was also the beginning of 'heavy' industry in Canada.

The old Labatt's building in London, Ontario, recalls the days when unnamed beers and whiskies were produced by small, local brew-houses, later merged into fewer and larger companies. Photo by JOHN DE VISSER

There had been another seminal factor working since earliest days: the somewhat surprising flow of Canadian invention. Pioneer societies do not normally have time or mental energy to spare as they battle for the simple facts of, first, survival and, then, sufficiency; necessity is seldom, in truth, the mother of invention. Every inventor stands on the shoulders of another, to some degree, but nevertheless Canada is credited with the first development or application of basic ideas of world significance in many industries, including steamships, oil drilling, telephone and telegraph, water transport, agriculture, tunnelling, aviation and, in the present day, automation.

The world's first long-distance telephone call was made between Mount Pleasant and Brantford, Ontario, on August 3, 1876, as Alexander Graham Bell demonstrated to family and sceptical friends the seemingly magical powers of the instrument he had worked on during the previous summers at the family home, Tutelo Heights. Born in Scotland, dividing his adult life between Canada and the United States, Bell is an international hero but there's no doubt he conceived the idea of the telephone – the most important single scientific advance of the past century – at Brantford, and built the major part of the first crude instrument there. He had, from the very beginning, the concept of the entire telephone communications system, with central exchange and automatic switching. The first telephone exchange in the British Empire was opened in Hamilton in 1878, within ten years both Nova Scotia and New Brunswick had provincial telephone systems, and by the close of the the century there were more than 100,000 miles of telephone lines across the country. Bell is buried at Baddeck, Nova Scotia, where he spent his summers for thirty-six years.

Still curiously ungenerous to its heroes, Canada makes little of the major technological triumph achieved by John Molson in pioneer Montreal, almost a century earlier. An orphan immigrant from England, Molson established a small brewery and by 1786 was producing Molson's ale, a business remaining in continuous production on the same site since that date. But beer was drunk by the Pharoahs of Egypt. Molson's significant achievement was the designing and building and operating of the first steamship constructed totally in North America. Americans John Fitch and Robert Fulton had steamboats in the water a few years earlier, but Fitch's craft was impractical and Fulton's *Clermont* incorporated engines built by Boulton and Watt in England.

Molson's ship, the *Accommodation*, launched on August 19, 1809, was built entirely of Canadian materials, the castings for the engine being turned out by the Forges St Maurice, at Trois-Rivières. She was eighty-five feet long, driven by two side paddlewheels. On her first voyage to Quebec City that November she carried ten paying passengers and took thirty-six hours – the captain anchored her during the hours of darkness. In the War of 1812, Molson's second ship, *Swiftsure*, became the world's first known steamship ever used for trooping. Later he added the *Marsham, Car of Commerce* and *Lady Sherbrooke*, the latter named to honour the ruling Governor's consort.

The St Lawrence shipwrights scored another important first when the 182-foot paddlewheeler *Royal William*, built at Quebec, powered with 300 h.p. side-lever engines manufactured in Montreal by Bennett and Henderson, became the first ship to cross the Atlantic principally under steam power. The year was 1833; the qualification in her claim to fame is required because, until the necessary condensers were perfected the following year, it was essential to hold an ocean steamship under sail every fourth day while her boilers were scraped free of salt. Samuel Cunard of Halifax, who was one of the investors in the *Royal William*, went on to found the world's best-known shipping line. His *Britannia* in 1840 was the first royal mail steamer on the Atlantic.

Out of the first phase of the Industrial Revolution, that of steam power and machine production, came the second, that of electrical energy and technological refinement. Electric current had indeed been part of the first, with the development of the telegraph from the 1840s and the use of the Atlantic cable from 1866. (Reinforcements to deal with the Fenian border troubles of that summer were called for by the new cable.) In the 1880s electricity was being used to replace horse power on the tramways of Montreal and Toronto. And the electric light was both replacing the

An elegant cow-catcher on one of the first electric streetcars which were replacing horse power in Toronto and Montreal during the 1880s. Photo courtesy ONTARIO ARCHIVES

lamp in the home and making city streets garish with the glare of billboards. In the form of electric fireplaces, it was beginning to be used as a source of heat.

The development of the electric motor began to transform the character of industrial towns and factories as the new clean power ended the use of coal and the tall smoke stacks with their black, rolling plumes of smoke spreading dust and soot. The first Canadian factory to run on electric power was John Barber's paper mill at Georgetown, Ontario, in 1888. Electricity reached on to the farms, too, in the 1890s, cutting the demand for labour and freeing younger sons to pursue the mushrooming opportunities amid the bright lights of the seductive cities.

From the rivers pouring over the rim of the Canadian Shield to the mountain torrents of British Columbia, Canada was rich in water power. The Shield is an ill-drained plateau where summer's rain and winter's snow are soaked up in millions of acres of muskeg, impounded in innumerable lakes, and slowly carried by a maze of crooked rivers to the southern edge. Over that ancient, worn lip they drop abruptly by sheer fall and flashing rapids to the Great Lakes and the St Lawrence. From Thunder Bay to the Saguenay and Labrador were scores of places for dams; more were offered by the Ottawa, majestically stepping down from Abitibi to the St Lawrence, and in the massive plunge of waters over the precipice of Niagara.

In the late 1880s the first developments of hydro-electricity began for flour mills, dairies, factories, and all kinds of established light industries. In Peterborough, Ontario, for instance, the long plunge of the Otonabee from Lake Katchiwano to Little Lake, which had led to the building of the first water-wheel mill of Adam Scott, was now harnessed by three dams providing the hydro-electricity that was to furnish power for the second industrial growth of the city. This development was repeated across Quebec from Shawinigan to Chicoutimi, and spread westward to Manitoba, Alberta and the Pacific coast.

The new abundant power was of special importance for one new industry, paper-making. The growth of the cities and of the popularity of their newspapers as literacy increased with public school systems created a demand for cheaper paper from wood-pulp. Fifty years ago the Sunday edition of a single Chicago newspaper required the cutting of seventy-five acres of Canadian forest. For newsprint, pulp from white spruce was especially suited. The northern forest of Canada had by 1900 been stripped of nearly all its white and its red pine, but the even more abundant spruce had been left standing. It now became available to the wood-pulp business.

A new forest industry arose to take the place of the square timber and the lumber trade. Millions and then billions of dollars went into the new pulp mills from the Maritimes to Vancouver Island, and into hydro-plants to power them. Like the mines, the new trade fed the American market to the south, drawing on raw material from the Shield. Unlike the minerals, however, spruce was a renewable resource from which paper could be made as long as paper was in demand. The pulp-and-paper industry quickly rose into first place among all Canadian industries in value of exports, capital invested, wages paid and in consumption of electrical power.

In his *An Ode for the Canadian Confederacy*, New Brunswick poet Charles G.D. Roberts had begun, 'Awake, my country, the hour is great with change!' And, while he was still teaching at King's College in Windsor, Nova Scotia, the greatest harbinger of change, the internal combustion engine, was patented in practical form by Gotlieb Daimler. Here was a source of power that could be used to drive vehicles without the necessity of rails. Suddenly the locomotive powers of man were freed from the railway to use the ordinary road, or even the pathless air. The difficulties of creating such vehicles were many, but by the end of the century the automobile was well launched on its takeover from the horse and buggy, and as early as 1900 well-to-do enthusiasts in the Winnipeg Motor Club were making highly adventurous expeditions on the flat grasslands of the Red River Valley. On Cape Breton Island from 1901, Alexander Graham Bell, joined later by Canadians F.W. Baldwin and J.A.D. McCurdy, experimented first with man-carrying kites and then with powered flight until, on February 23, 1909, McCurdy flew the *Silver Dart* half a mile over the ice of Baddeck Bay. The motor car and the aeroplane were on their way.

The days when bags of flour bore the quaint labels of small firms disappeared with the industrial explosion – a few names such as Ogilvie's remained. Photo courtesy GLENBOW-ALBERTA INSTITUTE

In the story of the automobile in Canada no name outshines that of Robert Samuel McLaughlin who turned out his first car in Oshawa, Ontario, in 1907 and survived to his 101st year holding down his job as chairman of the board of General Motors of Canada almost till his last breath. Robert McLaughlin, Senior, had moved his carriage company into Oshawa from the nearby village of Enniskillen in 1876 and, by adherence to a policy of quality products at reasonable prices, was soon supplying the carriage and sleigh trade with no fewer than 143 models. The Maritimes preferred the surrey with the fringe on top, Quebec liked the Concord bodies and Westerners demanded the buckboard and democrat. Volume rose to over twenty-five thousand carriages a year.

The eldest son, Jack J., had graduated as a chemist at the University of Toronto and would go on to found the multi-million-dollar Canada Dry soft-drinks company. The second son, George, was already in the carriage trade and young Sam first tried hardware and had ideas of entering law. But, at age sixteen, he began as an apprentice in the family business, working six days a week from seven until seven. He was paid $3 a week, from which his father, 'the Governor,' deducted $2.50 for board and clothing. He was already a partner in the business at age thirty before he had the nerve to arrive at the factory as late as 8 a.m.

At Christmas 1899 the McLaughlin Carriage Company's plant on Oshawa's Simcoe Street burned down and the town instantly voted a long-term loan of $50,000 to keep the industry in local premises. Sixteen other towns vainly tried to tempt the McLaughlins away. Sales passed a million dollars a year in the new plant but Sam was taking note of the spluttering 'horseless carriages' so loathed by the Governor.

John R. Moodie, of Hamilton, had imported Canada's first gasoline car, a $1,000 Winton one-cylinder runabout, in the summer of 1898. He caused Toronto's first traffic jam by piling up frightened horses and their waggons and buggies for three blocks along Yonge Street. Clumsy battery-driven cars and steamers lurched and chuffed about, and John Craig Eaton, third son of the store founder, indicated the rewards of the rag trade by buying a Winton. The ranching Cochranes of Calgary had a Locomobile, and the first Packard arrived to stir the dignified dusts of Belleville. In 1904, the Ford Model c was being turned out in the border town of Walkerville, Ontario, to be followed by the 20 hp Model t, the 'flivver' or 'Tin Lizzie' of hallowed memory. Henry Ford, the one-time farm boy, aided by his Canadian lieutenant James Couzens, was realizing his dream to put everyman on wheels.

Sam McLaughlin gave his father the slip in the summer of 1906 and headed for the States to talk to William Crapo Durant, the brilliant if unstable auto tycoon, then the new boss of the Buick company. Durant gave the McLaughlins the Canadian rights to the 2-cylinder Model f Buick engine for a term of fifteen years and convinced them that only by volume production could the auto industry really pay off. The Oshawa plant turned out two hundred McLaughlin-Buicks in 1907 and at the outbreak of the First World War production had reached a thousand a year. Durant had shuffled Buick, Oldsmobile, Cadillac and other companies into General Motors Corporation and, at war's end, the McLaughlin company was swallowed too.

In the relentless game of numbers, where huge sums of capital were required for economic success, it was a fate that awaited a considerable fraction of Canadian industry. The Canadian 'market' was to remain at the traditional one-tenth of the American. From the days of the Elgin-Marcy Treaty, to Macdonald's high-tariff 'National Policy,' to Goldwin Smith's intellectual advocacy of complete commercial union, Canadians had to choose between the tart flavours of industrial nationalism and the tempting sweets of American economic plenty and high 'standard of living.' They are still struggling with that decision today.

From the prosperous carriage and sleigh business owned by Robert Samuel McLaughlin, evolved many of Canada's first motor cars. Photo courtesy PUBLIC ARCHIVES OF CANADA

Chapter Eighteen
The giants of Ottawa

It will intrigue the modern reader to learn that one of the main reasons why Ottawa was selected as the capital of Canada was because of its comparative safety from military attack by the United States. When Sir Edmund Head, the Governor-General of the united provinces of the Canadas East and West, privately recommended the rough-and-ready lumber town to Queen Victoria in 1857, he wrote: 'Its distance from the frontier is such as to protect it from any marauding party, or even from a regular attack, unless Montreal and Kingston, which flank the approach to it, were previously occupied by the enemy.' Toronto, another of the claimant cities, Sir Edmund wrote, 'lay open to U.S. attack in the event of war.' The Queen had been asked to choose the capital because the so-called united provinces, the Roman Catholic French and the Protestant British, were deadlocked on that issue – and on just about every other issue of importance too. Lord Durham's dream had faded and the reality remained of 'two nations warring within the bosom of a single state.'

Fear of the American giant had caused the development of the town on the Ottawa in the first place. After the War of 1812, Britain decided to construct the Rideau Canal between the Ottawa River and Lake Ontario to provide an alternate route between Upper and Lower Canada, avoiding that section of the St Lawrence where hostile guns could halt river traffic. Lieutenant-Colonel John By was sent out with his Royal Engineers in 1826 to build the canal, and a settlement, Bytown, grew up about the northern entrance, where the Rideau joined the historic Ottawa. Plans were drawn for elaborate moated fortifications to stand on Barrack Hill, now occupied by the Parliament Buildings.

The two basic threats to the Canadian union – the racial and religious differences between Quebec and the rest, and the spectre of absorption by the United States – thus hovered over the laying of the foundation stones of Ottawa's soaring towers and spires. Before Thomas Fuller's romantic buildings were finished, the Irish-American Fenian raiders armed with leftover Civil War weapons were crossing the border, and it was being suggested in Washington that the United States should seize Canada as payment of damages arising from British collaboration with the defeated Southern Confederacy. These immediate fevers would, of course, subside but the nervous patient would continue to break into a sweat at every loud noise or chill wind from the south.

As the 181 members of the first House of Commons met in the autumn of 1867, in the afterglow of the Confederation achievement, their speeches rang with brave hope that the government would now rise above 'the petty politics of the past.' The provisions of that remarkable document, the British North America Act, now in effect the Canadian constitution, seemed to bridge the divisive gulfs. 'In our Confederation,' said Quebec's George-Etienne Cartier, 'there will be Catholics and Protestants, English, French, Irish and Scotch, and each by his efforts and success will add to the prosperity of the Dominion, to the glory of the new Confederation. We are of different races, not to quarrel, but to work together for the common welfare.'

That was well said by the descendant of Jacques Cartier, and sincerely echoed by leaders from the Atlantic shore to the Great Lakes – and, later, from the Prairies and the far Pacific coast – but human ingenuity and imagination, regrettably, had not then, nor yet, solved or surmounted the problems imposed by blood and geography. Within the lawful bounds of the democratic nation state, they may well be insoluble.

Among the fifteen men who have so far risen to lead the Canadian nation only those few are assessed as great who have accepted this fact, who have made compromise their policy, who have followed more than led. They have, in broad terms, handed on the quintessential Canadian problems intact to their successors, counting it success that the bombs with the sizzling fuses didn't

The logs opposite of Thomas Fuller's Houses of Parliament remind us that Ottawa was once a lumber town, chosen as capital because of its remoteness from the American border. Photo courtesy of ONTARIO MINISTRY OF INDUSTRY AND TOURISM

blow up in their hands. They did, indeed, guide the nation on a steady and profitable course but they took endless pains not to rock the boat. And the federal electorate has wholeheartedly approved of this, returning these men again and again to the seat of power, even giving one of them the endurance record for prime ministers under the British Crown. In looking at some of them here we hold up a clouded mirror to ourselves.

There are two quite remarkable facts about the Prime Ministers of Canada: they have been drawn for a hundred years from several racial stocks and sects, from farm and city, from backgrounds of wealth and poverty, and yet all have been found to be honourable men – there are few countries that can boast as much; secondly, with an international reputation for grey caution, Canada has several times chosen a leader who for sheer flair and colour could sustain a period novel. Among them perhaps the outstanding figure was the charming, bibulous, small-town lawyer in the fancy waistcoat who was invited by Governor-General Monck to choose and lead the first federal government.

John Alexander Macdonald had not been among the early advocates of Confederation – he was neither prophet nor mystic – but when he had taken the idea he had quickly become the only man who could bring it to reality, the 'principal architect of union.' In the Privy Council chamber at 11 a.m. on that July 1st, 1867, after the oaths of office had been administered, Lord Monck announced the Queen's pleasure that Macdonald be created a Knight Commander of the Bath. Among his selected coalition cabinet, Ontario's William Howland and William McDougall, Quebec's Cartier and Alexander Galt, Nova Scotia's Charles Tupper, and New Brunswick's Leonard Tilley were made mere Companions of the Bath. It provides an instant measure of Macdonald the consummate politician to recall that on his recommendation five of them were soon sporting titles and two of them – Cartier and Tupper – were raised to the superior baronetage.

From his earliest days as Conservative member for Kingston (his first ministerial job came at age thirty-two in 1847), Macdonald had grasped the paramount rule of Canadian politics and had established a relationship of mutual trust with Quebec that was to last until his death. When Nova Scotia's great tribune, Joseph Howe, was bent on withdrawing his province from the federation, it was the infinitely patient and beguiling Macdonald who, instead, got the Maritimer into his cabinet. 'Confederation,' Macdonald said, 'is only yet in the gristle, and it will require five years more before it hardens into bone.' He raised procrastination to an art and they began calling him 'Old Tomorrow.'

Tall, gangling, beaky, black curls flopping about his neck, a bantering, deprecating smile on his full lips, he looked more like a provincial theatrical manager than a statesman. He was blest with that rarest of political talents: a sense of humour. An American Senator's wife once found herself chatting with a thin backwoodsy fellow who offered that he was from Canada. She remarked that she had heard about 'a smart man up there,' one John A. Macdonald, but that he was 'a regular rascal.' Her acquaintance solemnly agreed. 'Why do the Canadians keep such a man in power?' the woman asked, 'They say he's a real scalawag.' 'Well,' came the answer, 'they can't seem to get on without him.' At this point the Senator came up and introduced his wife formally to Macdonald. The Prime Minister laughed and soothed the lady's confusion. 'Don't apologize,' he said. 'All you have said is perfectly true and well known at home.'

Canadians first came to know Macdonald as the lawyer who pleaded for Nils von Schoultz, the Polish revolutionary who led a mini-invasion of Canada by about two hundred Americans across the St Lawrence at Prescott in November 1838. When the attackers surrendered they were roped together and marched to Fort Henry at Kingston. One of the captives had a list in his pocket of influential Canadians who were to have been executed. Macdonald advised Schoultz to ask for mercy but the Pole disdained to do so and was hanged on the glacis of the fort. Macdonald had drawn up a will in which Schoultz left £400 to the dependents of the militiamen who had been killed in the skirmish.

The previous year of the Mackenzie and Papineau rebellions, Macdonald had shouldered his

Despite an international reputation for grey caution,
Canada has several times chosen colourful leaders like
the charming, small-town lawyer, John A. Macdonald.
Photo courtesy PUBLIC ARCHIVES OF CANADA

musket as a member of the Kingston militia to defend the Crown. Born in Glasgow, the year of Waterloo, a true-blue loyalty remained with him all his life. He believed that close association with Britain was Canada's best guarantee against annexation by the United States. He won his last election by declaiming, 'A British subject I was born, a British subject I will die.'

The immigrant Macdonalds in Kingston had lived in near-poverty and the Prime Minister was to say later: 'I had no boyhood. From the age of fifteen I had to earn my own living.' Articled to lawyer George McKenzie, he worked in Napanee and then in the idyllic scenic village of Hallowell, now incorporated in the Prince Edward County centre, Picton. During Kingston's brief years of capital glory, his law office on Quarry Street became increasingly a focal point for both municipal and provincial affairs. Although drawn into the ruling establishment of his time, Macdonald never really 'joined the club' in adopting the socially approved attitudes and appearances. His Celtic temperament was passionately aroused one moment, and casual and relaxed the next. On the floor of Parliament, he once shouted at Oliver Mowat (later Sir Oliver, Premier of Ontario): 'You damned pup, I'll slap your chops for you.' His legal experience allowed him insight into human frailty and he used his knowledge of human nature to the full.

When the Earl of Dufferin, then Governor-General, addressed McGill University students in Greek, a press report made much of the fact that his Lordship spoke 'without mispronouncing a word or making the slightest grammatical solecism.' Macdonald confessed cheerfully that he had supplied that comment to the papers. 'But,' remonstrated a colleague, 'you don't know any Greek!' The Prime Minister grinned: 'Perhaps not. But I know a little about politics.' As it happened, it fell to Lord Dufferin to restore confidence after the 'Pacific Scandal' drove Macdonald temporarily from office, and to reassure British Columbia that the cross-country railroad, promised by Macdonald to draw the colony into the federation, would get built.

It is said of Macdonald that he would buy votes but that votes could not buy him. Pressed for funds in the election of 1872, with appalling frankness or foolishness, he sent an open telegram to Sir Hugh Allan, head of the combine then attempting to build the railway: 'I must have another ten thousand. Do not fail. Answer today.' Allan sent the contribution, and the Conservatives won a narrow victory. Early the following year a solicitor's clerk stole a handful of documents – including the telegram – and sold them for $5000 to the gleeful Liberals. Hounded in the House, deserted by erstwhile friends, Macdonald resigned. His career appeared over.

It is quite possible he had sent the fateful telegram while drunk. In seeking the reasons for Macdonald's compulsive drinking, sympathetic biographers note that his life was marked with sorrow and shock. When he was only seven, he had seen his younger brother James die in convulsions. His first-born son, John Alexander, died as an infant after a fall, and his wife Isabella died young after a long, harrowing illness. After he remarried, at fifty-two, his second wife Agnes had a retarded daughter, Mary; when Mary was a grown woman, the Prime Minister would go home from a wracking day in Parliament and read her fairy stories. These personal sorrows could have made many embrace the bottle but even as a young man, before marriage, Macdonald seemed to be an eager victim of what long-suffering Celtic women call 'the failin' in their men. His father, an amiable loser, had 'the failin.'

Certainly, Macdonald was known to be drunk in the House of Commons, drunk in his office, drunk on the hustings. He drank whisky, gin, port and sherry by the bottle. It was an age when many homes and shops kept an open whisky keg, to be replenished from the grocer at 25 cents a gallon. Macdonald loved to stand toping at the saloon bar, regaling his cronies with vulgar jokes, laced with flashes of his satirical wit. When George Brown publicly accused the Prime Minister of drunkenness, the irrepressible Macdonald was even able to turn that to political account. 'The electors of Canada,' he scoffed, 'would rather any day have John A. drunk than George Brown sober.' They would, too.

When Dr George Grant, Principal of Queen's University, told Macdonald, 'I've always supported you when I believed you were right,' the Prime Minister cracked back, 'That's no use to me.

It was workmen such as these Ukrainians, seen in 1909 at Crowsnest Pass, who helped build Canada with their hands and whose efforts remain largely unsung. Photo courtesy GLENBOW-ALBERTA INSTITUTE

I want men who will support me when I'm wrong.' He was sadly wrong – the biggest mistake of his career – when he swayed his cabinet to confirm the execution for treason of the crazed Louis Riel, following the crushing of the 1885 Métis rebellion in the Northwest. With his inner vision of the vital importance of the Crown in Canada, Macdonald had insisted: 'He shall hang though every dog in Quebec should bark in his favour.'

In the cold realism of politics, Macdonald actually owed the continuance of his own public life to Riel. The Canadian Pacific Railway Company, now led by George Stephen, the president of the Bank of Montreal, was on the verge of bankruptcy; it had poured money into track-laying across the incredibly difficult Canadian Shield and the endless plains. Parliament refused to provide more funds. Macdonald had repeated his promises to British Columbians that a railroad would link them to the East and he knew that 'The day the CPR busts, the Conservative Party busts the day after.'

The shots fired at Duck Lake, Saskatchewan, on March 26, 1885, when Riel's half-breeds killed a dozen men of a Royal North-West Mounted Police patrol, broke the deadlock. The CPR's Van Horne offered to rush Dominion troops to the scene in eleven days; the rebellion was put down at Batoche, and a grateful Parliament sanctioned another loan of $22.5 million to complete the railroad.

In 1886 Sir John and Lady Macdonald rode a special train in triumph across the country he had done so much to create. For part of the trip, they sat on a risky platform on the front of the locomotive, by the belching smokestack. His surviving son, Hugh, was already living in the West and would become Premier of Manitoba.

In a career that would not be believed in fiction, often inebriated, always inspired, John Macdonald had drawn up the fine print of Confederation, held the confidence of Quebec, fended off the too-eager embrace of the Americans, laid the foundation of an independent foreign policy, and stitched his unlikely nation together with his improbable, scandal-ridden but absolutely vital railway. He died with his boots on, just three months after winning yet another election.

It is altogether fitting that the next 'giant' at Ottawa was a French Canadian, Liberal rather than Tory, a man for all seasons and sects, who was to hold the country's confidence through four consecutive elections, a record never excelled. Wilfrid Laurier was born in 1841 in St Lin, now Laurentides, forty miles north of Montreal, on the Achigan River – his family home is now preserved as a national shrine. He was a member of the federal Parliament continuously for forty-five years, and leader of the Liberal Party for thirty-two. Although he vainly fought the ageing Macdonald, Laurier brought into the political arena a panache to match the appeal of 'Old Tomorrow,' an inspired vision of Canada as an independent bicultural nation, and the same subtle gift for governing.

Despite his apostasy and megalomania, Louis Riel was being raised in death to the status of a French Canadian hero. His execution at Regina hardened the *nationalisme* then growing in Quebec to offset the ever-swelling majority of British and other Protestants in the country. Honoré Mercier, soon to be Premier of Quebec, was the fieriest orator at a mass protest meeting in Montreal's Champs de Mars on November 22, 1885, but Wilfrid Laurier, then forty-four, threw some kerosene on the flames by shouting that if he had lived on the banks of the Saskatchewan he would have shouldered a musket with the Métis. For a former Minister of the Crown for Inland Revenue, that must have run close to sedition but Laurier, the most persuasive of men, blest with a devastating charm, was within a dozen years to be knighted by Queen Victoria at her Diamond Jubilee and welcomed into her imperial Privy Council.

His outburst had been one of genuine passion but Laurier's true greatness was that, when it counted in ultimate councils, he steadfastly put the nation first and considerations of race and language in their proper perspective. He proved that a Canadian who happened to be French could not only command and protect Quebec but collaborate openly with the English-speaking

By racing troops to the Riel Rebellion in 1885, William van Horne proved the efficiency and value of the railway to a grateful Parliament who voted the necessary funds to complete it. Photo courtesy CANADIAN PACIFIC

majority for the general good of all. In this direction lay the only long-term hope for the complete fulfilment of the Canadian promise.

As a boy of eleven, Laurier had been placed for a period in a Protestant school, and boarded with a Scottish Presbyterian family. His schoolmaster, Alexander Maclean, was fond of quoting the great English poets, and in two years Laurier picked up a flawless knowledge of English, embellished with a lilting poetic elegance. After a further seven years with the French classics at L'Assomption College, he went into law at McGill. He was valedictorian for his graduating class in 1864: 'I pledge my honour that I will give the whole of my life to the cause of conciliation, harmony and concord amongst the different elements of this country of ours.'

Tall and slight, courtly, Laurier had that touch of the exotic to make him stand out in any crowd. When his fair hair turned silver, a nimbus around his balding dome, he carried it high like a banner and was known as 'the knight of the white plume.' Following a group of premiers who had begun life as gritty stonemasons and printers, he added refreshing style and grace to politics.

He had risen as a natural leader of the *Rouges*, the left-wing democrats who decided it was time to curb the power the priests had exercised over French Canada since the seventeenth century. The *Bleus*, the Quebec conservatives, with the open support of the *ultramontane* Bishop Bourget, were moving towards the formation of a Roman Catholic party. The priests urged that the religious orders should have immunity from the law, and said it was sinful for a Roman Catholic to be a Liberal. They feared, basically, the atheistic liberalism that had flooded France after the revolution a century earlier. Laurier argued in a memorable speech that the moderate *Rouges* sought to follow the example of the great British Liberals like Fox and Russell who were not anti-religious. He insisted upon the right of French Canadians to make up their own minds on political issues, without intimidation from the church. He was under no illusions: 'The moment I shall accept office,' he once wrote, ' ... It will be a war with the clergy, a war of every day, of every moment ... I will be denounced as antichrist.'

But it was a war that he would win. The entire Roman Catholic heirarchy campaigned against him in 1896 when he upheld the exclusive right of the Manitoba government to control education within its provincial borders – even though the point at issue was the abolishing of separate Catholic schools. Provincial rights would be doubly precious to an out-weighted Quebec in the swiftly growing nation and, in any case, Laurier was sure he could bring sweet reason to bear to get a better deal for the Catholic minorities in the West than would ever be ensured by federal coercion. He did, too, and although neither Catholics nor Protestants were entirely satisfied, they accepted his compromise happily enough, after some grumbles. That was the art of ruling Canada.

Laurier was bilingual in the widest sense. He could not only stir imperial conferences with his eloquence, but he could crack jokes with a sure grasp of local values. At a political rally in Moose Jaw, Saskatchewan, the Liberal candidate's daughter made the traditional presentation of a bouquet and Sir Wilfrid, a champion political baby-kisser, rewarded her with the equally traditional kiss. This time, though, the flower girl was a strikingly beautiful young woman of eighteen. Someone called out: 'I'm going to tell your wife.' Laurier didn't hesitate. 'When I started this trip,' he said, 'I promised my wife I would kiss only babies and flower girls up to the age of eight. But, you know as well as I do that they grow 'em big out West.'

It was Laurier, adroitly avoiding any commitment to an imperial parliament and thus moving Canada along the road toward full independence, who offered the British and the other British colonies the trading system that became known as 'imperial preference,' and later as 'Commonwealth preference.' In some forms, it persists today.

Laurier did agree that Canada would help defend the Empire when it was endangered – but he did not consider the Boer Rebellion in South Africa as such a threat. The British immigrants then flooding into Ontario and the West thought differently. Laurier tried desperately to find the healing compromise, and ruled that the government would not *send* troops but would equip and

The government lured settlers with generous offers and colourful brochures which neglected to mention water, food and fuel shortages or the hail, prairie fire, gophers and mosquitoes that plagued the pioneers. Photo courtesy PUBLIC ARCHIVES OF CANADA

transport a contingent of volunteers. Seventy-three hundred Canadians fought in South Africa; it was the nation's first military adventure abroad, although the troops operated under British command.

The Canadians won high praise in the field, three of them being awarded the Victoria Cross, the highest decoration for valour, in a single action at Leliefontein. But the smell of British gunpowder was too much for the black-bearded Henri Bourassa, a grandson of Louis-Joseph Papineau, who began to draw about him the latter-day *patriotes*. He didn't hesitate to fan the old embers of racial and religious hysteria in an attempt to supplant Laurier as the idol of Quebec.

When unmistakable war clouds were gathering in Europe, the Canadian government was pressed to contribute funds to help Britain keep abreast of the German battleship programme. It was the era when the balance of power was expressed in huge armour-plated warships. Laurier decided, instead, to begin the creation of a separate Canadian Navy with five cruisers and six destroyers. In a bitter by-election fight in Quebec, Bourassa's separatist party sent members in phony uniforms to rural farmhouses listing all men of military age; they told the *habitants*: 'Those who disembowelled your fathers on the Plains of Abraham are asking you today to go and get killed for them.' Laurier's man lost the by-election but the Prime Minister would not be intimidated and the Naval Bill went through.

Before any ships could be built, however, Laurier, at seventy, had been thrown out of office, and when the First World War arrived as predicted, Canada had to face it with two ancient training cruisers, only one of which was fit to put to sea. The Liberals had gone down to defeat in an election that turned on the visceral issue of the American threat. A 'free trader' by instinct and principle, Laurier responded warmly when U.S. President William Howard Taft offered in 1911 to reduce the barriers to north-south continental trade, without the usual demand that Canada drop its preferential tariff system favouring Empire countries. It was a revival of the bogey-word 'Reciprocity' – which had a meaning close to 'annexation' in many Canadian minds. Sir Clifford Sifton, the man most responsible for the peopling of the prairies, led a group of eighteen Liberal rebels against his chief, and the Bourassa party hammered at the Quebec grass-roots with war-scare politics.

When his enemies closed on him, Laurier looked back on the fifty years since his stirring dedication at the McGill convocation and summed up the heartbreak course of Canadian statesmanship: 'I am branded in Quebec as a traitor to the French, and in Ontario as a traitor to the English. In Quebec I am branded as a jingo and in Ontario as a separatist. In Quebec I am attacked as an imperialist and in Ontario as an anti-imperialist.' He paused. 'I am neither. I am a Canadian.'

Laurier bequeathed the country more than a credo. In 1900 he had taken into his Department of Labour, on the advice of Sir William Mulock, an earnest, short, pudgy social worker known to his few friends as Rex King. Torn between Ottawa and a lucrative career as a consultant (while 600,000 Canadians served in the First World War, King was earning $20,000 a year as a labour adviser to the Rockefellers), he was pushed into politics by a grandfather who had died thirteen years before he was born. The influence of ghosts was to pervade his whole career.

His parents had been plain Mr. and Mrs. John King, but his strong-willed mother had named her first son William Lyon Mackenzie, to keep alive the name of her father, the rebel leader of 1837. King now encouraged the use of the double-barrelled name, Mackenzie King, and confided to his diary that 'somehow I believe God has a great work for me in this Dominion, maybe at some time to be its Prime Minister.'

King had to wait until the long-suffering Robert Laird Borden was broken by the wrenching schisms of the wartime conscription crisis, and his successor, Arthur Meighen, defeated by the temporary entry on the national scene of the farmers' Progressive Party. King had followed Laurier as leader of the Liberals in 1919 and now, on December 6, 1921, a few days short of his forty-seventh birthday, he took the reins of power with a majority of just a single seat. That he could govern with that margin for almost four years in his first ministry, weighing the consequences of every phrase of every sentence, gave notice to the country that here was the greatest hard-core politician of them all.

With not a shred of the style or flair of a Macdonald or a Laurier, with an appearance homely at best and an ineffably unctuous and boring speaking manner, with no understanding of the French Canadian mind or language, King seemed surely doomed to a one-term rule. But, instead, he was to hold power from 1921 until 1930 (except for a few weeks) and from 1935 until his resignation in 1948. Then he handed over a vibrant going concern to his carefully selected heir, Louis St Laurent, who promptly won the Liberals a further nine years in office.

The acid-tongued lawyer Meighen said that King held on to office 'like a lobster with lockjaw,' and that he was 'the most contemptible charlatan ever to darken the annals of Canadian politics.' But King always packed too many guns for Meighen. His amazing political dexterity is seen in the Byng constitutional squabble. When the Liberals could win only 101 seats to the Conservatives' 116 in the election of 1925, King attempted to carry on with hoped-for support from the rump of Progressives. He staggered along until the following June, when finally the Liberals lost a crucial test in the House by one vote. King then asked the Governor-General, Viscount Byng of Vimy, to dissolve Parliament and order a new election. The gruff soldier refused, arguing that it was only a few months since the Liberals had tried and failed to win the country's confidence; instead, Byng sent for Meighan, waiting in the wings, and invited him to try to form a government.

Meighen appeared to have won, but his triumph was short-lived. King wrecked his attempts to rule with a masterly display of parliamentary skill and constitutional confusion, and the Conservatives quickly lost control of the House. Now it was Meighen's turn to resign and seek a dissolution; this time, the Governor-General acquiesced, to allow Meighen a chance to ask the country for a clear majority. But the voters hearkened to King's furious charge that Lord Byng had treated Canada like some 'banana colony' in rejecting the advice of his Prime Minister (that is, in refusing King a new bid); in the election that followed in the fall of 1926, the Liberals squeezed back with 116 seats to only 91 for Meighen's Conservatives. King was in the saddle for another four years.

He was not an innovator but King was infinitely skilful in sifting the gold out of mines opened by others. The gruff Nova Scotian Borden, underrated in the Canadian record, had lifted Canada at a bound to the *de facto* status of an independent nation by demanding a separate Canadian seat at the peace conference after the war. Canada had formed its own army abroad – the Canadian Corps, under General Arthur Currie – and had suffered sixty thousand dead; that was an expensive and valid ticket of admission that could not be denied. During the war, Borden had teamed with South Africa's Jan Smuts to demand from British Prime Minister David Lloyd George 'all existing powers of self-government ... full recognition of the Dominions as autonomous nations.' With the stage thus set, King was able to smoothly rebuff Lloyd George when London asked for an expression of Canadian support during a threatening incident between British and Turkish forces at Chanak on the Dardanelles. In 1923, King sent his Quebec 'viceroy' Ernest Lapointe to sign a fishery treaty with the United States, without British participation.

No doubt King thought often of his maternal grandfather's humiliation by the forces of the Crown, and he was at times notably cool to the British establishment. At the Imperial Conferences of 1923 and 1926, he was the sour apple who rejected even the loosest kind of Empire consultation, fearing that Canada might find itself morally committed to joint action when its own particular interests were not involved. The mighty men of Empire looked down their aristocratic noses at the pawky colonial isolationist and refrained from pointing out that the Motherland and the rest of the Dominions had played some sort of role in the allied victory in the recent war – and who, they might also have asked, would stand between Canada and any future European enemy that might arise? Lord Curzon did forget himself so far as to call King 'obstinate and stupid' – but Curzon was not haunted by the spectre of conscription and its supposed giant-killing power in Canada.

Better than any man before him, or since, King knew the levers of Canadian power. He even

threatened that he might not attend any more London conferences if their purpose was to try to get the Dominions to commit themselves to policies in advance. The 1926 conference found a face-saving resolution which declared that each self-governing member of the Empire family was now 'master of its destiny.' From there, it was only a step to the Statute of Westminster of 1931 which formally cemented the independence of the Dominions.

The Liberals were out of office from 1930 to 1935, the worst five years of modern Canadian history, and it is difficult to put aside the thought that King had engineered the eclipse. Personally, he allowed it to be understood he had done just that, to allow his Tory opponents to commit political suicide in the Great Depression. The financial crash of 1929 rocked Canada no less than other states, and every province was dismayed at lengthening queues of unemployed. Frustration and anger mounted and there was exactly the kind of breakdown of untrammeled capitalism that King had predicted in his book, *Industry and Humanity*, written in 1918. He had argued then for a new partnership between business and labour, with the state stepping in where necessary to insist on policies beneficial to all classes. When the claims of industry and humanity were opposed, industry must give way.

Dr King (Ph.D., Harvard, 1909) was perhaps the only politician in power in the world precisely trained to initiate the required rethinking of national economic ethics. The decision he took, however, was to accuse the Tories of fomenting the whole thing. The Conservative premiers of several provinces were urging him to raise taxes to provide them with money to pay the dole. There was an election due in the summer of 1930 and, in the last day of the outgoing Parliament, King rose and with one brutal sentence assured his defeat at the ballot box. 'With regard to giving moneys out of the Federal Treasury to any Tory government in this country for these alleged unemployment purposes while those governments are situated as they are today with policies diametrically opposed to those of this Government, I would not give them a five-cent piece.'

It was his usual soporific style, but this time his meaning was ruthlessly clear. The 'five-cent speech' sent ragged jobless men pouring into the voting booths to vote for Richard Bedford Bennett, the millionaire from Calgary, who used 220 booming words per minute (by stopwatch count) to prove that he would beat the Depression, 'or perish in the attempt.' He didn't beat it, nor did he perish. When King surged back to power in 1935 on the crest of improving times, Bennett soon joined his boyhood friend Lord Beaverbrook in England and the Beaver had him enobled as Viscount Bennett of Mickleham, Calgary and Hopewell (N.B.). He died in his bathtub, at seventy-seven, far from the scene of his Canadian anguish.

King had once informed Parliament that there was a real world and an imaginary world and that statesmen must operate in the real one. But King himself, seemingly the most prosaic of men, believed absolutely in the imaginary one, also. It is perhaps the most sensational single fact in the century of Canadian national politics that the man who was Prime Minister far longer than any other was a practising spiritualist, listening to unseen voices, certain that he was in touch with the dead – even with his deceased terrier. During his years of comparative idleness in Opposition, King slipped more completely into his community of ghosts, visiting spiritual 'mediums' here and abroad in circumstances of strict secrecy.

When this information became public after King's death in 1950, the great majority of Canadians to whom he had become a father-figure, representing all that was upright and worthy in the maturing nation, were stunned and unnerved. Had King really been taking advice from so-called spirits on the life-and-death issues of the Second World War and the testing questions of the postwar period? In one instance at least, concerning the possibility of conflict in Asia, the answer appeared to be 'yes.' There was also the unsettling presence of King's 'folly' – the baffling ruins at Kingsmere, his country place in the Gatineau. Here on a hilltop, King had patiently assembled pieces of mismatched masonry from wrecked Ottawa buildings until he had constructed something like the ruin of a mediaeval abbey. He never explained its meaning or purpose to anyone.

King never married and his relationship with his mother was of paramount importance to him;

The study of Mackenzie King, the pragmatic prime minister who believed in spiritualism. His mother's portrait in the background is still lit by a glowing lamp, as it was in his day. Photo by JOHN DE VISSER

at her request, he had given up a girl he wished to marry in Chicago. When he was already Minister of Labour, he wrote of his mother: 'It is like coming near to an angel to be with her ... the more I think and see of her the more I love her and the greater do I believe her to be.'

Isabel King was the thirteenth child of William Lyon Mackenzie, born during his years of poverty and exile in the United States. Her knowledge of her father's defeat did not deter her from marrying John King, a middle-class lawyer from Berlin (later Kitchener), Ontario, whose father had taken up arms in 1837 against the rebels. But she imbued her eldest son – she called him Billy – with her version of the Mackenzie spirit and, at university, King was writing in his diary, 'His mantle has fallen upon me and it shall be taken up and worn.' He actually did write things like that in his diary.

Isabel King died in 1917 and her son kept a large portrait of her in his study with a lamp always glowing beside it; it is still there today, the lamp still burning. When he was elected as leader of the Liberal Party in 1919, at age forty-five, he informed his diary: 'It is to His work that I am called. The dear loved ones know and are about, they are alive and with me in the great everlasting Now and Here.' It is clear he led an unhappy, unhealthy emotional life and that he sought some ease from frustrations in secret visits to prostitutes. He did not have the balancing ascetism of the monk – he several times tried to summon up enough courage to marry. 'I cannot live that cruel life without a home and someone to love and be loved by ... ' His mentor Wilfrid Laurier tried to find him a wife, introducing a suitable rich young widow.

Even the bluff warmth of a male friend seemed denied to King. He had carried forward to Ottawa one intimate from student days, Henry Albert Harper, installing him as his assistant and as the virtual editor of the new *Labour Gazette*. When Harper was drowned in the Ottawa River trying unsuccessfully to save a girl who had fallen through the ice, King had him memorialized in the statue of Sir Galahad that still stands on Parliament Hill, and then, five years after the event, honoured him in a touching but curious memoir, *The Secret of Heroism*. The book was as much about King as about Harper and so close was the author identified with the subject's heroism, patriotism, devotion to the common man, that one influential reviewer in the Toronto *Globe* referred to the title as *The Secret of Success* . Although in later years Ernest Lapointe was close enough to King to call him 'Rex,' and Franklin D. Roosevelt called him 'Mackenzie,' King had no intimates – except his succession of terriers, all named 'Pat.'

King treasured his wartime association with Roosevelt and worked hard to create the legend of Canada, the North American nation of British loyalty, acting as a broker and bridge between the old world and the new. In 1938, at Queen's University in Kingston, President Roosevelt had assured grateful Canadians the United States would 'not stand idly by' if Canadian soil was threatened by anyone. King had visited Adolf Hitler the previous year and had written him off as a 'simple sort of peasant;' the Liberals had, in a word, left Canada defenceless – ten naval ships, fourteen tanks, twenty-nine Bren guns. In 1940, the President and the Prime Minister made continental defence official, in an agreement signed at Ogdensburg. By then, of course, Canada was a belligerent, and thus the Americans could be seen inching towards active participation. The swapping of fifty old moth-balled U.S. destroyers for the loan of bases in Newfoundland and the Caribbean, arranged through Canadian offices, accelerated the slide. In 1941, nine months before the Japanese attack on Pearl Harbour, King and Roosevelt signed the Hyde Park Declaration which brought the two countries into close association industrially and financially.

While King was always mesmerized by the political dangers of conscription in Quebec, it was his fraternal deals with Roosevelt which turned out to be the time-bombs of his administration. With the great majority of his own cabinet, probably the best and most selfless ever assembled in Canada, demanding conscription as the only fair method of reinforcing a national army engaged in a fight to the death, King was finally pushed quailing over the brink in 1944. He had predicted that to enforce conscription in Quebec 'we would have to ... use our tanks and rifles against our own people.' In the event, nearly 13,000 Home Defence troops were ordered overseas, only 2,500 reached the front lines where sixty-nine of them lost their lives – in a total of 41,992 Canadian war dead. And the dreaded uprising in Quebec did not, of course, occur. Some windows were broken, in recruiting offices and banks, a few flags burnt, and even Bourassa's old *patriote* paper, *Le Devoir*, dismissed the rioters mostly as youngsters out for a lark.

In Louis St Laurent, King had found another true Canadian patriot; in supporting the conscription decision, he had put the nation as a whole above any sectional interest. Once he assumed leadership himself, advised particularly by Lester Bowles Pearson in External Affairs, St Laurent brushed the ghosts of the old 'Little Canada' policies aside and, in a series of audacious strokes, took Canada out into the select company of international powers. When he saw the Security Council of the United Nations strangled by the Communist veto, St Laurent proposed a North Atlantic Alliance, to put fighting teeth into the keeping of the peace. Canada was committing troops, including French Canadians, to fight abroad without a plebiscite, without even a single flag being trampled under. He had told Quebec to forget 'the illusive dream of a French Canadian state in North America.' It seemed, in those dimming days, that most of his compatriots were listening. When he called his first election, he was returned with the largest majority given any man since Confederation. Canada was before the world in its new maturity.

PART VI

The cycle of change

EPILOGUE
The middle age of a middle power

As a very prosperous and slightly smug Canada ran breathlessly to the celebration of its first century as a federated nation, there was little time or temper for a quiet contemplation of the journey that had been made, or qualitative assessment of the position that had been reached. Yet because of changing and coalescing elements in the national body, it was not merely a celebration, but also a climax of Canadian history. It was a major moment in the Canadian experience which came into focus, shone and passed. The aftermath is the uncertain present, and the obscure future.

Only a Scrooge, surely, would question that the nation had risen to new heights, to a new stature in its vigorous middle age. Under the new 'instant' flag of red maple leaf, the country was bustling with centenary sports meetings, picnics, concerts, ringing with self-congratulatory chimes, opening commemorative schools, libraries, centres for the performing arts, irrigation dams and comfort stations, and on Montreal's

An ancient piece of trade silver in the form of a beaver symbolizes the heritage passed from earlier generations of Canadians to those of the present who face the new challenges of the nation. Photo by TIM SAUNDERS

river islets there was the gay and glittering, vastly expensive, national birthday present of Expo 1967 to prove that Canada could do just about everything as well as, if not better than, anybody. That's how it seemed anyway, in the domestic newspapers and in the television shows as Canadian editors and commentators were swept away by the tide of press-agentry that washes over all world's fairs.

At the very least, it was English-speaking Canada's great courtship gift to Quebec – the inspiration was Montreal's but the tab was Ottawa's – even though Quebec's enthusiasm for the Confederation centennial ceremonies was decidedly cool. Wooing, or placating, French Canada had been for some years (and would continue to be) the highest priority of Canadian federal business. It would proceed even to the point of requiring bilingualism for significant advancement in the national public service; given the English lack of facility with other tongues, this seemed to be tantamount to inviting perpetual governance by minority.

When the great of the world made procession to Montreal – sixty kings, presidents, premiers and an emperor – they were met by Canada's own international celebrity, Prime Minister Lester Bowles Pearson, Nobel Prize-winner for his diplomacy in establishing the United Nations Emergency Force between the warring Jews and Arabs in 1956. With his scrubbed smiling face, his bow-tied 'Call me Mike' appeal, Pearson seemed the personification of Canada's sincere, if schoolmasterish, entry in the high-stakes game of international power politics. If the dream of leading a block of middle (that is, non-nuclear) powers was evanescent, the visitors were too polite to say so – all except France's Charles de Gaulle who did his weighty best to try to dismember the nation with his cry, '*Vive le Québec! Vive le Québec libre!*'

The centennial brought, too, an avalanche of books, sponsored by national, provincial, even county and municipal authorities, which seemed to record in numbing detail every town meeting for a hundred years from Heart's Content, Newfoundland, to Ucluelet, British Columbia, but which seldom attempted to illuminate or examine. There were commissioned murals, sculpture, plays, poems and an opera. There was, also (and possibly quite rightly), a subsidized history of the bagpipes in Canada – after all, we have had six Scottish prime ministers.

But beyond all these passing pursuits and pleasures, it was a climax in Canadian history because Canada had, almost surreptitiously, slipped over the brink of change and was firmly set upon a new and exhilarating course. There was no lack of pilots to warn of rocks and storms ahead, but the nation was caught with the impulse to take a chance for once and run not walk into its destiny.

Giddy with novelty, the electors gave the prime ministership to Pierre Elliott Trudeau, a fiftyish Montreal millionaire bachelor who had only three years' experience of government but who wore sandals, chains, sideburns, smoked glasses, all the furniture of the new thing, who danced the boogaloo and who was seen with film stars on his arm.

There had never been *anyone* in high office in the Kingdom of Canada like Pierre Trudeau. The fact that the 'swinging' mask concealed the most polished and pragmatic mind, French or British, ever to electrify the House of Commons would be revealed in due course.

So also would be revealed a lack of sensitivity, a personal hardness, which his critics termed arrogant. Verbal cleverness in putting opponents down, and an uncompromising personal attitude, were perhaps defects in one playing the essentially conciliatory role of Prime Minister of Canada. In the light of the growing demand for independence for Quebec, these qualities might or might not be helpful. Trudeau's government did continue and step up Pearson's attempts to appease Quebec and, in 1969, Parliament passed the Official Languages Act to implement the recommendations of the Royal Commission on Bilingualism and Biculturalism (the title reflects the jargon this strained and artificial exercise produced). Separatist opinion was wholly unimpressed and unaffected. Could it be that Trudeau, like John Diefenbaker, was to be a martyr to one indivisible Canada?

Change was nowhere more obvious than in the military. A country founded on conquest, held against invasion by plucky arms, proud of its record in the two world-wide conflicts of the twentieth century, was sidling into a semi-pacifist role, exphazizing the supplying of police for any U.N. intervention between warring states. The victors of Vimy Ridge, the men of Dieppe and the Walcheren were seen striving to be avuncular referees in armbands and coloured berets from the Vale of Kashmir to the Pyramids of Gizeh. The fact that its men were peremptorily ordered out of the Middle East in 1967 by the Egyptian dictator to clear the zone for the resumption of war did not noticeably diminish Ottawa's ardour.

A much-advertised review of foreign policy appeared to result mostly in a reduction of forces committed to defend the Western alliance and an expansion of effort to win the friendship of the Communist East. Whether this hint of a shift in emphasis would ameliorate Canada's position as a buffer trans-polar land between the two great ideologically opposed powers, only time could tell. But, realistically, the security and sovereign integrity of Canada rested ultimately on the neighbourly arms of the United States, as it had done since the decline of British power.

Within the nation itself there was the same striving and restlessness; on the university campus, on the streets, Canadians were in no way exempt from the passions of the times. But the brief newscasts and sensational headlines shouting of rejection of authority, of dissatisfaction with contemporary standards, of the 'drug sub-culture,' tended to conceal the truth about the Canadian condition in the 1970s. There was change, true, and welcome, but men still slept quietly in their beds. Women kept their homes. Children went to school. The roads were open. Civil men went without arms. The police were reasonably humane, protective and helpful, certainly not hostile and repressive. Careers were open to talent. The pursuit of fun, or the enjoyment of the arts, was open to all. In short, Canadian society remained civilized; in the homelier ways, one of the world's more civilized societies.

Next, the Canadian state remained a working state. The laws were generally upheld. Their reform was constant. The courts were held in reasonable respect. Public criticism was both free and effective. No complaint need go unheard. The government services were usually competent and considerate. The temper of government was unusually open and responsive, and government proceeded almost always by persuasion in preference to coercion. A blander, more liberal, regime, had not been known in Canada before, and was rare elsewhere in the world.

Yet, partly because life was for most Canadians a liberating experience, partly because life itself is change, and change brings conflict, there were deep disharmonies in Canadian society. The resentment of inequality caused by class was passing; class itself was changed, as education and taxation tended to diminish the transmission of wealth and opportunity from generation to generation. The growth of affluence made equality more possible, even if affluence itself made more conspicuous and more painful to bear the poverty of those who remained poor.

The resentments expressed were rather those of groups than classes. In Quebec, for example, the response of many, particularly of young people in Montreal, was the assertion that the French were a colonized people, exploited by Anglo-American capital for its own enrichment. Some of them, a lunatic fringe, exploded bombs to try to coerce opinion – a throwback to the anarchists of the nineteenth century. Eventually this led to kidnapping and murder.

The violence was to be suppressed in October 1970

by the proclamation of the War Measures Act, which gives the federal government unlimited authority to suppress subversive or violent agitation. But the discontent both grew and clarified. The Liberal government of Jean Lesage in Quebec set out to make the French masters in their own house, the province of Quebec. It was not enough; neither was the demand of the Union Nationale, under Daniel Johnson as premier from 1966 to 1970, for equality or independence.

In 1968, René Lévesque, a member of Lesage's cabinet, founded with some able colleagues, Claude Morin and Jacques Parizeau, a separatist party, soon to be called the Parti Québécois. Its aim was nothing less than total independence for Quebec, with special relations with Canada. In 1976, the P.Q would win a large majority in the Quebec legislature. Whatever happened in consequence, English-French relations could never be the same again.

As the national reassessment continued, the Indians of Canada, for their part, found spokesmen, both among themselves and among European Canadians, who declared the place of Indians in Canadian society intolerable. What seemed to emerge was that Indians were being stirred to protest against the recognition given native rights in existing treaties, and also to seek guarantees of their special position in certain parts of the country – Quebec (particularly in the James Bay area), the Maritimes, British Columbia and along the pipeline corridors of the North-West Territories. The effect was to bring into question both the past settlements and the ground of any future settlement.

Much federal money continues to be spent on research, judicial hearings and lawsuits, to the benefit of students and of lawyers. The issues are: will Indians come into the mainstream of Canadian life or will they be given their own separate enclaves, rights and privileges within the general body of Canada? Whatever the final decisions may be, one thing is clear: here, too, things can never be the same again.

Prairie farmers, British Columbia loggers and fishermen, and their ever-widening business and intellectual communities, holding their own regional views of the Canadian ideal, argued hotly that they were neglected and disregarded by an Ottawa deafened by uproars from Quebec. This behaviour was, of course, familiar enough. What was new in Alberta and British Columbia – not in well-balanced but limited Manitoba, not in Saskatchewan, still the great wheat farm – was a strong sense that the provincial economies were on the verge of adding to the primary industries of agriculture and fruit growing, of oil raising and timber felling, secondary industries and their own financial centres. The founding of the Bank of British Columbia was a symbol of this hope of economic maturity.

Backed by a steady increase in population, these hopes caused the two most western provinces to give added weight to the voice of the West. In the mid-1970s, as Conservatism seemed poised for a return to popularity, a determined effort was made to tempt (or even cajole) the Albertan Premier, Peter Lougheed, to Ottawa. While he was not to be drawn from his prosperous province, another Albertan, the younger Joseph Clark, from High River, was chosen as leader of the federal Tories. These several omens foreshadowed the time when the population and wealth of Ontario and Quebec might be balanced by those of the two provinces on either side of the Rockies.

In one sense, that of ultimate disharmony, the most disturbing agitation was that for women's liberation – liberation from the role that the wider society of which Canada was but a part had determined for women, particularly in the laws governing marriage and property. Even more constricting, perhaps, were the customs and male assumptions which limited opportunities for women to work in paid jobs, to make careers for themselves, and to rise to the top of their professions.

The movement was, in fact, a wave from Europe and the United States. But it had its own Canadian sources and channels. From the days early in the century in which Grace Hoodless had founded the Women's Institute for mutual help among women, in which Nellie McClung, Theresa Casgrain, and Janey Canuck battled for the vote for women, the roles and place of women in Canadian society had increased and grown. Women had become persons in law, full citizens, and capable of considerable careers in the professions and in industry. But acceptance by men of the new roles, laws and social customs, lagged far behind the actual changes, clogging and thwarting the final breaking of the ancient chrysalis. Women liberationists demanded the final breakthrough that would allow any woman personal independence, the means and the opportunity to make her way in the world, and full acceptance of her separate personality, free of the customary bonds of sex. It was asking much of a society still basically conservative.

When the first fury of the women's liberation brigade was spent, the great battlefront had broken against the hills and hollows of the ingrained custom of a patriarchal society and the sinewy tortuosities of man-made law. It had become a series of slow sieges of particular points and of skirmishes against such things as the misuse of feminine charms in advertising. Careers for independent women were perhaps made easier, or would be, and the property of married couples would be shared equally. Here, as in the other changes of the time, a quarter century of affluence made possible what would not be possible in hard times. In the brutalities of a depression, many working women might again go to the wall.

Canada, then, stood poised between the achievements of the past and the demands of the future. In the achievements lay the hope of meeting the demands. What Canada had become was earnest of what it might be.

It was, for example, re-equipping itself as a modern technological society. Such a society rests on the accumulation and analysis of information on a scale beyond the powers of human hand and brain. Only mechanical means powered by electronic impulse can now handle the information needed. In the capitals of government and the centres of business, therefore, computers in ever-growing numbers worked as tirelessly as the spin of the globe to do the task of counting, storing, retrieving the information without which government was blind and business inept. Research, the preoccupation yesterday of the scholar and the scientist, had moved to the centre of the world's affairs.

To know what to do requires the power to do it. Canada, rich in coal and oil and water power, now was turning even to the powers locked in the nucleus of the atom, the strange powers of repulsion and attraction that held matter in the bonds of energy. At Point Douglas in Ontario the first of Canada's thermo-nuclear power plants was already feeding electrical energy into the grid in 1967. Its many difficulties as the first of such thermo-nuclear plants, the Canadian heavy-water kind, were being overcome, and a similar and larger plant was building at Pickering. With the new hydro-electric complexes at Churchill Falls in Labrador, Manicouagan in Quebec, Portage Mountain in northern British Columbia, and the plants along the Nelson River in Manitoba, Canada was powering itself from its northern waters and the rich uranium ores of the Shield with a giant's strength to exploit the elements, as well as creating a dwarf's finesse to weave the sophisticated wares of the transistor, the laser and the infra-nuclear world.

Much of the work of the future would be the old labour of the mine, the forest and the field, but here, too, modern technology and engineering were changing both the materials sought and the means to handle them. The shovel and the wheelbarrow were almost objects of archaeology. The refining of uranium ore at Port Hope had become almost as exquisite a matter as the distillation of the elixir of life, – although there would be a price to pay in the careless disposal of radio-active wastes. Nothing for nothing was still the Canadian axiom.

The ancient and basic life of farming was changing no less, responding to all forms of technology. Chickens were reared on assembly lines, hogs artificially bred, harvesting and threshing combined in ever more elaborate machines. Even the cow was semi-mechanized. The vastness of the total effort was shown in the long lines of canned foods on the shelves of the supermarkets, the long pythons of the grain trains gliding through the forests of the Shield or the clefts of the Rockies to the many-cylindered terminal elevators of Thunder Bay or Vancouver.

The harvesting of the forests, grown wild on the folds of the Shield or the slopes of the Rockies, underwent a transformation of methods not less far-reaching. Long gone were the axe, the cross-cut saw, the great steam tractors and puffing-billy locomotives of the beginning of the century. Power saws to fell and lop and cut, steel cable to haul, and caterpillar tractors to move over any terrain that would bear their wide-spread weight, these had made getting the timber out of the bush a swift, all-season business. And when the saw logs and wood-pulp billets came to the mills they moved to different fates than in the old sawmills with their shrieking saws and the old pulp mills with their nauseous fumes. According to kind and quality, the billet moved swiftly through the digesting ovens to come out pulp, ready for baking into papers of all qualities, into cardboard for containers of infinite variety, or into plastics drawn from cellulose. Saw logs might emerge as beams, planks, boards as of old, or be sliced paper-thin on whirring chisels to make plywood or veneer, the chips to make wallboard or other composites. Many an ancient industry had been remade and diversified. Nothing could have meant more for Canada with its millions of square miles of forest lands fit for little other use.

On the ocean fisheries, a similar process was in train. The old trade of sail and line, of net and salt, had like the small farm become a trap of poverty. People would not suffer, nor government allow, such poverty as had scarred the emaciated outposts of Newfoundland and Nova Scotia. Many moved inland to the factories and the mines. Those who continued in the fisheries had to find capital, by co-operative action and government help, to buy large fishing trawlers with sonar, radar, power services and deep-water drags, if they were to take fish in the quantity that alone would pay. So the dories rotted on the beaches, the schooners became nags of the sea till the sea claimed their shapely, slattern hulls, and a few trim, costly trawlers ploughed the banks with stern efficiency.

The obvious booming health of the Canadian economy beckoned to surplus populations abroad and the influx of immigrants began to match the human tides of the turn of the century. In the decade after the end of the Second World War, two million 'New Canadians' arrived and, this time, most of them stayed, soon accumulating enough savings to send for relatives still in the homelands. Many of these people, eager to enjoy the vaunted North American 'standard of living,' came from eastern Europe, and from Italy and Holland, thus further thinning the old British-French balancing percentages in the population and hastening the development of the pervasive 'melting pot' society and culture so characteristic of the United States.

Fear of total absorption into that culture, as heralded by the already large American business holdings in the country, was never far from the surface of Canadian thought, particularly among the upper levels of the federal public service and in the universities. Was there indeed to be a true Canadian identity and cultural achievement, outside the bucolic *habitant* novel and the Group of Seven painters? At smart cocktail parties in the high-rise apartment blocks now spiking the cities it was wryly amusing to comment that Canada had been blest with British political wisdom, French culture and American know-how but had somehow finished up with British know-how, French political wisdom and American culture.

Canada should by rights have a thriving native literature. Few countries are richer, for instance, in the literature of exploration and travel, from Lescarbot's *Nova Francia* and Champlain's *Voyages*, through the *Relations* of the Jesuit missionaries to the traveller's tales of Kalm, Hearne, Mackenzie, the explorers like Hind and Palliser and the geologists like J.B. Tyrell. But it is all a report on Canada; it does not by imagination interpret and make familiar the land. The descriptive pioneer writing of immigrants Anna Jameson, Susanna Moodie and many similar in the nineteenth century was basically of this kind.

Much of the early French Canadian writing informs, sometimes with feeling, but it is not itself feeling. It is really a literature of nostalgia, what critic Edmund Wilson termed the 'seigneurial' literature. Even the one haunting tale of the central years, Peter Mitchell's *The Yellow Briar*, is a tale merely, lacking both plot and character study. Of imaginative insight, social concern, personal characterization, the Canadian writer was rarely capable. There were, of course, precious exceptions – among older writers of our times such as Bliss Carman, Robertson Davies, E.J. Pratt, Hugh MacLennan, Morley Callaghan – but the best-known of all, humorist Stephen Leacock, was English-born if Ontario-bred, and as literature his work was perhaps supercilious and even tawdry. Ethel Wilson, superbly evocative novelist of Vancouver, had roots in South Africa and England. Malcolm Lowry, brooding drunken genius, was an Englishman, setting foot in Canada at age thirty.

Among younger novelists however, Canada was beginning to produce more work of unquestionable Canadian authenticity and of imaginative range and insight: Roger Lemelin, Margaret Laurence, W.O. Mitchell, Margaret Atwood, Marie-Claire Blais, Mordecai Richler. Their best work is valid literature, uncomplicated by any concern with nationality, or national achievement. It stands on its own feet. Neither did it require aid from the state.

On the crest of the sustained postwar boom, with surplus revenues pouring into the tax coffers, the time, however, was deemed ripe to try to accelerate change in the cultural scene also. If the artists – the writers, painters, composers, playwrights, choreographers – were already there, perhaps what was needed was the elevation of public taste? With due regard for the Canadian precedent, a royal commission was set up in 1949 to investigate, analyse and report.

It had, of course, a fulsome title but everybody called it the Massey Commission, from its well-known chairman, Vincent Massey, former history lecturer and later chancellor of the University of Toronto, president of the Massey-Harris farm implements company, first Canadian Minister to Washington, the wartime High Commissioner in London, holder of the select British distinction Companion of Honour. It was not exactly a surprise that Massey's report in 1951 did find the fragile arts in danger of drowning under the cross-border torrents but what was new, even revolutionary, even unconstitutional, was his main recommendation that federal tax money be doled out to strengthen the universities on a provincial per capita basis and that a copy of the British Council be set up to 'encourage' the arts, letters, humanities and social sciences. The recommendations soon had the force of law.

By the clauses of the British North America Act, education was the exclusive field of the provinces – and Ottawa was soon snubbed by Quebec's *nationaliste* Premier Maurice Duplessis who ordered the universities of his province to refuse the money. The use of federal money to assist universities by grants was a few years later ended as an invasion of a provincial responsibility. But aid to research in the arts and social sciences was achieved anyway by another result of the Massey Commission, the Canada Council. That body was funded at the outset by a clever allotment of a windfall $50 million in death duties from the estates of two of the last of the old multi-millionaires, a redistribution of wealth that the possessors had not chosen themselves to give in patronage.

Vincent Massey went on to serve for two terms as the first native-born Governor-General, and his Canada Council began its experiment of the force-feeding of the arts with public funds. The lead was eagerly followed by lookalike provincial and even municipal agencies. No one really supposed that genius could be purchased, but after the Canada Council's first full score years of life, it had become so omnipresent as a banker for the national culture machine that many critics drew attention to a falling-away of previously inadequate, but at least voluntary, community support. Certainly, it became an accepted fact that most of the nation's best-known theatres (in both languages), all of its symphony orchestras, its domestic opera and ballet, could not continue at anything like present levels without tax support, and might indeed be forced to close without it.

With an estimated one-third of all Canadian cultural activity (admittedly, a difficult measure to take with any exactitude, but including an increasing amount of book, magazine and even newspaper publishing) being bankrolled by the state, some further questions were asked with growing frequency. Was the outpouring of public money on the arts bringing significant benefit to the broad mass of the citizenry who willy-nilly paid by far the greater portion of the bill, or did it rather confer a special benefit on a much smaller (if highly vocal) group whose cultural needs or aspirations outran their willingness or ability to pay for them?

Could all future governments be trusted to refrain from covertly or openly manipulating the propaganda instruments the public treasuries were funding? If our higher culture remained dependent upon government grant, what would the position be in a recession or depression? The politician in a democracy who seeks to retain his seat of power must finally be responsive to the majority.

With some heartening exceptions, the majority of Canadians seem as yet little changed in their cultural preferences and perceptions. It is still the imported Broadway hit that packs the Canadian theatre; it is the American, and occasionally the British, television entertainment that wins the home audience; it is mostly the sensational American 'bestseller' that is read. No matter how the sophisticate may wring his hands, the battle remains to be won and the winning cannot be soon. Perhaps a long-term answer lies in the upgrading of instruction in the schools, with exposure to the more esoteric arts in the earliest grades, and in the encouragement of regional arts centres built and run with the maximum of grass-roots support and participation.

While these many problems – cultural, commercial, constitutional – vexed and disturbed Canada's middle age, it was entirely clear that the age of easy grandiloquence and easy progress based on the sale of natural resources was over. From Laurier to Trudeau marked the transition from a simple frontier society, graced by its comparatively few professional and learned folk, but plain-minded, hard-working, spottily puritanical and capable of rowdiness, to a society drained of eagerness, sceptical, cynical, nourishing a deepening sense of frustration or loss. Not only was there no magic any more; neither was there any verity or any simplicity. Canadian society had matured, all too quickly, to a maturity all too shallow and all too brittle. In such a condition, the country faced possible division into English and French states, absorption by a reluctant even unwilling United States, and the quick withering of the Canadian evanescence of the twentieth century.

So, at least, it seemed in the hurrying years that followed the centennial euphoria. What was there in the Canadian experience to trigger such a fall? The bright sun clouded in its arc. This land, these people, the things done, the fields cleared and cities built, would remain and carry on. The people would die and come again. But would there remain any trace, any fragrance, of the thing called Canadian and loved as such for six generations of men and women who sought no other name, no other experience than the making of Canada?

Part VI

A Chronology of Canada

No one-volume story about Canada can be definitive and in this book, furthermore, the usual regimen of dates and detailed documentation, the campaign records of the wars, have been deliberately set aside in favour of a narrative "story approach." This will perhaps nettle the scholar but will, hopefully, catch and hold the attention of those to whom the genuinely interesting Canadian chronicle has too often been just a dusty duty. To fill any gaps, and to succour the student faced with the inevitable history "projects," the authors offer the following thousand-year chronology.

*986   Bjarni Herjólfsson sights northeastern coasts.

1001   Leif Eiriksson discovers Helluland, Markland, Vinland.

1004   Thorvaldr Eiriksson sails to Vinland.

1007   Thorsteinn Eiriksson attempts to reach Vinland but fails.

1011-13   Thorfinnr Karlsefni and wife, Gudridr, attempt to colonize Vinland, and their son, Snorri, is born.

1014-15   Freydis, half sister of Leif Eiriksson, makes second abortive colonization attempt in Vinland.

1480   Bristol traders send ships into western sea, possibly sighting eastern coasts.

1497   John Cabot plants first English flag in Canada on Cape Breton.

1498   John Cabot vanishes on second western voyage.

1500-1   Gaspar Corte-Real traces the east coast to Labrador, and is lost at sea.

1502   Miguel Corte-Real reaches Newfoundland, and is also lost.

1524   Giovanni de Verrazzano, with a French commission, visits eastern coasts.

1525   Estevão Gomes reaches Cape Breton.

1527   Englishman John Rut in Newfoundland and Labrador.

1534   Jacques Cartier raises French flag on Gaspé Penninsula.

1535   Cartier on second voyage, reaches sites of Quebec and Montreal.

1541   The Sieur de Roberval (and Cartier) attempt colonization of Quebec.

1576   Martin Frobisher reaches Baffin Island, seeking North-West Passage; repeats voyage the next two years.

1578   Marquis de la Roche appointed Viceroy of New France.

1578   Sir Francis Drake claims Pacific coast for Queen Elizabeth I as 'New Albion.'

1583   Sir Humphrey Gilbert lays formal claim to Newfoundland (still thought to be the mainland); establishes Anglican Church.

1585-6-7   John Davis makes his three Arctic voyages.

1600   Pierre Chauvin and Pontgravé begin fur trade at Tadoussac.

1602   George Weymouth explores around Baffin Bay.

1603   The Sieur de Monts and Samuel Champlain at Quebec.

1604   St. John River (N.B.) discovered and named.

1604   De Monts and Champlain establish settlement on island in the St. Croix River, Bay of Fundy.

1605   Port Royal (Annapolis Royal, N.S.) founded; granted to the Sieur de Poutrincourt.

1606   John Knight's expedition disappears in Labrador.

1608   Champlain establishes Quebec *Habitation*.

1609   Champlain ascends the Richelieu to Lake Champlain.

1610-11   Henry Hudson discovers his inland sea, or bay, and is set adrift by mutineers.

1612-13   Welshman Sir Thomas Button seeks the North-West Passage from Hudson Bay, taking possession of hinterland for England.

1613   Champlain explores the Ottawa River.

1615   Récollet friars arrive from France.

1615-16   Robert Bylot and William Baffin explore the eastern Arctic seaways.

1617   Louis Hébert, the 'first farmer,' brings family to New France.

1619   Danish Jens Munck spends a disastrous winter in Hudson Bay.

1621   Sir William Alexander granted Nova Scotia by James VI.

1628   David Kirke captures French colonizing fleet en route to Quebec.

1629   Kirke brothers capture Quebec, held by England for four years.

1631-32   Luke Fox(e) and Thomas James broaden knowledge of Hudson Bay area.

1639   Ursuline nuns arrive at Quebec.

1642   The Sieur de Maisonneuve founds Montreal as missionary outpost.

1649-50   Jesuits Brébeuf and Lalement martyred by the Iroquois.

1663   Royal government instituted by Louis XIV.

* The chronology of the Viking voyages is impossible to establish with certainty and a margin of error of up to ten years in some cases must be accepted.

233

1665	Marquis de Tracy brings the Carignan-Salières Regiment to Quebec.
1670	Hudson's Bay Company is chartered by Charles II.
1672	The Comte de Frontenac appointed Governor of New France (first term).
1673	Louis Jolliet and Père Marquette discover the Mississippi.
1680	The Sieur de la Salle builds Fort Crèvecoeur on the Illinois.
1682	La Salle descends to the mouth of the Mississippi.
1689	Frontenac returns as Governor of New France; massacre by Indians at Lachine.
1690	Frontenac defends Quebec against Sir William Phips.
1690	Henry Kelsey of HBC reaches site of Saskatoon.
1697	Le Moyne d'Iberville captures York Factory.
1701	Cadillac builds the first fort at Detroit.
1710	Port Royal, Acadia, captured by the British.
1713	Acadia and Hudson Bay territories surrendered to Great Britain by Treaty of Utrecht.
1717	Fort Churchill built by Hudson's Bay Company.
1731-39	La Vérendryes establish a chain of trading and defence posts in the Prairies while searching for the Western Sea.
1745	Louisbourg, Cape Breton, captured by New Englanders; restored to the French, 1748.
1749	Edward Cornwallis founds fortress of Halifax.
1754	Anthony Henday sees the Canadian Rockies.
1755	The expulsion of the Acadians.
1758	Louisbourg taken by General Amherst.
1759	General James Wolfe captures Quebec.
1763	Canada passes to Great Britain by Treaty of Paris.
1768	Sir Guy Carleton (later, Lord Dorchester) appointed Governor.
1771	Samuel Hearne goes overland to the Arctic Ocean.
1774	Quebec Act makes Catholics eligible for public office, safeguards religion, extends boundaries down the Ohio and Mississippi.
1774	Americans invite Canadians to join the War of Independence.
1775	Americans capture Montreal, fail to take Quebec.
1779	Foundation of the North West Company.
1781	American Revolution succeeds with fall of Yorktown.
1785	Saint John, N.B., first Canadian city to be incorporated by royal charter.
1787	Charles Inglis appointed Anglican Bishop of Nova Scotia.
1788	Captain James Cook spends a month at Nootka, B.C.
1789	Alexander Mackenzie's expedition to the Arctic Ocean.
1791	Constitutional Act creates Provinces of Upper and Lower Canada.
1792	John Graves Simcoe, first Governor of Upper Canada, chooses Newark (Niagara-on-the-Lake) as capital.
1792	Captain Vancouver charts Vancouver Island, names it Burrard Inlet.
1793	Alexander Mackenzie reaches the Pacific by land.
1794	Simcoe moves his capital to York (Toronto).
1803	Lord Selkirk sends Scottish settlers to Prince Edward Island.
1807	David Thompson explores the Columbia River.
1808	Simon Fraser descends the Fraser River to the Pacific.
1809	John Molson builds first steamship at Montreal.
1811-12	Selkirk acquires 45 million acres along Red River and establishes nucleus settlement of Manitoba.
1812-14	War with the United States; successful defence against invasion on Niagara Peninsula and the St. Lawrence.
1816	Governor Semple of Red River Colony killed by Métis in the 'fur wars.'
1817	Rush-Bagot Agreement with U.S. limits armaments on Great Lakes and St. Lawrence.
1817	Montreal and York (Toronto) linked by regular stage coach.
1819-22 (and 25-27)	Sir John Franklin explores the Arctic coasts.
1821	Merger of Hudson's Bay and North West Companies.
1825	Lachine Canal opened at Montreal.
1829	Opening of the Welland Canal, bypassing Niagara Falls.
1832	Opening of the Rideau Canal, Ottawa-Kingston.

1836	First Canadian railroad connects La Prairie and St. Jean, Que.
1837	Papineau and Mackenzie Rebellions.
1839	Dr. John Strachan appointed Anglican Bishop of Toronto.
1839	Lord Durham's Report recommends unification (done 1841) and opens door to responsible government.
1843	Victoria, Vancouver Island, founded.
1845	Franklin lost in effort to pass through North-West Passage.
1846	The Canada-U.S.A. border continued along 49th parallel to the Pacific.
1846	City of Hamilton incorporated.
1848	Responsible government established in Nova Scotia.
1848	City of Fredericton incorporated.
1849	Annexation Manifesto (Montreal) proposes union with the United States.
1849	Mobs in Montreal burn the Houses of Parliament.
1849	Reciprocity offered by Canada to United States.
1849	Vancouver Island created a Crown Colony.
1851	First postage stamps issued in Canada.
1853	Grand Trunk Railway to link Lake Huron and Atlantic.
1854	Clergy Reserves are secularized, seigneurial system abolished.
1857	James Miller Williams brings in first successful oil well.
1858	Gold rush in British Columbia begins.
1864	Confederation conferences at Charlottetown and Quebec.
1866	Fenian raids on Canada.
1866	Colonies of Vancouver Island and British Columbia united.
1867	Dominion of Canada inaugurated with Sir John A. Macdonald as first prime minister.
1868	Assassination of D'Arcy McGee.
1870	Canada takes over Rupert's Land and Manitoba established as a province.
1870	First Riel Rebellion.
1871	British Columbia joins the Dominion.
1873	Prince Edward Island joins the Dominion.
1873	City of Winnipeg incorporated.
1874	North-West Mounted Police organized.
1876	Alexander Graham Bell first demonstrates telephone (Brantford, Ont.).
1879	'National Policy' of tariffs adopted to encourage Canadian industry.
1880	Britain transfers title to the Arctic islands to Canada.
1881	Canadian Pacific Railway construction begun; last spike driven 1885.
1884	Discovery of copper and nickel at Sudbury, Ont.
1885	Second Riel Rebellion; militia brought by rail from east crushes Métis at Batoche, Sask.
1886	City of Vancouver incorporated.
1892	Discovery of lead, zinc and silver at Kimberley, B.C.
1893	First Canadian auto produced.
1896	Sir Wilfrid Laurier becomes first French-Canadian prime minister; western Canada opened to immigration.
1896	Gold discovered on the Klondike River, Yukon.
1899-1902	Canadian volunteers fight in South African Boer Rebellion.
1900-13	Peak of railway expansion; three transcontinental lines.
1901	Coal and steel production begins at Sydney, N.S.
1903	Silver discovered at Cobalt, Ont.
1903	City of Regina incorporated.
1904	Marquis rust-resistant spring wheat introduced.
1905	Provinces of Alberta and Saskatchewan are formed.
1906	City of Saskatoon incorporated.
1908	Prince of Wales (George V) visits Quebec for tercentenary celebrations.
1909	Gold found at Porcupine, Ont.
1911	A Reciprocity Agreement proposed by U.S. defeated.
1914-18	Canadian Expeditionary Force serves in World War I.
1919	Prime Minister Robert Borden insists that Canada sign the Treaty of Versailles on its own behalf; Canada becomes independent member of League of Nations.
1921	William Lyon Mackenzie King begins his first period as prime minister.
1921	Frederick G. Banting discovers insulin.
1927	First foreign legation established (Washington).
1930	Gilbert LaBine discovers radium at Great Bear Lake.
1931	Statute of Westminster formally confirms independence of British Dominions.
1936	Oil begins to flow from Turner Valley, Alta.
1939-45	More than one million Canadians serve in World War II.

1940	Commonwealth Air Training Plan begins on one hundred Canadian airfields.	**1954**	St. Lawrence Seaway construction begins with American collaboration.
1944	RCMP ship *St. Roch* sails the North-West Passage in 86 days.	**1954**	Labrador iron ore reaches Sept Iles by new railroad.
1945	Russian spy ring uncovered in Ottawa.	**1957**	Lester B. Pearson (prime minister, 1963-68) wins Nobel Peace Prize; Canadian forces begin UN peace-keeping assignments.
1945	Canada becomes charter member of the United Nations Organization, as elective member of the Security Council.	**1957**	NORAD combined U.S.-Canadian air-command, organized for instant continental defence.
1947	Oil in huge quantities tapped at Leduc, Alta.	**1960**	Prime Minister John Diefenbaker (1957-63) brings in Bill of Rights.
1948	Prime Minister King retires after creating longevity record for British parliamentary leaders.	**1964**	Unification of armed forces by Paul T. Hellyer, Minister of National Defence.
1949	Newfoundland joins the Dominion as tenth province.	**1965**	Maple leaf emblem proclaimed as official Canadian flag.
1949	Louis St. Laurent, second French-Canadian prime minister, leads Canada into NATO alliance; abolishes appeals to British Privy Council.	**1967**	Centennial of Confederation celebrated at World's Fair (Expo), Montreal; visited by sixty heads of state.
1950-53	Canada fights in Korea to repel Communist agression.	**1968**	Pierre Elliott Trudeau becomes Liberal leader and prime minister; Canada moves into its second century as a federated state.
1951	Canadian Brigade and air units join NATO allies in Germany.	**1976**	Parti Québécois wins Quebec provincial election on separatist platform.
1952	Vincent Massey becomes first Canadian appointed as Governor-General.		

Bibliography

Amundsen, Roald. *The Northwest Passage.* New York: Dutton, 1906.
   My Life as an Explorer. London: Heinemann, 1927.
Archer, John H. and Koester, Charles B. *Footprints in Time. A Source Book in the History of Saskatchewan.* Toronto: House of Grant, 1965.

Babcock, W. H. *Legendary Islands of the Atlantic.* New York: American Geographical Society, 1922.
Back, Captain George. *Narrative of an Expedition in H.M.S. Terror in 1836-37.* London: Murray, 1838.
Backman, Brian and Phil. *Bluenose.* Toronto: McClelland & Stewart, 1965.
Berton, Pierre. *The Mysterious North.* New York: Knopf, 1956.
   The Great Railway. (2 vols.) Toronto: McClelland & Stewart, 1970.
   Klondike. Toronto: McClelland & Stewart, 1958.
   My Country. Toronto: McClelland & Stewart, 1976.
Bird, Will R. *These Are the Maritimes.* Toronto: Ryerson Press, 1959.
Bishop, Morris. *Champlain: The Life of Fortitude.* New York: Knopf, 1948.
Bolger, Francis W. P. *Prince Edward Island and Confederation.* Charlottetown: St. Dunstan's University Press, 1964.
Borden, Henry. ed. *Robert Laird Borden: His Memoirs.* Toronto: Macmillan, 1938.
Bowes, G. E., ed. *Peace River Chronicles.* Vancouver: Prescott Publishing, 1963.

Brebner, J. B. *Explorers of North America, 1492-1806.* New York: Macmillan, 1933.
   North Atlantic Triangle. Toronto: Ryerson Press, 1945.
   Canada, a Modern History. Ann Arbor: University of Michigan Press, 1960.
Broadfoot, Barry. *Ten Lost Years, 1929-1939.* Toronto: Doubleday, 1973.
Buchan, John. ed. *British America.* Boston: Houghton, Mifflin, 1923.
Burpee, L. J. *Pathfinders of the Great Plains.* Toronto: Glasgow, Brook, 1914.

Callbeck, Lorne C. *Cradle of Confederation.* Fredericton: Brunswick Press, 1964.
   Cambridge History of the British Empire. (Vol. VI) Cambridge: Cambridge University Press, 1930.
Cameron, Alex A. and Tordarson, Leo. *Prairie Progress.* Toronto: Dent, 1954.
Careless, J. M. S. *Brown of the Globe.* (2 Vols.) Toronto: Macmillan, 1959.
   Canada, a Story of Challenge. Toronto: Macmillan, 1963.
   The Union of the Canadas, 1841-1857. Toronto: McClelland & Stewart, 1967.
Carrington, Philip. *The Anglican Church in Canada.* Toronto: Collins, 1963.
Cashman, A. W. *The Edmonton Story.* Edmonton: Institute of Applied Art, 1956.

Chadwick, St. John. *Newfoundland, Island into Province*. London: Cambridge University Press, 1967.

Clark, A. H. *Three Centuries and the Island*. Toronto: University of Toronto Press, 1959.
Acadia, the Geography of Early Nova Scotia to 1760. Madison: University of Wisconsin Press, 1968.

Clark, S. D. *The Developing Canadian Community*. Toronto: University of Toronto Press, 1962.

Collins, Robert. *A Great Way To Go, the Automobile in Canada*. Toronto: Ryerson Press, 1969.

Cowan, Helen I. *British Emigration to British North America: The First Hundred Years*. Revised. Toronto: University of Toronto Press, 1961.

Cowan, John. *Canada's Governors-General*. Toronto: York Publishing, 1965.

Craig, Gerald M., ed. *Early Travellers in the Canadas, 1791-1867*. Toronto: Macmillan, 1955.
Upper Canada, 1784-1841. Toronto: McClelland & Stewart, 1963.

Creighton, D. G. *John A. Macdonald*. (2 Vols.) Toronto: Macmillan, 1955.
Dominion of the North. Toronto: Macmillan, 1944.
The Empire of the St. Lawrence. Toronto: Macmillan, 1956.
Canada's First Century. Toronto: Macmillan, 1970.
Towards the Discovery of Canada. Toronto: Macmillan, 1972.

Crouse, Nellis M. *The Search for the North Pole*. New York: Smith, 1947.

Cruikshank, E. A., ed. *The Settlement of the United Empire Loyalists in 1784*. Toronto: Ontario Historical Society, 1934.

Dafoe, John W. *Clifford Sifton in Relation to his Times*. Toronto, Macmillan, 1931.
Canada: an American Nation. New York: Columbia University Press, 1935.

Davidson, C. G. *The Northwest Company*. Berkeley: University of California Press, 1918.

Dawson, R. McG. *W. L. Mackenzie King, a Political Biography*. Toronto: University of Toronto Press, 1958.

Debenham, Frank. *The Polar Regions*. London: Benn, 1930.

De Boilieu, Lambert. *Recollections of Labrador Life*. Toronto: Ryerson Press, 1969.

De Fronsac, Viscount. *Rise of the United Empire Loyalists*. Kingston: British Whig Publishing, 1906.

Dollier de Casson, François. *History of Montreal, 1640-1672*. Toronto: Dent, 1928.

Donaldson, Gordon. *Fifteen Men*. Toronto: Doubleday, 1969.

Doughty, Arthur G. *The Acadian Exiles*. Toronto: Glasgow, Brook, 1916.

Duncan, Dorothy. *Bluenose, a Portrait of Nova Scotia*. New York: Harper, 1942.

Eastman, S. Mack. *Church and State in Early Canada*. Edinburgh: The University Press, 1915.

Eccles, W. J. *Frontenac: The Courtier Governor*. Toronto: McClelland & Stewart, 1959.
Canada under Louis XIV, 1663-1701. Toronto: McClelland & Stewart, 1964.

Eggleston, Wilfrid. *The Queen's Choice*. Ottawa: Queen's Printer, 1961.

Eifert, V. S. *Louis Jolliet, Explorer of Rivers*. New York: Dodd, Mead, 1961.

Fairley, T. C. *Sverdrup's Arctic Adventure*. Toronto: Longman, 1959.

Farb, Peter. *Man's Rise to Civilization as Shown by the Indians of North America*. New York: Dutton, 1968.

Ferns, H. S. and Ostry, B. *The Age of Mackenzie King*. London: Heinemann, 1955.

Firth, Edith G., ed. *The Town of York, 1793-1815*. Toronto: University of Toronto Press, 1962.

Franklin, Sir John. *Narrative of a Journey to the Shores of the Polar Sea in 1819-22*. London: Murray, 1823.

Freuchen, Peter. *Book of the Eskimos*. New York: World Publishing, 1961.

Freuchen, Peter and Salomonsen, Finn. *The Arctic Year*. New York: Putnam, 1958.

Gibbon, John Murray. *Steel of Empire*. New York: Bobbs-Merrill, 1935.

Glazebrook, G. P. de T. *Canadian External Relations: an Historical Study to 1914*. Toronto: Oxford University Press, 1942.
A History of Transportation in Canada. Toronto: Ryerson Press, 1938.
Life in Ontario. Toronto: University of Toronto Press, 1968.

Guillet, E. C. *Early Life in Upper Canada*. Toronto: Ontario Publishing Co., 1933.
The Great Migration. Toronto: Nelson, 1937.

Guillet, Edwin and Mary. *The Pathfinders of North America*. Toronto: Macmillan, 1957.

Hale, Katherine. *Toronto, Romance of a Great City*. Toronto: Cassell, 1956.

Hall, Charles F. *Arctic Researches, and Life among the Esquimaux*. New York: Harper, 1865.
Narrative of the North Polar Expedition, U. S. Ship Polaris. Washington: Government Printing Office, 1876.

Hamil, Fred Coyne. *Lake Erie Baron*. Toronto: Macmillan, 1955.

Hannon, Leslie F. *Canada at War*. Toronto: McClelland & Stewart, 1968.
Forts of Canada. Toronto: McClelland & Stewart, 1969.

Harrington, Richard. *The Face of the Arctic*. New York: Schuman, 1952.

Havighurst, Walter. *Long Ships Passing: the Story of the Great Lakes*. New York: Macmillan, 1942.

Hearne, Samuel. *A Journey to the Northern Ocean*. Toronto: Macmillan, 1958.

Henderson, John. *Great Men of Canada*. Toronto: Southam Press, 1928.

Herrington, W. S. *Pioneer Life Among the Loyalists in Upper Canada*. Toronto: Macmillan, 1915.

Higinbotham, John D. *When the West was Young*. Toronto: Ryerson Press, 1933.

Hill, Douglas. *The Opening of the Canadian West*. London: Heinemann, 1967.

Holland, Vivian. ed. *Into A Nation*. Toronto: Canadian Council of Churches, 1966.

Hood, M. McIntyre. *Oshawa, Canada's Motor City*. Oshawa: McLaughlin Public Library Board, 1969.

Horwood, Harold. *Newfoundland*. Toronto: Macmillan, 1969.

Howay, F. W. *British Columbia, the Making of a Province*. Toronto: Ryerson Press, 1928.

Hunt, G. T. *The Wars of the Iroquois*. Madison: University of Wisconsin Press, 1940.

Hutchison, Bruce. *The Unknown Country: Canada and her People*. Toronto: Longman, 1942.
The Incredible Canadian. Toronto: Longman, 1952.
Canada: Tomorrow's Giant. Toronto: Longman, 1957.
MacDonald to Pearson. Toronto: Longman, 1967.

Innis, H. A. *The Fur Trade in Canada*. Toronto: University of Toronto Press, 1930.

Jackson, Frederick. *A Thousand Days in the Arctic*. New York: Harper, 1899.

Jenness, Diamond. *The People of the Twilight.* Toronto: Macmillan, 1928.

    The Indians of Canada. Ottawa: The Queen's Printer, 1932.

Johnson, F. Henry. *A Brief History of Canadian Education.* Toronto: McGraw-Hill, 1968.

Jones, Gwyn. *The Norse Atlantic Saga.* London: Oxford University Press, 1964.

Kane, Dr. E. K. *Arctic Explorations.* Philadelphia: Childs & Peterson, 1856.

Keating, Bern. *The Grand Banks.* New York: Rand McNally, 1968.

Kenton, Edna. ed. *Jesuit Relations and Allied Documents: Travels and Exploration of Jesuit Missionaries in North America, 1620-1791.* Toronto: McClelland & Stewart, 1963.

Kerr, D. G. G. and Davidson, R. I. K. *Canada: A Visual History.* Toronto: Nelson, 1966.

Kerr, D. G. G. and Gibson, J. A. *Sir Edmund Head: A Scholarly Governor.* Toronto: University of Toronto Press, 1954.

Kyte, E. C., ed. *Old Toronto.* Toronto: Macmillan, 1954.

Laut, A. C. *Conquests of the Great Northwest.* New York: Moffat, Yard, 1911.

Leechman, Douglas. *Native Tribes of Canada.* Toronto: Gage, 1956.

Lescarbot, Marc. *History of New France.* Toronto: Champlain Society, 1907.

Liddell, Ken E. *Alberta Revisited.* Toronto: Ryerson Press, 1960.

Locke, George H. *Builders of the Canadian Commonwealth.* Toronto: Ryerson Press, 1923.

Lower, A. R. M. *Colony to Nation.* Toronto: Longman, 1946.

    Canada, Nation and Neighbour. Toronto: Longman, 1952.

    Canadians in the Making. Toronto: Longman, 1958.

Ludwig, Emil. *Mackenzie King.* Toronto: Macmillan, 1944.

Lunn, Richard and Janet. *The County, the First Hundred Years of Loyalist Prince Edward.* Picton, Ontario: Prince Edward County Council, 1967.

MacEwan, Grant. *Between the Red and the Rockies.* Toronto: University of Toronto Press, 1952.

MacEwan, Grant and Foran, Maxwell. *West to the Sea.* Toronto: McGraw-Hill, 1968.

MacGregor, James G. *Edmonton Trader.* Toronto: McClelland & Stewart, 1963.

    Edmonton, a History. Edmonton: Hurtig, 1967.

McInnis, Edgar. *The Unguarded Frontier.* New York: Doubleday, 1942.

    Canada, a Political and Social History. Toronto: Holt, Rinehart and Winston, 1959.

Mackay, Douglas. *Honourable Company: a History of the Hudson's Bay Company.* Toronto: McClelland & Stewart, 1966.

Mackenzie, Sir Alexander. *Voyages from Montreal through the Continent of North America to the Frozen and Pacific Oceans in 1789 and 1793.* (2 Vols.) Toronto: Radisson Society, 1927.

MacNutt, W. S. *The Atlantic Provinces.* Toronto: McClelland & Stewart, 1965.

Markham, Sir Clements. *The Lands of Silence.* Cambridge: Cambridge University Press, 1921.

Marquis, T. G. *The Jesuit Missions.* Toronto: Glasgow, Brook, 1916.

Martin, Chester. *Lord Selkirk's Work in Canada.* Toronto: Oxford University Press, 1916.

Martyr, Peter. *De Orbe Novo.* (2 Vols.) Edited by F. A. MacNutt. New York: G. P. Putnam's Sons, 1912.

Massey, Vincent. *What's Past is Prologue.* Toronto: Macmillan, 1963.

Mirsky, J. *To the North! The Story of Arctic Exploration.* New York: Viking Press, 1934.

Moody, Dr. J. P. *Arctic Doctor.* New York: Dodd, Mead, 1955.

Morley, Alan. *Vancouver, from Milltown to Metropolis.* Vancouver: Mitchell Press, 1961.

Morton, A. S. *A History of the Canadian West to 1870-71.* Toronto: Nelson, 1939.

Morton, W. L. *The Critical Years.* Toronto: McClelland & Stewart, 1964.

    The Kingdom of Canada. Toronto: McClelland & Stewart, 1969.

    The Canadian Identity. Toronto: University of Toronto Press, 1961.

    The Progressive Party in Canada. Revised ed. Toronto: University of Toronto Press, 1967.

    Manitoba: A History. Toronto: University of Toronto Press, 1957.

Mowat, Farley. *Canada North Now.* Toronto: McClelland & Stewart, 1976.

    The Polar Passion. Toronto: McClelland & Stewart, 1967.

    Westviking. Toronto: Little, Brown and Co., 1965.

Mowat, Grace H. *The Diverting History of a Loyalist Town.* St. Andrews, N. B.: Charlotte County Cottage Craft, 1932.

Munro, Wm. B. *Crusaders of New France.* Toronto: Glasgow, Brook, 1918.

Nansen, F. *Arctic Exploration in Early Times.* London: Heinemann, 1911.

Neatby, H. Blair. *W. L. Mackenzie King.* (Vol. 2) Toronto: University of Toronto Press, 1963.

Neatby, Hilda. *Quebec, the Revolutionary Age, 1760-1791.* Toronto: McClelland & Stewart, 1966.

Neatby, L. H. *The Conquest of the Last Frontier.* Toronto: Longman, 1966.

New, C. W. *Lord Durham.* London: Oxford University Press, 1929.

Nute, G. L. *Caesars of the Wilderness.* New York: Appleton-Century, 1943.

Oleson, T. J. *Early Voyages and Northern Approaches.* Toronto: McClelland & Stewart, 1964.

Ormsby, Margaret A. *British Columbia: A History.* Toronto: Macmillan, 1958.

Pain, S. Q. *Three Miles of Gold, the Story of Kirkland Lake.* Toronto: Ryerson Press, 1960.

Parker, John P. *Cape Breton Ships and Men.* Toronto: McLeod, 1967.

Parkman, Francis. *La Salle and the Discovery of the Great West.* Boston: Little, Brown, 1913.

    The Old Regime in Canada. Boston: Little, Brown, 1909.

    A Half-Century of Conflict. Boston: Little, Brown, 1909.

Parry, Sir Edward. *Journal of a Voyage for the Discovery of the N. W. Passage in 1819-20.* London: Murray, 1921.

Partridge, B. *Amundsen, the Splendid Norseman.* New York: Stokes, 1929.

Peary, R. E. *Nearest the Pole.* London: Hutchinson, 1907.

Pollard, W. C. *Pioneering in the Prairie West.* Toronto: Nelson, 1926.

Raddall, Thomas H. *Halifax, Warden of the North.* Toronto: McClelland & Stewart, 1948.

    Path of Destiny. Toronto: Doubleday, 1957.

Rasmussen, Knud. *Across Arctic America.* New York: Putnam, 1927.

Reaman, G. Elmore. *The Trail of the Black Walnut.* Toronto: McClelland & Stewart, 1957.

Reed, C. B. *The First Great Canadian, Sieur D'Iberville.* Chicago: McClung, 1910.

Rich, E. E. *History of the Hudson's Bay Company, 1670-1870.* (2 Vols.) London: Hudson's Bay Record Society, 1958-1959.
The Fur Trade and the Northwest to 1857. Toronto: McClelland & Stewart, 1967.

Ross, Alexander. *The Red River Settlement.* Edmonton: Hurtig, 1972.

Ross, A. H. D. *Ottawa, Past and Present.* Toronto: Musson, 1927.

Scadding, Henry. *Toronto of Old.* Toronto: Oxford University Press, 1966.

Shipley, J. W. *Pulp and Paper-making in Canada.* Toronto: Longman, 1929.

Siegfried, André. *Canada.* New York: Harcourt Brace, 1937.

Sissons, C. B. *Church and State in Canadian Education.* Toronto: Ryerson Press, 1959.

Skelton, Isabel. *The Backswoodswoman.* Toronto: Ryerson Press, 1924.

Skelton, O. D. *The Life and Letters of Sir Wilfrid Laurier.* (2 Vols.) London: Oxford University Press, 1922.

Smith, W. L. *Pioneers of Old Ontario.* Toronto: Morang, 1923.

Southworth, John Van Duyn. *Age of Sails.* New York: Twayne, 1968.

Spicer, Stanley T. *Masters of Sail.* Toronto: Ryerson Press, 1968.

Stacey, C. P. *A Very Double Life, the Private World of Mackenzie King.* Toronto: Macmillan, 1976.

Stanley, G. F. G. *New France, the Last Phase, 1744-1760.* Toronto: McClelland & Stewart, 1968.
The Birth of Western Canada. Toronto: University of Toronto Press, 1960.
Canada's Soldiers. Toronto: Macmillan, 1960.

Stark, J. H. *Loyalists of Massachusetts.* Boston: Start, 1910.

Stefansson, V. *The Friendly Arctic.* New York: Macmillan, 1921.
Hunters of the Great North. New York: Harcourt, Brace, 1922.
Great Adventures and Explorations. New York: Dial Press, 1947.

Stewart, Walter. *Shrug: Trudeau in Power.* Toronto: New Press, 1971.

Story, Norah. *Oxford Companion to Canadian History & Literature.* Toronto: Oxford University Press, 1967.

Svensson, Sam. *Sails Through the Centuries.* New York: Macmillan, 1962.

Sverdrup, Otto. *New Land.* London: Longman, 1904.

Swayze, Fred. *The Fighting Lemoynes.* Toronto: Ryerson Press, 1958.

Symington, Fraser. *The Canadian Indian.* Toronto: McClelland & Stewart, 1969.

Thomson, Don W. *Men and Meridians, the History of Surveying and Mapping in Canada.* Ottawa: The Queen's Printer, 1966.

Tracy, F. B. *Tercentenary History of Canada.* (Vol. 1). Toronto: Collier, 1908.

Van Steen, Marcus. *Governor Simcoe and his Lady.* Toronto: Hodder and Stoughton, 1968.

Wade, Mason. *The French Canadian.* Toronto: Macmillan, 1968.

Wallace, Frederick W. *Wooden Ships and Iron Men.* Toronto: Hodder and Stoughton, 1923.
In the Wake of Wind Ships. Toronto: Hodder and Stoughton, 1927.

Wallace, W. Stewart. *Macmillan Dictionary of Canadian Biography.* Revised ed. Toronto: Macmillan, 1963.

Walsh, H. H. *The Christian Church in Canada.* Toronto: Ryerson Press, 1956.

Warburton, A. B. *History of Prince Edward Island.* New Brunswick: Barnes & Co. Ltd., 1923.

Warner, D. F. *The Idea of Continental Union.* Louisville: University of Kentucky Press, 1960.

Waterston, Elizabeth. *Canadian Portraits: Pioneers in Agriculture.* Toronto: Clarke, Irwin, 1957.

Weems, J. E. *The Race for the Pole.* New York: Holt, 1959.

Whitelaw, Wm. Menzies. *The Maritimes and Canada Before Confederation.* Toronto: Oxford University Press, 1934.

Wilkinson, Doug. *Land of the Long Day.* Toronto: Clarke, Irwin, 1966.

Willson, Beckles. *Nova Scotia.* Toronto: McClelland & Goodchild, 1911.

Wilson, Douglas J. *The Church Grows in Canada.* Toronto: Ryerson Press, 1966.

Woodcock, George. *Canada and Canadians.* Toronto: Oxford University Press, 1970.

Woodley, E. C. *Canada's Romantic Heritage.* Toronto: Dent, 1940.

Wright, Esther Clark. *The Saint John River.* Toronto: McClelland & Stewart, 1949.
Blomidon Rose. Toronto: Ryerson Press, 1957.

Wong, George M. *The Rise and Fall of New France.* (Vol. 1). Toronto: Macmillan, 1928.

Wrong, G. M. and Langton, H. H., eds. *Chronicles of Canada.* (33 Vols.) Toronto: Glasgow, Brook, 1914-16.

Index